BEYOND THE GOALPOST

BY
ANDY RUSSELL

CONTENTS

Foreword Written By Franco Harris
Introduction: The Pursuit Of Adventure

DEDICATION

This book is dedicated to my dear friend and business partner, Sam Zacharias, who helped me start and maintain my business while playing football all those years and who "managed" our eight consecutive trips around the world, opening up opportunities we *never dreamed possible*. Sam has always been extraordinarily supportive and helpful, backing me in whatever challenge I pursued: *business, charitable efforts and wilderness adventures.*

Foreword

By FRANCO HARRIS

For a number of us, our first taste of adventure started with sports. Remember the first time you rode your bike across town to your little league baseball game or the many times in high school when you would take the team bus to unknown hostile territory? These early experiences required the fortitude to venture into the unknown. In retrospect they seem small—but back then those were big steps, first steps in a lifelong journey toward adventure and challenge!

I did not have the opportunity to travel while I was growing up even though my parents came from different parts of the world and my father was still in the Army. But I didn't have to travel to experience the international flavor of the world; it was all around me. Just about every American military man in our neighborhood had married a woman from a foreign country. We had neighbors from Germany, Japan, the Philippines, South America, France, and of course, Italy. Through time, most of them were sent to other military bases around the world. Why we weren't sent anywhere else I don't know, but believe me, I was ready to travel!

After high school, I went to Penn State on a football scholarship. The summer after my sophomore year, I had a job working for Mr. Water Conti at Conti's Cross Keys Inn in Bucks County. During this time my mother had gone to Italy to see her family. On the spur of the moment, I decided that I was going to Italy to connect with her and to meet the rest of my family. All alone, I flew to Frankfurt, Germany where I visited with some of my childhood friends who were stationed there. From Germany I took the train to Pisa, Italy to meet my mother. It was a great experience and I knew instantly that I would return.

There is no doubt that football has afforded me the opportunity to travel. After my second year in the NFL I was invited to visit the troops in Korea. At that time Seoul was still under Marshall Law and at night I saw a lot of military activity. That trip also presented me with the honor of meeting General Colin Powell. I have been back to Korea twice since then.

As the saying goes, Life is an adventure. My friend Andy Russell has made this his mantra and has personally taken it to an extraordinary level. Life offers us such great opportunities if we only take the initiative. Some people find adventure by furthering humanitarian causes; some find adventure in their professional careers; and some find adventure in scaling new heights ... literally! I would have to say that Andy seeks out adventure and has found it in all aspects of his life.

No doubt that sports has opened up my life as it has done for so many. I hope that everyone can find "that something" that will open up their lives in the way that Andy describes it. Even though I have been to Italy (numerous times), Austria, Kuwait, England, Japan, Korea, Guam, Nicaragua, Costa Rica, Mexico and Canada, Andy has given me new inspiration to keep exploring the world around me; to keep an open mind to new challenges; and to keep going.

Thanks Andy. You were our captain and our leader when we were with the Steelers and you led by example; you set the bar high and we rose together to achieve much. I'm delighted that you continue to inspire us today.

I can't wait for tomorrow ....

Introduction
THE PURSUIT OF ADVENTURE

I have already written two books about my experiences in football (from high school, college to professional) and what strikes me is that I have, almost all my life, been attracted to athletic challenges, adventure and possibly even danger, although that would have been an unconscious attraction. The reason I have decided to write a third book is simple—it's a genre that I feel most comfortable with and, for me, it's about the joy of writing and telling a story that is meaningful to me and, hopefully, the reader also enjoys these stories—yes, writing one's experiences can be difficult but I love the challenge. It also forces me to try to understand what it was that drove me as a young child, and to recall who were my mentors during my growth from an infant to an adult and especially ask myself why I was so driven to pursue what many would consider dangerous sporting activities—i.e., professional football, mountain climbing, wilderness canoeing, cave exploring, etc.

Part of this need, I suspect, is the realization that I am getting old, (now 68), and I have that need to tell my children, grandchildren and my dear friends (there are so many), how I think about life, how lucky I have been, and what a positive influence they have all been—I am indebted to all of them. If one can write his legacy (and I know that has to be earned) this book would be my attempt to define me to myself. Obviously, there are many who would not care, and their interest in this book would only be the fact that I was a member of the Steelers in those glorious days of the 70's—otherwise they'd have no interest—I understand and can appreciate that. Knowing that, I have included many stories about the Steelers amazing transformation from a consistent loser in the 60's to the incredibly successful 70's.

I am sure that my children and their children (my grandchildren) think they know me and, for the most part, they probably do, but this book, in a way, is an effort to explain their old man or grandpa (the grandkids call me "Geema") in a little more detail. How was I raised? Who were my mentors, (many outstanding friends, teachers and coaches) and what did they preach? When did I see the light, if I ever did? Where did the most meaningful experiences occur? The questions go on and on and yet I feel compelled to answer as many as I can and I hope that many of the chapters will do just that.

Obviously, our lives are hugely impacted by where we come from and how we were raised and I feel so fortunate to have had wonderful parents who taught me the old school values (hard work, determination, dedication, focus, respect, attitude and a refusal to quit—these and other attributes will be repeated often through many chapters) and passed on to me their love of seeing this so interesting world. My world has also been shaped by the people that I have known and I feel very lucky to have had such good teammates and mentors, who helped me on my journey.

The chapters in this book range from Steeler experiences to travel experiences to personal letters sent to important people in my life to deeply personal experiences I have had growing up. The best way to describe the various chapters is that they are eclectic, some having no connection or relation to other chapters—just something that I found interesting, such as our two trips to Costa Rica and Alaska including the guides we met along the way.

For those Super Steelers fans there are a number of chapters that deal with experiences had on and off the field with my so professional, disciplined, driven and exceptional teammates.

Chapter 1

A VERY LUCKY LIFE

Reflecting back on my life I am constantly amazed at the number of favorable things that have happened to me, on my journey through life, and the wonderful people and events that have impacted my life so positively. Not only have I had an enormous amount of good fortune but I have also been astounded at the serendipitous nature of life, where seemingly unrelated events, people and incidents, have come together in such unbelievably balanced, synchronistic and fortuitous ways that I just have to believe that I have been, bottom line, extraordinarily lucky.

But, just maybe, one can get very lucky by following a couple of basic tenets: the power of thinking positively (always maintaining a good attitude) and coupling that with working hard—paying the price. Good things tend to happen when you expect them to happen and when you combine that with quality preparation with enormous effort (something all of my fine coaches over the years always stressed), not that I have always paid that price but when I haven't I have learned my lesson.

In my perspective, my life's journey has been full of wonderful adventures, fascinating people and exciting challenges, some met successfully and others not, but almost always worthwhile. It also is clear to me that I have been lucky to be born into a great family, to have had great life partners (wives)—Cindy, my second wife, a true soulmate whose interests are almost exactly like mine (spending time with family and friends, working out, climbing, hiking, skiing, biking and traveling and some business) and Nancy, my first wife, who always supported me, was a fabulous mother of our children, being there for them when I was flying around the world chasing my dreams, trying to earn a living—two great children and seven beautiful grandchildren, and to be surrounded by outstanding friends and partners,

1

both on a personal and professional level, both sports and business. Now that's a lucky guy!

Perhaps my experience is not significantly different than the average American growing up in the 40's and 50's—after all this is a great country and opportunities were in abundance. We all, I'm sure, can think back and remember events and lessons taught by parents and mentors that have hugely benefited our lives. But, in addition, we also can remember amazing coincidences, symbiotic happenings, that have come together in an almost unfathomably coordinated way that without a lot of effort have turned out to impact our lives in a hugely positive way and we have to believe in and give credit to plain old good luck or is it fate? Sometimes it's all about being in the right place at the right time combined with busting one's butt to make the grade.

Looking back, what were some of these lucky events that I have found so beneficial? This chapter is not about patting my self on the back for having had the sense to follow the direction of my parents or the teachings of so many fine coaches and mentors. It is not about my own journey to find the right course, or the correct amount of energy required of a certain challenge. Obviously, I could have ignored the advice of my mentors and chosen to do things my way but I didn't— thank goodness I learned to appreciate the value of accepting their wisdom. But rather, it is my way of saying thank you to all those wonderful family members, friends, teachers, coaches and mentors (yes, I'm repeating myself) who have had such a profound and positive influence on my life.

So, when it comes to numbering my lucky events, first and foremost, was having the good fortune to have been born to a Mom and Dad who not only loved me but also taught me the old school values that have been so helpful in dealing with life's challenges: values such as the importance of being honest, independent, frugal (waste not), disciplined, unrelenting and understanding that we have to pay the price (hard work), and, perhaps most important, the value of having a good attitude. I don't mean to suggest that there haven't been times that I failed to follow these ethics but, in each case that I haven't, it was clearly wrong and often had devastatingly negative repercussions, sometimes badly hurting people that I care deeply about and devastating my own psyche. Many of the following chapters will repeat (remember Hemingway believed that writers to make their point should repeat, repeat and repeat) those old school values because I believe they are so important.

Obviously, we can all debate the benefits of various philosophies and I certainly don't want to seem too preachy here, since I'm sure my parents weren't perfect, failing to teach me some other valuable lessons—qualities like patience (Coach Noll always told me that I was too impatient, too impulsive, too aggressive), often unwilling to accept well meant criticism (sometimes I resisted my great coaches advice and direction), and always maintaining a sense of humor—not always my strengths.

Also, I certainly don't want to suggest that I know any amazing secrets to happiness or success. These are simple ideas, stuff that most of our parents I'm sure tried to pass on, and so this chapter isn't to suggest that I know something you, reader, don't but instead this chapter can possibly serve as a reminder to all of us about what it takes to have a rewarding life. We know these things but tend some times to forget them or not truly appreciate and underestimate their influence and power.

When I am asked what one attribute that I have noticed that happy, successful people have (I do not judge success by money but by the quality of one's family life, one's lust for life, one's ability to establish meaningful relationships (friends), and accomplishments in whatever their chosen field is), I believe that there is one consistent trait they all have (at least in those successful people I have been fortunate enough to meet and get to know) and that is just plain old having a good *Attitude*.

People who have great attitudes, (those who are upbeat, enthusiastic, happy, positive, and open), are often the people who are best liked and most successful. In my own career, I have noticed how often I have been able to improve upon my performance, get along with people better, just by forcing myself (yes, sometimes I resist) to have a good attitude, certainly something we all should be able to control or to manufacture when needed.

As a young kid I learned quickly from my parents that bad attitudes would not be tolerated; as they totally outlawed any complaining whatsoever—complain about anything, regardless of how justifiable, and they'd give me something to really complain about—a spanking. Of course, I couldn't complain about that or I'd get another spanking.

Of course, you can't blame or criticize someone who was raised differently, being allowed to complain when it might have been appropriate or at least smart to do so. More modern child raising techniques recommend that children be treated more like adults, teaching them how to make good judgments and decisions, without the fear of a spanking.

Of course, asking a three year old if they want to take their medicine is probably not a good idea—it shouldn't be an option. However, our children were certainly encouraged, at times, to give their opinion, to voice an alternative solution or make recommendations and often their ideas were better than ours. But they certainly understood the word *NO*, a word that so many of today's parents seem to have trouble defining to their children.

My sweet mother, Esther, a women's liberation advocate long before it became fashionable, taught me to respect women and appreciate that they could be an equal partner. Despite being a reasonably attractive and healthy lady, she stressed something that seems to be contrary to what so many parents preach today—she taught me that it is not at all important what you look like (that being handsome or well dressed is of absolutely no value and certainly not a goal). She believed what you do, what you accomplish, what kind of an attitude you have and how you treat people are the only things that really matter. She preached that physical attractiveness was simply genetic and not something someone should feel good about—of course, maybe that was her way of teaching me not to be so concerned about my teenage acne.

She also preached that it wasn't important what you owned (expensive homes, cars, or clothes)—that possessions should only be necessities and had nothing to do with the quality of one's person. Today, not surprisingly after my sweet mother's lectures, I find myself pretty much a minimalist—rarely shopping for anything and disliking it when I do. Obviously, if there were more people like me out there our retail economy would suffer badly—I just never shop, unless it's for buying gifts for other people. I am absolutely not into "stuff—clothes, cars, homes, etc." I do, on the other hand, believe in spending money to seek out adventures, experiences and challenges with family and friends.

But most importantly, she taught me to believe in myself, to believe that I could achieve whatever goals I set assuming I dedicated myself.

Your basic, *Think Big, Work Hard and Have a Dream* ethic and you will be rewarded—maybe not with money but with self respect. Obviously, none of us will accomplish all of our goals but believing in one's abilities is critical when competing at almost any level and certainly there have been times in my life where I have failed to remain confident—like when the Steelers lost 16 straight games (the 1969 1-13 season and the first 3 games of the 1970 season).

My father, William Mair Russell II, who emigrated from Glasgow, Scotland at the age of 11 with his tough parents (his Dad, my grandfather, had operated the Glasgow Steel Mill's open hearth furnace), was all business—teaching my brother, Will, and me the value of hard work, always stressing the importance of concentrating on one's tasks and completing the job—total commitment and effort will overcome a lot of things, like competing against someone smarter and more talented. It is amazing what good things will happen when you just work to exhaustion, make no excuses, and have a good attitude.

Naturally, my first wife Nancy and I tried to pass on these values to our two children, Andy and Amy, and I think we were successful—they've both turned out great and found their own unique paths.

I'll never forget when my son, his freshman year at Dartmouth, called to say, "Dad, guess how many guys on my football team maxed the College Board SAT exam?"

Not ever imagining that it would even be possible to max those so difficult tests (having done poorly myself), I replied, "You're kidding—I have no idea."

"Well, there are three guys on my team who maxed the SATs but, you know what Dad, I think I can do as well in our classes as them."

"How are you going to do that?" I said.

"I'll just have to work harder," was the terse reply and, sure enough, he had the top grades in a number of his classes, proving to himself, I'm sure, that nothing beats just plain old hard work.

My daughter, Amy, went on a 30-day National Outdoor Leadership (NOLS) program in Alaska where she hiked long miles every day, sleeping and eating on the ground, not having a shower or washing her hair for that entire time, and she loved it—not wanting to come out when it was all over. When she had been cold, hungry and tired, she had forced herself to have a good attitude and, guess what; it had worked, giving her a true appreciation of the values of her difficult

5

experience, savoring the challenges, and appreciating the support of her colleagues. She is a lot like her Dad.

I realize that those were very different, simpler times (in my case, the 1940's, my kids the '60's and 70's). It was also a much safer world, before the days of terrorists, child abusers, and drug pushers, and other various weirdos (or at least before such behavior was chronicled so closely by our media, understandably badly frightening many parents).

For example, one of my parents' major goals was for me to become independent, to be capable of making my own decisions, finding my own path, to become self reliant—to be a leader, not a follower (at least not the kind of person that would be overly influenced by his peers, especially their bad ideas).

For example, when I was eight years old, living in Detroit at the time, we would often visit a cabin owned by my grandparents (on my mother's side, Guy and Mimi Blackinton) on the shore of Lake Huron, in Michigan. Behind the cottage was a dense forest, a wilderness to me, to explore. My father taught me how to swing an axe and off I went into the woods, alone, carrying my axe, told to bring back some firewood for the fireplace. When I had asked when I should return, they said, "Just get back before dark"—it was just after lunch.

After collecting a small pile of kindling, I set it aside and, after finding a beautiful patch of land in an opening in the forest, began trying to build a log cabin deep in the forest. I took old fallen trees, 5 to 7 inches in diameter, and cut them in logs about 7 feet long, notching them on each end about a foot from the end. Working away, totally absorbed in what I was doing, enjoying immensely the feel of swinging an axe, over and over, placing the logs in a square (I figured I could fill up the large space between the logs with mud) I didn't notice it getting dark.

This small little "cabin" became a secret project as I returned every day over our weeks' stay but after four or five days my parents became curious and asked what I was doing, spending so much time in the woods by myself. When I explained that I was building a log cabin they naturally wanted to see it and I proudly showed them the half completed, so called, cabin (around four or five logs high, granted a very rudimentary structure).

They praised me for my industriousness but, unfortunately, we left before I could finish that project. The following year they sold the lake house and I never returned—maybe, some other young person discovered and finished my "cabin." My point here is that very few parents today would allow their eight year old to disappear into the woods with an axe by himself for four or five hours without worrying—times today are certainly different.

When I was nine, living in Evanston, Illinois, my parents would allow me to walk to downtown Evanston (miles away) to go to the movies (25 cents) by myself. I can remember to this day being absolutely riveted when I saw Burt Lancaster portray the famous Native American athlete, Jim Thorpe, hoping someday to be like him, a successful athlete. My parents would go on to fuel my love of sports by giving me photo albums of famous sporting events, like the Olympics, and I dreamed constantly of what it would be like to compete in the decathlon as one of the world's most well rounded athletes, an event I never even tried, despite going out for track and running (a relatively poor 10.7 second 100 yard dash, causing me to either be last or tied for last in all the events—probably wind aided and down hill), shot putting, high jumping 5'11", and broad jumping (20'10")—putting me in a very mediocre category. Isn't it surprising, here at age 68, that I can still remember those numbers—just goes to show you that you can never overestimate a former jocks ego.

When we moved to Pelham Manor in Westchester County, New York, my mother would take me on the train into Manhattan to visit the public Library, reading me excerpts about our Native Americans, surviving in the wild that enthralled me. Finally, after learning the ropes (ten years old) she suggested I go into Manhattan by myself—after all, I knew where to get off the train (Grand Central Station) and how to find my way to my favorite spots—the library and an Indian Artifacts store called Puma Craft. So off I went on my own little adventure, sightseeing alone as a ten year old in Manhattan. It is hard to imagine letting one's child do that today—I wouldn't.

A few years later my mother, knowing how much I loved to climb things (anything—trees, roofs, jungle gyms), suggested that after church service (we were Unitarians) we drive over to the New Jersey Palisades (on the Hudson River) where I could climb the cliffs while she read the Sunday paper. After climbing nearly an hour, hanging by my finger nails, starting to feel the extreme exposure to a fall, definitely becoming afraid (hey, I was only 11 years old with no ropes or technical climbing training), I glanced down toward where my mother was sitting and saw a line of cars backed up for miles and a policeman frantically waving me down.

At the police station, where my mother and I had been taken after our "arrest," (for potentially causing a rock slide) my mother proudly, and wrongly, told the officer that "my son is a very good climber and he would not have dislodged any rocks down onto the cars below." They gave us a slap on the wrist and sent us home. However, I realized that I might easily have dislodged a rock slide, possibly hurting some people and that, perhaps, I should be more careful in the future, despite my sweet mother's encouragement.

But my parents really set the gauge on the independence goal when they told me, at the age of 15, that I should go to Europe by myself and bicycle from Glasgow, Scotland to Naples, Italy. Granted, for part of the trip (from Amsterdam to Milan), I would join the son, Jan Hein Vlasman, of a Dutch family (his father had been killed by the Nazis) our family had befriended and helped by sending food and money.

When I asked my parents how long they thought the trip would take, they "estimated" two and half months. Dad told me that he would give me $400 in American Express traveler's checks for the journey but that I would have to work in a factory the following summer to pay him back. When I asked what would happen if I ran out of money, he said, "Get a job." When I asked what if there are no jobs he said, smiling at me, "you'll starve." But, in fairness, he did give me a list of phone numbers of contacts through out Europe (none were in cities where I traveled) of people who worked in his company, Monsanto, in case I needed help in an emergency—I proudly never called any of them, nor did I need to.

When I asked if I could take a buddy of mine with me they agreed but doubted that any of the other parents (we were living in St. Louis at the time) would allow such a trip. Surprisingly I found that one of my good friends, and football teammate, Jack Schneider, was allowed to join me and we took a boat from Montreal to Southampton, England and a bus to Glasgow, bought two bikes for approximately $36 each (with no gears—too expensive) and bicycled down through Great Britain, took a boat to Rotterdam, rode a train to Amsterdam where we joined up with the two Dutch boys and rode our bikes down through Germany, Switzerland, over the Alps, to Milan, Italy where the Dutch boys left on their bikes for the French Rivera and we sold our bikes at a public square (for $10 each), and finally hitchhiking down to Naples just in time to catch our boat home.

For me it was an epic journey (granted, only for me), one that changed me forever, teaching me responsibility, accountability, independence, self reliance and giving me the confidence to make my own decisions, lead not follow. I'm sure I made my share of mistakes on that trip but for the most part it was a grand experience. Arriving home I gave my Dad $150 that I had left over—can you imagine traveling today through Europe on a two and a half month trip for only $250—that's about $3.33 per day for all travel expenses, transportation, lodging and food. We never ate in a restaurant, buying a loaf of bread and some cheese at the local markets. We slept mostly in Youth Hostels but often had to sleep on the hay stacks in barns or on the ground.

One of the reasons that trip was so helpful in teaching me that I could find my way in the world was that I had a very smart, older brother, Will, (who was not invited to go on such a trip because my parents didn't think he needed it) and he would most often have the answers to any of our parents questions. Naturally I began to defer to his judgment, always letting him make our decisions, appreciating his intelligence, questioning my own. As often happens in families, the younger child, plays the role of the family comedian and I questioned my ability to make key decisions—that trip through Europe removed that doubt—for me that journey was an odyssey, changing my life, giving me greater confidence in my own ability to make quality decisions.

When I was a freshman at the University of Missouri, (I was there on an athletic scholarship), struggling to survive the rigors of freshman football and still complete my studies, I received a rare call (I was allowed no more than a once a month phone call and no more than four minutes because of the expense of long distance calling—hey my parents were Scottish and proud of it) from my dear mother. It was a short conversation that went something like this, "Hi Dear, good news, your father has just been promoted to Vice President of Monsanto Overseas, we'll be moving to Brussels, Belgium, we'll be gone about ten years, but you can call once every two months but no more than three minutes because long distance is just so expensive, good luck, bye, bye," and she hung up.

When I hung up that phone I realized why my parents had wanted me to grow up so self reliant and independent—they knew this day would come. I knew then that I just couldn't screw up and fail in football (lose my scholarship) or flunk my courses—it was time to get serious in my life. My parents moving to Europe my freshman year in college would necessitate my being independent; being able to make my own decisions, to make the right choices, pick the friends who would inspire me and not get me in trouble and I had discovered, through trial and error, that I was ready.

One of the lessons that my life has taught me is that hard is good, easy is bad, and that you don't have to have fun to have fun! Do something really difficult, meet the challenge, and finish the deal, complete the exhausting effort and you will feel very good about it, proud to your core. Do something easy, something of no significance, or of a frivolous nature; or if you do something difficult you stop because it hurts or because its too exhausting and you will not feel good about yourself. I have had wonderful coaches and mentors, who have taught me to never give up, play hurt, pay the price, and give every bit of energy you have to achieve the goal. Those phrases may seem trite but only because they are so true—follow those rules and life will be fun and rewarding. They certainly made me a believer.

That's not to say that the challenge has to be a physical one. Certainly doing a difficult mental test (i.e., developing a business plan and then executing it, painting a painting, sculpting, writing a book, developing new ideas, efforts that take an enormous amount of time, can still give one that great feeling of having done something difficult/challenging/meaningful/worthwhile—a natural high.

Recently I had a relatively insignificant experience that nevertheless, to me, once again, reminded me that attitude is sometimes the key to dealing with life's challenges, to create, in one's mind, the right way to think about something. I was climbing Maroon Peak (the taller of the two Maroon Peaks) outside of Aspen. Post football, I had decided (along with my pal Ray Mansfield) that we would replace football with "adventure travel." We had done a number of outdoor "gut tests," proving, at least to ourselves, that we were still vital, young enough to push our bodies to it's limit—much the way we had during our fourteen year NFL careers.

One of those "gut tests" was climbing four 14,000-foot mountains in one day. I had read an account of a young man who had climbed all of Colorado's 14,000-foot mountains in 14 straight days. For those who "conquer" all of those 54 mountains you can claim the "Grand Slam," something accomplished mostly by locals, (people who live in Colorado).

Since we were playing in the Denver Bronco's Alumni golf tournament that September, I suggested to Ray that we try another gut test—to climb the four 14ers in a single day (actually the young man who had done all 54 in 14 straight days (the record is now 11), had done seven that day but it looked doable for Ray and I to climb those four, as they were near Vail, a place where we would be playing golf.

So, following our round of golf in Denver, we drove up into the mountains, spending the night in Breckinridge (not far from these four, (named Democrat, Lincoln, Bross and Cameron) and found ourselves, the next morning at 4:30 am, driving up to the high mountain "trailhead" in our Lincoln Town car. As we drove up a bumpy jeep trail we passed numerous campsites, full of campers still asleep, all having 4-wheel drive vehicles, unlike our sleek freebie.

We climbed those four mountains, taking about 12 hours and loving every minute of it. We had sunlight, rain, hail and a major blizzard all during those 12 hours and it tested every bit of our resolve. When we finished Ray took off his soaking wet climbing pants, threw them in the trunk and slammed it shut, putting on his warm, dry sweat pants—unfortunately, he immediately recognized that the car keys were still in his climbing pants, now locked in the trunk. It was a classic case of the brain damage caused by high altitude and fatigue—the theory is that for every 1000 feet you are above 10,000 feet, you lose 10 points of your IQ and for Ray and me that put us in serious jeopardy.

As luck would have it, a few minutes later, some locals drove up in a pickup truck on a fishing trip, with a bag of tools and, thankfully, we were able to get into our trunk through the back seat, as, fortunately, we had opened the car doors prior to Ray's blunder. Driving back down to our Condo in Breckinridge, we both realized that mountain climbing could very well be the antidote for our post-football blahs.

11

This was a new challenge, one that may not require the athleticism of the NFL but certainly requiring the mental toughness and commitment required by our Steeler coaches.

So, flash forward fifteen years, (back to something that has reminded me of the value of having a good attitude), here I was climbing South Maroon, one of Colorado's more difficult mountains, up a semi-technical route (the north couloir), tethered to a guide's rope, struggling to work my way up in deep snow. We eventually summited but (and here's the good attitude story) on the way down the guide turned off on a route that seemed different than what we had come up. Despite my questioning his route, (it definitely seemed wrong to me) not wanting to go one step out of our way, since we were in the 11th hour of the climb, we pushed on down a steep slope towards what appeared to me to be a cliff.

The guide finally stopped, surveyed his surroundings, and informed me that we had gone the wrong way and that we would have to climb back up to reclaim the correct route. I mean you have to understand the situation. Here I had hired the guide primarily for his route finding knowledge. I was exhausted from a very difficult 11-hour effort and I had even questioned his route 30 minutes back up the mountain. I did not need another hour added to the climb. Thinking that I had every reason to be very pissed off, about to start a rant, criticizing his decisions and questioning whether I should even have to pay him, I remembered my family credo—Russell's never complain, ever, about anything.

So after he apologized, stifling my anger, trying hard to sound sincere, I forced myself to say, "Don't worry about it—this way makes it a better work out and God knows I need one." With that we both laughed and we climbed back up towards the correct route. Upon reaching the right path, after climbing at least another half hour straight up, the guide apologized once again. Still feeling the sting of irritation I again forced myself to have a good attitude and said, "Hey, this is great—I got to see more of this beautiful mountain this way."

The guide started praising me for having such a good attitude and, all of a sudden, everything was OK, I felt good—I had turned a negative into a positive, simply by forcing a good attitude, and, best of all, I actually started to believe my two little positives—better work

12

out and seeing more of the mountain. Why not believe in something positive than pick the negative?

This minor incident reminded me that the benefits of having a good attitude, even if it has to be manufactured, is still one of life's best kept secrets and I again appreciated those wonderful old school teachings of our parents, coaches and mentors. Hey, I'm not suggesting here that I always have a good attitude, about everything, often finding myself inordinately irritated by some trivial occurrence, usually discovering when analyzing it, that there was something else that was really bothering me.

Nor do I want to suggest that I am always totally self reliant, independent, as I often find myself relying upon my so very smart business partners (Jeff Kendall and Don Rea), allowing them to lead the way. But I will give myself some credit for being smart enough to pick such great partners.

Of course, if you're lucky enough to grow up with great parents and mentors, who teach you all those wonderful old school values, you really can't take too much credit for following those ethics and discovering that good things happen when you follow them. The credit goes to the teachers, the mentors who guided us.

Chapter 2

CLOSE TO THE EDGE

One of the reasons Ray Mansfield, my former teammate and best Steeler buddy and I chose wilderness adventures to test ourselves was that it made us feel so incredibly alive—very much like the game of football had? We had entered the NFL in the same year, 1963, and we both retired in 1976, 14 years later from the Steelers. Reflecting back on those outdoor tests, we were clearly attracted to both the challenges but, apparently, also the dangers, discovering that by facing them we would experience an enormous adrenaline rush.

Winston Churchill once said "that there is nothing more exhilarating than to be shot at without result." The world's greatest mountain climber, Reinhold Messner, has said that "without the possibility of losing one's life there can be no adventure."

I had learned the truth of Churchill's statement when in Vietnam, on a USO Tour; a sniper's bullet missed my skull by only a few inches. I had crawled back out of his line of sight, knowing that I had just been in a sniper's scope and, from approximately 200 meters he had probably only misjudged the shot by a tiny fraction of an inch. I had been enormously lucky and I found my heart pounding and I suddenly realized that I had never felt so alive. I could hear better, see better, smell better—all my senses were at their absolute maximum, far more intensely than I had ever experienced them on a football field.

That moment overwhelmed my senses. I was more exhilarated than I had ever been, because a Vietcong sniper had put me in his sights and fired, wanting to kill me. I would learn later that a number of people (some journalists), standing on their roofs or balconies in Saigon that very day had been killed by sniper fire. Obviously, it would be very absurd to go to a war zone to get one's adrenalin fix.

Later that night, reflecting on that experience, I realized that danger (risking one's life) can push our senses and our level of exhilaration to

14

new peaks. I sat there wondering, despite thinking that it would be hugely immature and naïve of me (as I had a wife and young boy who were totally dependent upon me), if there wasn't a part of me that had unknowingly chosen to come on this Vietnam USO Tour because I was attracted to the danger. I knew there were rockets being fired into Saigon on almost a daily basis and nearly everyone had predicted that there would be a Tet Offensive of a significant magnitude and yet I had signed up.

Granted, my exposure to these dangers was insignificant as compared to what our brave soldiers faced every day, but for a moment I felt quite stupid, understanding that I may have voluntarily put myself in a dangerous situation, where I had consciously believed that my only reason for being there was to thank our troops for their so spectacular service.

Regarding Reinhold Messner's point that adventure is really not possible without it being life threatening, I realized that I had never, at least consciously, sought danger at that level. Nevertheless, I realized that there had been a number of occasions on mountains and in canyons where the slightest misstep could have been disastrous—i.e., if a huge ice block broke loose, or a rock moved, a tripping or slipping on a narrow ledge could have all caused death.

However, what could be boring trips to professionals, like Mr. Messner, might be huge adventures to someone like me who is relatively new to the world's vast wildernesses and their challenges. After completing the fourteen 8000 meter peaks Reinhold had promised his mother that he would do no more serious climbing. But after a few years of staying away from the mountains, he cross country skied pulling a sled with his gear and food across the Antartic continent, a trip he would later say was dramatically more dangerous and difficult than climbing Everest.

Realizing that there must be something in my nature, and perhaps all of us, that is attracted to danger; I have tried to remember some of the times in my life where I had chosen to seek out risky situations. Granted, I'm sure we all did things as kids that were fairly irresponsible and potentially dangerous, but as a young boy, before my teens, I was always trying to climb the biggest and most difficult trees in the neighborhood, always pushing the limit, hanging from the top branch, wanting to go higher. All it would have taken was one weak branch to crack, one slip and I could have fallen and died or been badly injured.

Few of my friends would climb so high but there was something in my nature that always pushed me to go a little higher, perhaps, unconsciously, searching for a higher level of risk and, therefore, more excitement! Swing the swing as high as it will go, dive from the highest point, climb the steepest roof tops, or pick a fight with the neighborhood bully—there were many ways to get one's kicks as a youngster.

In my teens I apparently got my thrills in the world of sports, whether diving for loose balls on the basketball court, trying to avoid tacklers (I was a running back in high school and college) or throwing my head in front of a runner's knees (my linebacker job—we played both ways in those days), hoping to bring him down.

I realize that listing one's encounters with danger is a relatively frivolous effort in that many people will have had far more dangerous encounters (i.e., our soldiers in Iraq) and this isn't about competition for having had the wildest experiences—just making the point that danger, hopefully in a controlled environment, can be extraordinarily exhilarating. However, taking careless risks to get a high is just plain stupid (perhaps as dumb as taking drugs)—obviously one needs to be well trained and prepared.

I have realized that most of the serious risks I have taken over the years have had something to do with climbing—climbing up or down something (cliffs, mountains, mine shafts, caves, tunnels, roof tops, trees and below I have written about just a few of those experiences, some of which I must admit were more than a little irresponsible—lets say just plain stupid.

One of my more irrational moments (there are many) came in Switzerland, on the bicycle trip, with my St. Louis friend, Jack Schneider, when we were 15 years old and bicycling Glasgow, Scotland to Naples, Italy. We had stopped early at a youth hostel in a small town in Switzerland, high in the Alps, because of the steepness of the terrain—pacing ourselves for a tough, gearless bike climb the next day.

Wanting to experience these beautiful Alps first hand, I asked Jack to go on a short climb prior to dinner but we soon found ourselves blocked by a cliff. As we scrambled up the steep rocky wall (with no gear—a free climb), leading the way, I found myself on a small ledge (about fifty feet from the rocky floor below), a couple of yards across

16

from a small gully from which we could easily gain the top of the cliff. Realizing that I either had to jump across or climb back down, I finally got the nerve to leap across the void (maybe 5 feet) and barely made it. Afterwards, I sat there breathing hard (not from the exertion but from the fear), waiting for Jack to reach this same precarious point.

When Jack got to the ledge, he hesitated, like me not being comfortable with his position, but I encouraged him (perhaps irresponsibly) to leap across. Jack didn't like the look of this challenge but also didn't want to climb back down (a more difficult thing to do but less dangerous) so he finally jumped but he didn't quite jump far enough, landing somewhat precariously and began to tilt backwards, about to fall head first to the rocks below, but I frantically reached out to him with my left hand, as my right hand held tight to the rock wall and just barely caught him from falling, yanking him across the divide. We both laid there panting with relief, realizing that a disaster had almost occurred, our hearts were pumping. Fortunately, we found another way down.

Obviously, this wasn't a significant climbing challenge (real rock climbers could probably do it in their sleep) but, nevertheless, it provided my friend and me with a very scary moment, one significant enough to frighten us into an elevated emotional state—the kind that only comes after a facing a significant moment of danger, yes life threatening.

A few years later, I found myself leading (because I was the only one who had done a canoe trip before) a group of my high school buddies on a wilderness canoe adventure in the Boundary Waters Canoe Area in northern Minnesota. We were on our third day of a two week long canoe effort to penetrate all the way up through the land of lakes into Canada and we found ourselves with the option of portaging around rapids (carrying our backpacks and canoes) or shooting the rapids.

Naturally, I recommended (perhaps an unknown tendency to seek the more exciting option) that we shoot the rapids, despite being sixty miles from the nearest road, telephone or cabin. The first to go down, my buddy Jack in the front, always willing to accept my (perhaps foolish) challenges, we flew over the last drop, falling nearly five feet, resulting in our canoe turning over and ourselves being ejected from the canoe into the ice cold water.

The underhaul of the falls sucked us back down and I found myself being pulled beneath the small waterfall and taken down below where I could see the relic of an old sunken canoe ten feet below me. Just as I felt the power of the water releasing and about to start swimming back up and away from the falls, I felt my ankle and boot sucked into a crack in the rock ledge beneath the falls but, luckily, I was able to kick my foot upwards and avoid the potential trap, one that would have surely killed me, if caught even for more than a few seconds, as I had already been under for some time.

I arose to the surface gasping for air, knowing that I had just been very lucky, avoiding, once again, that freak accident that can end your life. Jack had had a similar experience but was also OK. The rest of the guys smartly decided to portage around the rapids. As we paddled away, Jack remarked, "I'm as pumped up as I was when I almost fell in Switzerland!" I too could feel the exhilaration, pulsing through my body.

During my college years I was less likely, due to the constant work out requirements of playing college football (for Dan Devine's Missouri Tigers), to seek out risky situations but even in those days I would somehow, on rare occasions, find those danger rushes.

For example, on the semester break my sophomore year, I convinced my college roommate and dear friend, Jim Card, a very gifted pitcher on the Missouri Baseball team, (one of the best teams in the USA in those days), to join me on a trip to Colorado to see some of my best high school friends who had gone to the University of Colorado in Boulder.

We drove out from Columbia, Missouri, without much money, in my parents old Buick (they had left it with me, as they had moved to Europe). On the way, Jim deftly talked a motel clerk into a lower rate, offering for us to sweep the parking lot and to sleep on the top of the beds so as not to disturb the sheets—we did both. Arriving in Boulder we met the two high school buddies, Mike Bottom and John McCullough, and they put us up in their apartment, sleeping on the floor.

The next morning John, Jim and I decided to explore into the mountains, despite being massively hung over (which, of course, is no excuse for our stupidity). So, John, Jim and I, (Mike was busy studying) drove up into the mountains and John, a strong basketball teammate in high school, suggested we park the car off the road, and climb up a steep slope, just to "discover" what was up there. Nearing the top of a fairly long and arduous slope (which took us nearly an hour to climb up through the snow) we discovered an old wooden mining shack that was unlocked. I had been told that most of Colorado's old mines were boarded up and locked shut.

Fascinated by this discovery, we entered the shack and found an open, square mining shaft going straight down, (about ten feet wide), and found an old wooden ladder going down, attached to the wall in the middle of the totally vertical shaft with thick wire cables hanging in the center of the shaft. How could we resist, despite it being a massively stupid idea, the adventure of climbing down that ladder, into the void, the darkness, seeking the mystery of where it would end?

Well, without much debate, we went down, praying that the ancient ladder wouldn't come loose, and occasionally breaking or passing broken wooden slats of the ladder—clearly a fall would cause us to fall hundreds of feet down the shaft—to us it was an endless pit with no bottom and our hearts were pounding. After all, the mine had probably been built in the mid 1800's and been closed for over 50 years with both the wooden beams (upon which the ladder was affixed) and the wooden ladder itself rotting away.

"Are you sure this is a good idea?" Jim asked, with his voice dripping in fearful sarcasm.

"I've read that because the air is relatively dry and stays nearly the same temperature year around that things do not deteriorate as rapidly down in these mines," I replied, praying that I had remembered that correctly.

After climbing cautiously about 100 feet down our flashlights discovered that we had reached a horizontal shaft, a tunnel penetrating into the rock, with narrow rail tracks heading deep into the mountain. Glad to be off the disintegrating ladder, we decided to walk back into this tunnel and did, probably no more than 300 meters, stopping occasionally to examine old pick axes and other discarded tools, and we eventually found an old mining cart sitting on the rail, obviously formally used to bring the ore to the vertical shaft. I tried shoving it a few yards down the track, picturing in my mind how the miners of those days got their exercise.

Deciding to return to the main vertical shaft (before finding the end of the horizontal shaft) we went further down finding a second horizontal tunnel down about another 200 feet.

When we had arrived at the second horizontal shaft I had climbed off the ladder first, crossing 5 or 6 feet with my feet on a large, wooden beam, (with my flashlight awkwardly stuck in my belt) holding with my hands on the upper beam above my head. Reaching the horizontal tunnel I waited for my comrades but as John crossed over with his back to the void, his foot slipped on a loose board (something that I had unknowingly avoided) and he teetered on the edge about to fall. Once again I was lucky to be in the right place at the right time, grabbing out for him and just being able to pull him over to the floor of the tunnel. Listening to the board, (which had fallen into the vertical shaft), bang its' way down for a long time before any silence, we knew we had just dodged another life threatening moment. It took us quite some time, understandably, to coax Jim across that same beam. In all there were three horizontal mining shafts before we reached the bottom one (the 4th), nearly one thousand feet down into the mine shaft, an exploration that had taken us nearly two hours and we were concerned that our flashlight batteries might burn out—not to mention the constant worry that the ladder would rip loose from the rotting beams.

Arriving at the bottom, finding the last horizontal tunnel we were anxious to return to the surface, (but not really enthusiastic about climbing back up that decaying ladder) we felt a breeze, as though there was an opening down the shaft. Curious, (how could there be wind blowing down the shaft—hoping there would be an "escape hatch,") we walked down the small tunnel seeking the source of the breeze and eventually, after hiking nearly a quarter of a mile down this shaft, ducking under low roofs and squeezing through smaller passages, we finally saw a glow (yes, the proverbial "Light at the End of the Tunnel") and we spilled out onto one of the mountain's side slopes that was relatively flat compared to those above and what we guessed was approximately a quarter of the way around the mountain (probably a couple of miles) to the west from where we had parked the car.

It was late, about 4:30 pm, and we were standing in snow a foot deep, insanely in our leather penny loafers (not exactly climbing boots), wondering if we should return to the mine and climb up that huge shaft or if we should stay outside and attempt, despite the deep snow, to find our way around the mountain, back to our car.

"Look, lets see if we can hike down and around and if we get lost we can always return, following our footprints in this deep snow, back to the safety of the mine shaft. I've heard that the temperature in the mines, even in winter, is always around 48 degrees, a level that would allow us to survive the night," John said.

"What have we got to lose—I sure don't think it would be real smart to go back in there and try climbing back up that frigging ladder," Jim replied.

So off we went, hiking down through even deeper snow drifts, miles from our car, attempting to intuitively figure out which way to go—it seemed logical that we should descend the slope and turn left (or south—of course, we didn't have a compass and it was rapidly getting dark) and hopefully we could find our way back to the highway and the car. After about a half hour hike, crossing a ice covered creek, we discovered what appeared to be an opening in the trees, presumably a road, covered with deep snow and we followed it about a quarter of a mile until coming upon a cabin, deep in the forest.

The cabin was dark, obviously no one was at home and there was no indication that the road had been used any time in the immediate past. We figured it was a summer cabin and rarely, if ever, visited in the winter. So, despite being pretty clean cut kids, who normally followed all the rules, (we did not commit crimes—like breaking in and entering), we entered the cabin through a window that had been left unlocked—at least there was no damage and, after all, this was an emergency, at least it felt like one to us.

The cabin was nicely decorated and we quickly decided who would sleep where and piled dozens of blankets onto the beds, as there was no heat in the cabin (they had obviously drained their pipes). Despite it being only around (7:00 pm) all three of us were exhausted, possibly from the tension of doing something so dumb and dangerous and fell right to sleep, not awaking until day break.

Discovering that the gas stove worked, and that there was some canned food in its' pantry, being very hungry, we decided to heat up some canned soup and pasta, needing to recover from our mental trauma caused by yesterday's mine challenge/insanity. Realizing that we were technically stealing, having broken into the house and eating their food, we decided to leave the owners a note of thanks and 20 dollars—(granted, we could not have found a motel and eaten for three people that cheap but we were on a very limited budget).

"Thank you very much for your unknowing hospitality. We were lost, it was dark and very cold, and the use of your beautiful cabin was the epitome of graciousness—frankly your cabin saved our butts. Please accept this small dollar token of our appreciation." Jim, always the clever wordsmith, wrote.

Leaving the house (locking their window and refolding all their blankets), we realized that we still needed to find our way back to our car. Not wanting to be forced to return to the mine and ascend that vertical shaft, we naturally decided to follow the snow covered road back through the trees in what we hoped would be the right direction. Unfortunately, we discovered we were in a small valley and the road soon climbed up a steep hill which wasn't great for our aching leg muscles.

Nearly an hour later we found ourselves post holeing in deep snow along what appeared to be a ridge line and we noticed, far down below, a highway (presumably the one we had taken the previous day to where we parked the car and hiked up to the entrance of the mine).

"Why don't we leave this road and climb down this slope directly down to the highway," John said.

"It looks awfully steep and nasty—the snow is so deep it might move, causing an avalanche," Jim rightly worried.

"Lets do it," I stupidly replied and down we went, running down a couple of hundred meters of snow at least three feet deep (with some larger drifts), falling, jumping, leaping, and laughing—covered with snow, we finally spilled out onto the highway (no cars) and, as we had avoided an avalanche, we high-fived each other, congratulated ourselves on having survived what for us was an amazing adventure. It took about twenty minutes for us to walk down the road and find our parked car covered in snow.

A few years later the same team of (yes, Dumb, Dumber and Dumbest—Jim, John and Andy were back at it)—trying to find adventurous experiences that would top the previous ones. This time we became spelunkers (cave explorers) and since we were on another semester break and all three of us back in St. Louis, we decided to try and find a cave that I had read about where no one, (at least at that time), had discovered the end of.

Missouri is a state with many caves, some with huge caverns, with enormous limestone stalactites and stalagmites, funneling through the limestone, some of which had never been fully explored. In fact one of the larger caves had provided a hideaway for the famous outlaw Jesse James. I had explored a few small caves but really never spent much time trying to find my way in a large, unexplored cave and certainly wasn't a knowledgeable spelunker, nor were we well equipped or prepared.

But being somewhat naïve and, yes, perhaps insanely driven towards adventure, we drove down looking for a cave known as the "Granny Baker Cave," named apparently after the woman who had owned the property where it was located. I had read about the cave in a book I had checked out of the library that identified the where-abouts of most of the caves in Missouri. No one had ever found the end of Granny Baker cave!

So, following the directions we headed southwest from St. Louis, towards Rolla, not having told anyone where we were going and after about an hour and a half drive (following a rather poor map) we found ourselves driving down a dirt road, reaching a point mentioned in the book and we started walking across a field, heading up into a wooded hill side.

After nearly an hour's search in the woods, climbing up through nasty underbrush and fallen limbs, (truly "bushwhacking," as there was no trail), in 90 degree plus weather, finding nothing resembling a cave, almost ready to quit the search, totally frustrated, we finally stumbled upon a very large opening (about 15 feet high and 50 feet wide) which looked more like an overhang near the bottom of a cliff than an entrance to a cave. However, after reading the book's description of the entrance we concluded that we had indeed found the Granny Baker Cave.

Were we prepared? Hardly, as we did not have any food, nor had we brought any climbing gear or any additional clothing. We were dressed in work out shorts, T- shirts and jogging shoes but in we went. Was this an adventure or just plain stupid? Probably it was a little bit of both. Frankly, we didn't have a clue about caves, not understanding where there might be potential dangers (collapsing roofs, deadly currents, getting lost, rabid bats, etc.)—we were total novices but happy to be out, facing another adventure. At least we weren't climbing a 1000 feet down an ancient ladder with rotten wooden slats.

So, we soon discovered a tunnel with a creek trickling out and we entered the cave which at that point had a roof nearly 20 feet high and the tunnel was nearly the same width. The water was cold and when we started about knee deep. We followed this tunnel probably about a quarter of a mile, which took about a half hour, stumbling along, before discovering a large room with multiple tunnels leading off in many different directions. We decided to continue following the water and soon (another couple of hundred yards) discovered that our tunnel was getting smaller and the water deeper.

About an hour later and about a mile or so further we were struggling to walk in water over our waists and the cave shaft had become even smaller—perhaps 12 feet wide and 10 feet high. Just about that time we were surprised to see a couple of bats fly by us at the speed of baseball going past your head—apparently they had heard us and had come to investigate who was invading their home, disturbing their peace. The bats did not hover above us but just blew by as though they were heading out of the cave. Soon there were others and one came so close that I felt its' soft wing brush my face.

"Do you think we should continue what with all these bats?—I've read that they often become rabid." Jim said.

"Let's keep going and see if we can find where these bats are coming from—they may have another large room," I suggested, ignoring Jim's concern.

So after walking nearly another half mile down this cavern the roof had dropped to just slightly above our heads by a foot or so. All of a sudden there were many bats, hanging on the roof of the cave, flapping their wings around us and squeaking like the rodents they are. Rounding another bend (there were many—hundreds) we now were in a very narrow cave with the water above our shoulders and the roof had lowered much nearer the water level. The problem with this was that this seemed to be the place where the bats lived and they were not happy with our invading their space, as they bombed around us. As ugly bats (aren't they called "flying rats?") hung only a few feet above our heads, unhappy that we had not found the "end of the tunnel," but unwilling to continue any further in the deeper water, facing angry bats, and the tunnel becoming smaller, we reluctantly turned around and headed back towards the large room we had discovered earlier.

Arriving back in this auditorium, seeing many bats flitting around near our heads, John and I decided to explore one of the other tunnels (the second largest one) that ran in a different direction than the one we had just exited.

"If you guys don't mind, I think I will just wait for you here—maybe sit down for awhile. That experience wore my butt out," Jim said.

"No problem—we'll explore this smaller cave and probably be back in no more than an hour—or two," I responded.

So, we left our buddy, sitting in the mud (or so we thought), and headed down the next biggest tunnel but in a slightly different direction than we had just returned from. This tunnel was much tighter and with less head room, but no water, and it wove around in various directions with a few sub tunnels going in even more directions.

"We should build some rock cairns so we know the way back," John suggested.

"Good idea, we sure don't want to get lost down here—it might be days before they discover our car and figure out that we're up here in Granny Baker," I replied, as we had told no one where we were going.

After squeezing, ducking, and climbing (at least there were no bats) through this shaft for about an hour, leaving cairns at every possible place where we might make the wrong turn, we angled up into a much smaller cavern that came to an abrupt end in a tiny room. We figured it was the end until we looked up, seeing a vertical shaft going straight up what appeared to be at least 30 feet higher with perhaps another horizontal cavern running off from above.

Naturally, since both John and I liked to climb, we decided to test ourselves by climbing up the "chimney" by jamming our feet against the other side and pushing ourselves up with our arms, grabbing onto whatever was available, helping us up. Finally, reaching the top we discovered that there was only a very narrow horizontal shaft which, with our fading flashlights, looked very hazardous. So, we decided to abort the mission, turn around and go back and get Jim to then exit from the Cave.

25

Upon arriving in the large room, (Jim had heard us coming for some time) Jim said, "Where the hell have you guys been? I've been sitting here on this pile of bat dung being bitten by beetles for well over an hour."

"Sorry about that but we found a climbing challenge that we just couldn't resist," I said.

So, we headed out, exiting the Granny Baker Cave about a half hour later, noticing bright red bites all over Jim's legs (he had clearly had an ugly time waiting for us). Later, back at the University, Jim, seeing his bites were swollen and infected, would be forced to go to the infirmary to get shots in fear of getting rabies. It was a good month before his legs cleared up but now, so many years later, I'm sure, having survived, he is glad that he had those two strange adventures with his two crazy buddies.

Many years later (in my late fifties, still trying to find acceptable levels of risk, near to the finish of climbing all of Colorado's fifty four 14,000 foot mountains, I was climbing Capital Peak, one of Colorado's top five most difficult 14,000+ foot peaks, with a guide, when we came to a place (down a small gully to work around a sub peak known as K2) when I immediately sensed danger—the gully, short and steep, was full of loose rocks, about 15 feet down to a cliff below, dropping nearly a thousand feet.

"Don't you think we should rope up here?" I asked.

"No, just follow me and put your feet where I put my feet," said the guide rather cavalierly.

Despite worrying that I was 210 lbs. and he was only about 150 lbs., which might have a different impact on the rocks, I followed him, feeling very vulnerable, worrying about a misstep and all of a sudden the rock beneath me (the same one the guide had stepped on) moved and slid down the gully. I frantically grabbed for the nearest rock, thinking that if it moved I was a dead man. Fortunately, that rock didn't move and I was able to continue on.

Moments later we reached the "crux" of the climb, a slab of rock, known as the "Knife Ridge," about fifty feet across, the ridge, in places, no wider than a few inches, falling steeply down hundreds of feet on either side but having numerous footholds of solid rock. Here the guide decided to rope me up but instead of crossing the Knife first himself and then belaying me off of a solid connection, he just jumped onto the other side of the wall, assuring me that "if you fall, you can't pull me up and over this ledge because of the leverage"—so, despite our weight difference, we were sort of belaying each other.

"I'm not worried about me falling, I'm worried about you falling," I said.

The guide didn't seem to appreciate my humor but we moved forward and gained the summit about a half hour later—I sat there sucking in deep breaths, feeling thankful that I had survived another frightening experience but worrying about the climb down. The following year I would read about a climbing instructor, a man who had climbed all 54 fourteen thousand foot peaks twice, giving a lecture on climbing safety to a group of teenagers, standing in that same gully, who had fallen to his death when the rocks he was standing on moved.

There was the time that I was climbing North Maroon, with my wife, Cindy (also a gung-ho climber) one of Colorado's most challenging mountains (another top five), and when I reached the so called "Crux," position, a narrow notch to climb up, maybe 20 feet above a small ledge (about two feet wide) with a drop of hundreds of feet below. I watched our guide climb up the "chimney" without being roped and I thought to myself that what he had done took absolutely no athletic ability. Having reached the top of the gully, the guide, preparing a belay, suggested I rope up but I said no and before he could object I began climbing up the notch.

This was clearly a case when my athletic ego had gotten in the way of my brain—the reason I had hired the guide in the first place was for safety (mostly to be sure of the route and dangerous crux positions) and here I was rejecting his advice, thinking I could do it without being roped up. Fortunately, I was lucky (no rocks moved) despite being so stupid. Cindy, who had started to cry but overcame her fear (one of life's great natural highs) although roped, also ignored the guides advice, finding her own way. Despite our stupidity, we both felt the exhilaration from climbing North Maroon and it stayed with us for weeks.

Rereading this chapter I realize that many readers might think that I wasn't a very caring person, putting many of my friends in extremely precarious positions. Obviously, the thrill of adventure had clouded my judgment and I was somewhat careless in not being better prepared, nor giving better guidance to my friends. Looking back, however, I am very happy that I had these adventures (granted nothing like climbing Everest, traversing the Antarctica or canoeing the Amazon) but to us city folk they were extremely stimulating. We had discovered that overcoming a fear can be an extraordinary adrenalin rush. Obviously, we were very fortunate that no one was badly hurt on any of our "adventures."

After reading this chapter to my son I asked him what he thought about it.

"Well, Dad, I have to admit that my first reaction to it was that if you had died in your teens, taking such crazy risks, that Amy (his sister) and I would never have been born and our children, your five grandchildren also wouldn't be here." Life is good!

Chapter 3

OUR MENTORS

We are lucky in our lives, if we find a mentor, someone usually older, who helps us find our unique way, that individualistic, all our own, this is our destiny, truly our blissful path—a person who pushes us to reach our potential but also supports and encourages us in times of stress and trouble.

Most of us, whether we appreciate it or not, find our first, and perhaps most powerful, mentors to be our parents. They guide us through all the trials and tribulations along our journey into adulthood and we often don't even understand, or appreciate, what powerful and positive forces they have been in our lives.

It is interesting how sons often follow their father's footsteps into their profession. My son was amazed at how many of his friends at Dartmouth became what their fathers are—doctors, lawyers, businessman, teachers, politicians, whatever. Clearly a majority chose their fathers professions. Is this because the fathers pushed them or encouraged them into their profession or is it just because they admired their fathers so much that they wanted to mimic them? Or is it because they want to finally get their father's approval, or is it because they are competitive and want to out perform, to be even more successful than their fathers, such motive resulting from some unresolved anger, insecurity or frustration or because they had a knack for being good at what their father was good at?

I'll stop playing amateur psychologist here but suffice it to say there are far too many possible motives to characterize here, but bottom line; our parents are powerful influences in our lives.

My dad, William Mair Russell, who immigrated across the ocean from Scotland when he was eleven years old, to move to Flint, Michigan made an enormous contribution to the way I think. He taught me how to work hard (we were required to do various chores around the house such as lawn mowing, weed picking, leaf raking, dish washing and keeping our beds neatly made each day and our rooms neatly set up—these were daily rituals that could not be shirked.

Granted, these weren't exactly difficult tasks but if I failed to perform them it would mean a spanking with Dad's favorite belt. So, he taught me about being responsible, about being someone that people could count on. Of course, being just a kid, I occasionally screwed up and neglected something but I certainly learned that there would be a consequence for bad behavior. He taught my brother and me early about accountability.

The even more powerful influence on my life was from my mother, Esther, whose constant message to her boys was for them to learn to become self reliant, independent, confidently able to deal with the real world out there on their own.

I certainly have to include my brother, Will, a person who always showed me the way, teaching me to stand up for my rights, to always remember to be fair and truthful in my dealings with other people. Will gave me a new appreciation for the word "determination." He redefined it, as he became one of the youngest people in the state of New York to become a licensed Ham Radio operator and learn to fly airplanes at an early age.

It is not necessary that your mentor be older, although that is the normal case. When I am asked to give a speech of a motivational nature to young people, I always stress the importance of being very careful who they pick as their friends, especially after they have left the family home, whether to go to work, to college or the military—on their own journey to finding themselves. It is almost certain that they will meet people who they find very attractive, or interesting, maybe even seductive, in their style or outspokenness or eccentric behavior, people who are rebellious, rejecting many of society's theories of proper behavior but some of those people should be avoided—being good at picking the right friends is critical.

Since most of us are generally raised with a lot of rules, (do this, don't do that, keep you nose clean, etc.) it can be exciting to meet someone who doesn't follow the rules, turning his or her back to the norm—beware of these people, they can entice you into a lot of trouble.

I'm not saying, that youngsters shouldn't question and test the wisdom of their elders and just blindly go follow every goal or value they have been taught but be careful—most of the old school values are still being passed on down, generation after generation, because they are so valid.

Society can, and does, get better as our children find new and improved ways to do things—important things like how to raise children (adjusting the degrees of freedom and discipline); the time spent with family versus career; how to be a good friend who can be counted on in times of need; helping our governments and our legislators to find that elusive perfect way of setting rules that govern our society and its people in the challenge of the care and feeding of all those living in our nation without restricting the freedoms of individual rights and expression—certainly daunting tasks.

These are complex issues and a good mentor will not ask you to not challenge tradition, to not question the norm and ask why—but he or she will ask you to respect the old school values that are so difficult to refute. These values are sometimes thought of as trite but only because they are so true and athletic challenges have reconfirmed to me the importance of the traditional values or attitudes.

Values or attitudes such as maintaining one's intensity; sustaining your concentration; being totally driven and disciplined; exerting maximum effort; refusing to quit when things get difficult or painful (playing hurt); striving to excel when things are going bad; and most importantly, never complaining and always having a good attitude— these concepts will take you a long way. Hey, we all know this stuff, right? But sometimes it's just good to remind ourselves of what it takes to enjoy this life.

A coach once told me that the key to success is to "Think big, work hard and have a dream," and yes, that was my mother's mantra. You can control all three and two, thinking big and having a dream are pretty much the same thing. But hey, it works—try it and remember the most important of the three is the "work hard."

How many people do you know who work seven days a week, 24 hours a day, with a good attitude who aren't happy, let alone successful? Yes, of course, there are people who get lucky, win big in Vegas or a lottery, receive a huge inheritance from their parents that they didn't earn—yes, things like that can happen but for the rest of us—we must do the best we can.

One of my key goals as an athlete was to leave the field believing that I gave every thing I had, that I gave the maximum effort, every single play—win or lose. It was a difficult goal, one that I never quite achieved, but it was certainly a worthwhile objective. There was always some play where I could have done more, tried harder, executed a technique better, anticipated a play more accurately, been more patient, etc. When you really care, you become a perfectionist. After a game I would tend to dwell on what I did wrong versus what I did right.

I also think we all have to be careful how we define success. Is success being rich or being famous? I don't think so. My definition of success is to reach a place in your life where you feel content, self-realized, and happy with where you find yourself. Granted, reaching this point in one's life can be very difficult. Chuck Noll, the brilliant Steelers coach used to tell us that, "life is a journey and you never arrive." What's important is the quality of the journey, not the destination or as some say, "There is no finish line." Others say that the "journey is the destination."

There are many people who are both rich and famous, who own a lot of fancy "stuff" (huge mansions, Corporate Jets, speedy cars, big yachts, expensive paintings, beautiful furniture, etc.), and have all the appearance of being successful but are still unhappy. I believe the reason they are unhappy is because they're too much about what they own and not enough about what they do. If you're not careful, what you own, will own you. Like they say, the two happiest days when you own a boat are the day you bought it and the day you sold it, the latter being the best.

When we are lying on our death beds I don't believe we will give a damn about what we owned—no, it will all be about the life experiences we have had, what we have accomplished and the people we have done it with: those who have loved and helped us, our mentors, and remembering our journey through the challenges and adventures of life, whatever they may have been—it won't be about the "stuff" we have owned.

Most of the successful athletes I have known were totally driven to succeed and worked hard to reach the levels they achieved. What caused these men to be so driven? Was it a lesson taught by a parent or a teacher or a coach or mentor? Or is it, as the Buddhists say, all about the devil ego, the need to separate oneself from the crowd, or just some aggressiveness, a combative instinct, that's part of their genetic makeup, something they were born with? I suspect it is a combination of all of the above and thank God for giving us strong egos, egos that push us to realize our abilities and potentials. I suspect, however, that ego driven experiences, particularly if driven by some deep seeded insecurity will probably be far less meaningful when we look back on our lives than some simple act of kindness or helping a child find his or her way.

Thinking back on my journey through childhood, high school, college and the business world, I realize just how fortunate I have been to have always found myself surrounded by super talented and driven people. These people always set a good example and pushed me to be better—of course I must give myself some credit. I was smart enough to choose the friends who challenged me to be better and consciously avoided those who tempted me to get in trouble.

Going through rush week for the fraternity program at Missouri University, prior to the start of my first college term, I met a person who would have a profound influence on my life. His name was Don Wainwright and, like me, he was entering the university on a football scholarship. His father had been a Sigma Chi, so Wainwright was what's known as a legacy. He was a good-looking fellow, sort of the Greek God type, tall, blond, handsome and muscled. He was a good student and also a decent jock—so, naturally, the fraternity was rushing him hard to join.

We stood there talking about the upcoming freshman football challenge and soon realized that we had a lot in common. When asked if I was going to join the Sigma Chi house, I told him that I thought that it seemed to me that it would be preferable to live in the college dorm room at least for the first semester so that we could concentrate on the two most important things in our life at that time—football and our studies. I believed we didn't need the hassle of fraternity hazing our first semester—that we would already be part of a team and we didn't need a second team (a pledge class) so soon. It would be better to avoid too much social life until we had these two, more important challenges under control. Amazingly, since we had only met a few hours before, we agreed to room together at the freshman dorm, at least through the first semester.

Well, that was one of the few times that I influenced Don's life but he would become a profound and powerful influence on mine. Wainwright wasn't a hugely gifted athlete, more the type that succeeds because of his attitude, his drive and effort. I realized the first day of the semester that Wainwright meant business and would demand that his roommate also make a total commitment.

After breakfast at the athletic dining hall, before our first afternoon practice, he urged me to meet him at our dorm room after my last class, so that we could get ourselves "psyched up and ready to rumble."

When I returned to our dorm room, I found Don banging his head against the wooden closet door. Noticing my arrival, he spun around and delivered a forearm shiver into the cement block wall. Moments later, sitting on the two beds positioned against each wall with only a five-foot aisle in between (the head of the beds abutting up against two small desks) facing each other, we tossed a football back and forth.

"Russ today is our first college football practice. We must go out there and give everything we have—go all out, execute the best damn practice we've ever had in our lives. It is critical that we impress the coaches the very first day that we are the kind of athletes they want—totally committed, willing to pay any price, driven to excel, and fearless," Don said.

"Don, it's just a practice—don't worry about it, we'll do just fine," I said.

"No, you don't understand, this is the moment I've been waiting for my entire life. We're going to kill ourselves today to show those coaches that we mean business—we will not be denied," Don said.

I sat there, throwing the ball back and forth, noticing that Don, far too stiff, was dropping too many, thinking to myself that I had selected a wild roommate, one who I would discover would push me to be the very best I was capable of. It was like living with your coach.

That day at practice, I watched Don drive himself to be successful, diving into runner's legs with absolutely no regard for his own safety, leaping for high passes, driving himself to exhaustion—it was clear to everyone that he was wild, maybe even a little nuts, totally unrelenting in his desire to prove his heart, if not his talent. Watching him make this absolutely total commitment inspired me, I think almost subliminally, and I began to try harder.

That night, sore and exhausted after a three-hour practice, sitting at our desks with our backs to each other, studying, I realized that I wasn't paying any attention to what I was reading and decided that I'd try to find a free hour the next day at the Library to complete the homework—I was just too tired to care.

As I pushed back my chair, Wainwright said, "Where do you think you're going Russell—get back at that desk and keep studying. We will study every night until 11:00 pm, or however much longer it takes to get our assignments done, and we will be the top student athletes on the team."

You might think I'd just tell him to go to hell, but, I could hear my mother, Esther (the top student in her high school class and at Oberlin College), imploring me to study harder, and I knew that Don was right—after all, it was unlikely I would ever make a living playing pro football (frankly, it had never occurred to me). I'd need that degree and studying harder was the way to get it.

Don and I both made the first team on that freshman squad (in those days first year players were not allowed to play varsity—not that we were ready to) and we both played reasonably well. When I scored two touchdowns in our opening game against Iowa State, running a punt and kickoff back on long runs, Wainwright, perhaps sensing my euphoria, couldn't resist commenting to me on the bus drive back to Columbia.

"Damn, Russell, I can't believe how lucky you are—you just aren't that tough. If it wasn't for the rest of us, busting our butts, to block for you, you wouldn't have done anything—don't forget it Buddy. This is a team game," he said.

"Hey, Don, I appreciate those efforts," I said, but I was soon thinking about a couple of good moves I had made to avoid the Iowa State tacklers.

Don and I became close friends and roomed together at the Sigma Chi house (we joined mid year). Towards the end of our first semester, as we were preparing for final exams, Don wanted to know how I was doing. When I explained that I was having trouble with algebra, he said, "Don't worry about it—we'll lock ourselves in the basement study room and I'll teach you the whole damn course in one weekend—it'll be a good refresher for me. Don was an engineering major and taking advanced algebra at the same time as I was taking the basic course.

The algebra final was at 7:40 am on Monday and Don and I went down to the fraternity's basement study room early Saturday morning. Don had a found a large blackboard, upon which he began writing basic algebraic formulas. He would then sit back and watch while I tried to solve the problems and I discovered that his patience was very short, finding myself covered with chalk as he frequently bounced the eraser off my head. He would then jump up and loudly explain algebraic logic as he forced my hand to rewrite the solution.

We worked all that night and all through the next day and that next night and Monday morning, having been awake for nearly 48 hours, I walked into that classroom, totally exhausted, but also confidant that I finally understood algebra. The professor was astounded when I answered every question correctly, maxing the final exam, getting the top grade on that final exam in the class, and moving my over all grade up from a D, prior to the test, to a B.

Don had berated me, insulted me, pushed me but never once, during that weekend was I ever distracted or bored. I now realize that in High School I was probably dealing with a problem of a lack of concentration, an attention deficit disorder that had caused me to do badly—I just didn't pay attention. The only place I had never lacked focus was playing sports. Don had made a game out of the learning process; challenging me much the way coaches had all my life. Guess what, all of a sudden, just by being forced to concentrate and focus, algebra became easy.

Obviously, anyone is blessed to find a friend like Don Wainwright, whose company, Wainwright Industries (an auto parts supplier to the auto industry), not surprisingly, won the highly prestigious 1994 small business category Malcolm Baldridge Award for top quality in the U.S. given by the U.S. National Institute of Standards and Technology—the only quality award that is actually awarded by the President of the U.S.

People like Don Wainwright help us keep focused on our goals and force us to give it our best. Where do you need friends and competent mentors the most? The classic, macho analogy, is to ask who, if you had to be in a foxhole in a battle for your life, would you want to be with you? Despite realizing that saying Marilyn Monroe is a cute answer, she certainly would not be the person you'd most want to have with you in such a life-threatening situation.

Having never been in a foxhole, pinned down by enemy fire, I can only imagine what it would feel like and, if, heaven forbid, I'm ever in that situation, I would want Don Wainwright in there with me as he's smart, tough, brave and resourceful. He also convinced me to finish our ROTC, causing me to spend two great years as a Lieutenant in the Army in Germany which I wouldn't trade for two more years in the NFL. Of course, Wainwright, forever the warrior, might draw unwanted fire at our position, so, maybe, I'd prefer to have Jim Card (another roommate and mentor), a thinker, who might find a way to do our job without getting blown-up. My other Mizzou teammate, Jack Musgrave, might figure out a way to "settle" the dispute and Jeff Kendall, my business partner for so many years, would figure out a way to negotiate a "win-win" resolution. Don Rea, on the other hand, would probably hold out for a lengthy battle of wits and my old pal, Sam Zacharias would make friends with the enemy, figure out their insurance needs, and we'd all be OK. For those of you readers that have actually been in a foxhole, men who have fought valiantly for our country, risking their lives please excuse my facetiousness—but I'd take any of my old buddies mentioned above in a tough situation.

But I will give myself some credit for having the sense to follow Wainwright's advice and stick to it. I had other friends who chose to go another direction, have a beer, chase the cute coeds rather than study and then wondered why they failed and were forced to leave school.

I had other friends in college who helped me be better. Once, after taking a whipping in ping-pong from one of my fraternity brothers who was a straight A student, he said, "Russell, you confuse me. You are one of the most naturally competitive people I have ever met in sports, whether it's on the football field, or just shooting hoops or even playing ping-pong, but when it comes to your scholastic challenges you don't care if someone beats you. Why don't you pick a friend and compete in the classroom?" To me that was a unique concept, feeling competitive in my studies, was something I had never considered.

So, my other Sigma Chi roommate, Jim Card, a great pitcher on Missouri's number one rated baseball team, also majoring in economics, and I decided to compete in the classroom. We studied together and then made small wagers as to whom would "win," have the best grade, on the next exam or essay. It definitely caused me to increase my focus and my intensity and, surprise, surprise, my grades jumped up from C+ to A–, all because I tried a little harder. Jim would often beat me but it still felt good to be in the game, trying hard and doing better.

Jim and I became friends with our English composition (writing) professor, Paul Doherty, and frequently visited him at his apartment where he would tell us stories about famous authors, such as Hemingway, Faulkner, Dostoyevsky and Twain. Paul, a good athlete himself, would amaze us with his ability to drop kick a football onto his bunk bed from across the room, a technique I was totally unable to master. Paul encouraged both of us to take more literature courses and to achieve more academically.

Another college friend who helped me learn how to study more effectively was Ron Lurie. Ron and I had played football together in high school (he was a year behind me) and he also came to Mizzou with an athletic scholarship. I knew that Ron was a very good student, basically your 4 point, top grade always but I only learned his secret when, as a senior in my final semester, we took the same course, Business Law A.

Ron and I sat right next to each other in the front row of the class and I noticed that he wrote constantly, taking profuse notes during the one hour lecture, whereas I would only write down what I thought was most important, omitting things I didn't believe were significant to the lecture—Lurie wrote everything down, everything.

Now Ron, a junior, was still forced to deal with football practice every day, whereas I was through with my college football (my last senior football year behind me) with my only requirement that I lift some weights to prepare for my first year with the Steelers. For some reason I felt that my most important task was to become a better student—at least prove to myself that without the demands of football practice (my previous excuse) that I could finally become a good student.

So, anyway, Lurie calls me and suggests that we get together to go over our notes and study together for the first exam, and I agreed. When we got together Ron, handing me his notebook, said, "Go to page 14, I'm a little shaky on that section. Surprised that he took the time to number his pages, I flipped to his notes and he began to reiterate those notes, verbatim, without error for the next five pages.

I was surprised, never thinking that the secret to achieving top grades was simply to memorize everything in great detail.

I would take that concept to another level, not only memorizing all my (now much more detailed notes) notebooks but also memorizing verbatim the explanations of key phrases, legal concepts, etc., from books in the library. When I would write in my "bluebook" I would put quotation marks on the explanation, and then put footnotes explaining where the expert's analysis came from at the bottom of the page. I was soon getting the top grade in the class, all because Ron Lurie taught me to memorize in great detail.

You know, one of the problems is that we all tend to want to work on what we are already good at, instead of working on what we are not good at. In football, athletes who were already good at catching the ball, but not so adept at running their routes, would work on catching the ball. Hey, it is human nature to want to feel good about what you are doing and to avoid doing what makes you feel uncomfortable. In my case, I needed to work harder on my scholastic challenges than on my athletic techniques, which, seemed to come much more naturally. Blocking and tackling were easy compared to solving algebraic formulae and memorizing Chemistry charts.

When I got into the business world, I met Pete Kalkus, a young Harvard Business School grad, while working at Oliver Tyrone Corporation, a Pittsburgh developer of major office towers. Kalkus was there to analyze new markets and do feasibility studies for new buildings. I was there to help manage office buildings, such as the old Oliver Building, (i.e., make sure the tenant's windows were cleaned on time—not exactly why I got my MBA). Peter, who left after the first year to become a top executive at DLJ Real Estate, taught me to think big, to climb out of the box, to dare to do something that my father hadn't done—to start my own business.

"Why would I start my own company—I'm doing just fine where I am?" I asked.

"Andy, let me make something perfectly clear—I believe in a basic principal that I think you should also subscribe to, which is that it is better to own a company than it is to work for a company."

"Why?"

"Because you can have more control over your life—greater freedom to chase your own goals," Peter said.

"Maybe, but remember I'm still playing football and how would the business survive when I'm off at training camp?"

"Look, you make your Steeler salary over 5-6 months right?"

"Yes."

"It's enough money to last you the entire year—right? Most people can't start their own businesses because they have to get a paycheck each month to pay their bills. You have the luxury of taking a chance for six months. If it doesn't work, what have you lost?" Kalkus said.

Finding his argument compelling I agreed to start my own business, a syndication company, get licensed by the SEC to sell securities, raising money for various DLJ real estate deals, put together by Pete Kalkus. It was scary stuff but turned out to be the right career move. That decision turned out to change my life in a significant way—what if I hadn't listened?

Just as in football, I was in for a long run of good luck, with tremendous teammates who helped me enormously. I definitely had the right partners (Sam Zacharias, Jeff Kendall and Don Rea) and their advice was often genius.

Sam would help me keep my business alive while I was off at training camp and practice. We would fly around the world many times with our pal Ray Mansfield, making presentations, seeking investors, networking (before we even knew the meaning of the word) and always having fun.

Don Rea, Chuck Gomulka, Steve Frobouck and Charlie Zappala would help me learn the investment banking business and we would ultimately grow to where our expertise and reputation was good enough to be selected as a lead underwriter for the Pa. Turnpike Commission and the new Pittsburgh Airport. Don Rea, Jeff Kendall and Steve McCarthy would show me how to build an operating company, Liberty Waste Services, which would grow large enough to be purchased by a public company, Allied Waste.

Don, who created some wonderful deals with his superb financial engineering skills, would show me how to stand up for what I believe in and when to draw a line in the sand and say, "no". Don had fought hard, against Charlie, Chuck and me, on many occasions, usually over whether we should agree to the opponent's, the other side's position, and would prove, over and over, that he was right to stick with his convictions on what was fair in negotiations with our business partners.

Jeff, a complete business super star, would drive himself unbelievably hard and close over 100 acquisitions in a ten year time span. This allowed Don to spend more time watching his sons play baseball at Duke and Pitt and gave me the opportunity to go with my bliss—to travel all over the world with old pals and to climb mountains. Jeff's success was a performance every bit as gutsy and impressive as any I had seen on the field.

Okay, so you can see that I've been blessed with good mentors, good partners and good friends—all in the same people. Be ever vigilant, choose your friends carefully and then listen to them.

If you'll bear with me I'd like to take this opportunity to thank just a few of those I haven't mentioned, people who have helped me on my journey and helped make it more meaningful and enjoyable—family, mentors and friends: people like Ray Mansfield, Chuck Puskar, Nancy Russell, Ed Tussey, Walt Bent, Bill Comfort, Jack Coleman, Tom Bob, Jerry Prado, Ernie Buchman, Ron Puntil, Chuck Queenan, Bob Arnold, Art Silverman, Carl Trosch, Tom Reich, Murray Litmans, Dick Simmons, Jerry Fogel, Bob Davis, Al Onofrio, Dan Devine, and Chuck Noll.

There are far too many people who have positively impacted my life, particularly in the world of athletics but I have already mentioned many of those above. In the end I have been enormously lucky to have so many wonderful mentors, coaches and friends who have helped me find my way. Thank you people, I'm forever indebted.

Chapter 4

THE SUPER BOWL YEARS

With our current team, having just won another Super Bowl last year (2008—for a Steelers six pack), hoping they can win another in '09, we still have to realize how difficult it is to win back to back championships, despite having all the ingredients to win, we all must remember just how difficult it is to go all the way. The Steelers of the 70's lost too many big games, games that we should have won but, for many reasons (failure to make the big play with the game on the line; key players being injured, player and coaching mistakes; etc.

Obviously we Steelers fans enter the 2009 season with extremely high expectations. Is this fair? We have an exciting new coach, Mike Tomlin, (the youngest coach to ever win a Super Bowl), will approach this coming season much as did Chuck Noll and Bill Cowher, with very high expectations—it is in their nature. Should we only be satisfied if the Steelers again go all the way to the Super Bowl Championship? Probably not but that's what people want and expect.

Those teams in the 70's spoiled us, winning those 4 out of 6 Super Bowls, having eleven players in the Pro Bowl in the same year (1975)—eight of us on the defense. We should be realistic in our expectations for this year's team. Lots of bad things can happen (like injuries, freak bounces of the ball—i.e., perhaps the ball will bounce the wrong direction this year, back into an opponents hands, instead of how last year it may have found a teammates hands, controversial officiating, etc.)

Our Steelers have Ben Roethlisberger, a strong, gun-slinging quarterback, much in the style of Terry Bradshaw, unafraid, daring to go deep, wanting the game on the line, in his hands (which now are adorned with two Super Bowl rings). In Hines Ward he has one of the best receivers the team has had since the great Lynn Swann,

John Stallworth, (both Hall of Famers) and Louis Lipps. The all-important offensive line should be improving which should help a highly motivated Willie Parker and Rashard Mendenhall rack up some more yards. That and the accompanying combination of quality back up receivers and strategic versatility all have the potential to consistently move the ball.

On the defensive side, always strong, they should be better than ever, (currently number One) especially if Troy Polamalu doesn't get hurt, as he is a great play maker, certainly in the league of former Safety greats, like All Pros Clendon Thomas, Mike Wagner, Donnie Shell, Glenn Edwards and Rod Woodson.

Coach Tomlin has the coaching assistants who have the technical expertise to again take the team all the way. Talk about a team that is poised—these guys have all the tools necessary to win it all once again.

Of course, standing in their way is a lot of also very good teams. Today's NFL is better balanced than those of the 70's. It is nearly impossible to predict who will win in the NFL today. For example, no one predicted a few years ago that the four Super Bowl winners (Indianapolis Colts, Baltimore Ravens, New England Patriots, and Tampa Bay Buccaneers) would win—none were picked to be even close to being the Super Bowl Champs. This year, 2009, we might again be surprised which team may emerge as the best—but it's still possible that it could be our Stillers.

I understand and appreciate that the current players are tired of reading about the 70's team and don't want to hear about those teams. The ring they won in 2008, after an amazing string of victories, is all theirs. If they are able to survive all the threats to their journey to the top once again, from injuries, mistakes (turnovers), breaks, etc. they will earn a third coveted World Championship ring and it will be all their own.

What was it like back in the 70's after emerging from those terrible 60's? Those of us who played in the 60's (five of us made it to the first Super Bowl—Mansfield, Walden, Bleier, Davis & me) had to deal with the knowledge of how awful we had been (i.e. during a 4 year stretch we had 41 losses out of 56 games, going 1-13 in 1969) and were, just like the fans, ecstatic over the transformation of the team—from a perennial loser to a team very difficult to beat.

Frankly, the old 60's players, were hard to convince, just not able to believe that we had come so far, always expecting that something bad would happen causing us to lose the big game (the ball would bounce the wrong way—after so many losses it becomes hard to believe that you can win). But those young super stars (Greene, Bradshaw, Ham, Wagner, J.T. Thomas, Edwards, Blount, Bleier, Greenwood, White, Holmes, Webster, Harris, Swann, Stallworth and Lambert—well, just too many to mention) had none of those psychological scars, and they were convinced that we could win every game.

What made those teams so special? Chuck Noll, who had assured us we would improve as we learned better techniques, with greater discipline and concentration, finally put together the athletes he wanted in 1972, clearly the quintessential turn-around year, going from perennial loser to a team tough to beat, finally winning our first Division Championship and winning our first ever playoff game against Oakland, with Franco's amazing Immaculate Reception. I believe we were a better team than the Miami Dolphins, who defeated us in the AFC Championship game, but we just didn't get the job done—no excuses and I give Miami credit for their victory.

The following year, 1973, with a cast of wonderful players we once again made the playoffs but were badly beaten by a very good Oakland team—we just hadn't learned what it takes. We weren't making the big plays with the game on the line, defensively or offensively.

Getting ready for that next season, 1974, few experts picked the Steelers to go all the way. But the Steelers had built a dominant defense that could hold the game close until our offense found its rhythm. Our well-balanced offense, with the running game moving the sticks even on third and mid long (normally passing downs—taking enormous pressure off Terry) and a passing game in synch, had a solid year and we again made the playoffs. Of course, you know what happened. We went on to win the Steelers first Super Bowl Championship, beating the Vikings in New Orleans in Super Bowl IX.

Probably the single most important game in the Steeler franchise history was the big playoff win that year against a great Oakland team (who had just defeated the World Champion Miami Dolphins) in Oakland.

With Dwight White and Ernie Holmes playing perhaps their finest games ever (Oakland liked to run to their left, behind All Pros

Upshaw and Shell to our right side) our defense stopped their vaunted running attack and our offense, playing nearly mistake free, scored the points we needed. The key play in that game was Jack Ham's magnificent interception of Kenny Stabler's pass late in the game—assuring us the win. Kenny, perhaps one of the most under-rated quarterbacks of all time (he was phenomenal) having beaten Miami in the final seconds of their game, had winked at me from their huddle, as though he was saying that he was going to do the same thing again—win in the last few seconds, but Hammer made his all time great play.

Flying back to Pittsburgh, celebrating on the flight home, euphoric over that win, it finally dawned on us that we were really capable of winning the whole enchilada, of finally climbing to the top of the mountain (to us the Super Bowl was Mount Everest)—but we truly believed we could climb it.

What was so special about that team? First and foremost, Coach Noll, clearly a genius, and his great staff, understanding all aspects of the game, had taught us that success is in the details, how to work together, to be a team, without petty jealousies, pulling for each other, staying out after practice to help each other perfect our techniques— we all liked and respected each other.

Second, we had a lot of talent at virtually every position. Somehow Coach Noll had taken a group of athletes with widely diverse person-alities (from the eccentricity of Frenchy Fuqua and L.C. Greenwood to Joe Greene's passion for winning, to the cool, awesome compe-tence of Jack Ham, to the hardnosed discipline of young rookie, Jack Lambert to the brilliance of Terry Bradshaw, Franco Harris, Lynn Swann and John Stallworth) and forged us into a symbiotic team, one that would bleed for each other and never give up.

People often ask who the leaders were, often assuming that it might be the middle linebacker or the quarterback. Actually I think leadership is often misunderstood in professional football. It is rare that anyone would voice meaningful, inspirational comments in the huddle or off the field—we were all too busy focusing on our own responsibilities. Sure, players would occasionally pat someone on the back, make an impassioned plea to the team and himself to give it everything but most often leadership was by example only, showing the way, with effort, discipline, class and dignity.

My own judgment of the leaders of those teams is that every player demonstrated leadership in his own unique way, as watching a backup playing hurt on the special teams could inspire a starter.

The key thread, that kept those teams together, was Chuck Noll, seemingly always able to blend the talent with the personalities, rarely saying the wrong thing, keeping us intensely focused, ignoring all distractions (i.e., media). Coach was a great leader and I think it was powerful that we all could tell that his leadership had nothing to do with his own ego, only wanting us to be successful and reach our potential.

I think the players from those teams truly appreciate how difficult it is to go all the way and are far less critical of today's team than probably the average fan. We should have won even more, for example in 1976 (possibly our best team) we were beaten by Oakland when both Rocky Bleier and Franco Harris (both 1000 yard rushers that year) were injured and not able to play in that game. Of course that is our offense's excuse and a good one but we have no excuse for the bad defense we played (perhaps we tried too hard). Bad things can happen that can cause great teams to be beaten.

Unlike the 70's, today's team must deal with salary caps, free agency, new rules, realities (i.e., money) that pull teams apart. The Steelers of the 70's would never have stayed together in today's world, never have won four out of six Super Bowls. It was a wonderful time, but one that is almost impossible to duplicate. Lets appreciate today's team for what they are, an extraordinary group of quality athletes and driven personalities, all striving for the same objective—their next Super Bowl win.

Chapter 5

A MOUNTAIN SLAM

The word "Slam" is often used in many sporting references. Athletes sometimes say that they "slammed" an opponent or, when the effort was relatively easy, that it was a "slam dunk." The word is even used in some card games, referring to a Grand Slam, when the player has won all or most of the cards.

The word graduates to the superlative when we talk about a "Grand Slam," in athletics, where the athlete has won a series of important events, most notably, the winning of the four major PGA events: The Masters, U.S. Open, British Open and the PGA Championship, most recently accomplished by Tiger Woods (although nit-pickers like to point out that he did not do it all in the same year—as though Tiger's task was made easier doing it consecutively over two years).

Tennis also has its Grand Slam where the winner wins a year's Australian Open, Wimbledon, French Open and U.S. Opens—the four Pro Tennis majors. Being the dominant Number One player in the world Roger Federer, despite his brilliance, has not been able to win the tennis Grand Slam. Obviously, those are spectacular golfing and tennis achievements—to win against all the best competitors in the world without any help from teammates in the most difficult and pressure packed events.

In the world of mountain climbing there are two major challenges (sometimes referred to as Grand Slams), the most difficult becoming a member of the club (currently some 14 men) who have climbed the world's fourteen 8000-meter (24,800+ feet) peaks (such peaks as Everest, Annapurna, Nanga Parbat and K2—all 14 being in the Himalayas, ranging from Pakistan, Afghanistan up to Nepal). There are not very many climbers even attempting those mountains because first of all you have to be a world class climber (with all the experience, technical skills and superb conditioning) and secondly you have to be willing to risk your life (primary dangers being killer weather conditions, unstable ice or rock, unpredictable avalanches or unseen glacial crevices—obviously, Tiger Woods has enormous "technical" skill but certainly doesn't risk his life every time he tees it up.

It also helps if you are wealthy (as these expeditions are not inexpensive) or such a climbing celebrity (i.e., Reinhold Messner, arguably the world's greatest climber and the first to climb the 14 Himalayan giants—without oxygen) that sporting companies pay you to promote their gear.

Another major mountain challenge, which is significantly easier than the 8000 meter challenge above, is the so called "Seven Summits" challenge—climbing the highest mountain in all seven Continents: (Kilimanjaro in Africa, McKinley (Denali) in North American (Alaska), Acconcagua in South America (Argentina), Elbrus in Europe, Kosciuszko in Australia, the Vinson Massif in the Antarctica and finally Everest in Asia. This challenge, except for the money and time required to get to these places, is more reachable by the common man or woman, as even Everest isn't considered especially technical but, granted, is still incredibly difficult from a physical challenge (wellness) standpoint (the lack of oxygen, total exhaustion, acute mountain sickness, pulmonary and cerebral edema), avalanche danger and unbelievably dangerous weather. On all those mountains, excepting Kosciuszko, one is definitely putting their life at risk, especially trying to climb Everest, as well as Mt. McKinley, Acconcagua, Vinson Massif and even Kilimanjaro, as an American climber died of pulmonary edema during our family climb of that mountain.

Granted, the so called Seven Summits are not considered any where near as dangerous as the fourteen 8,000 meter peaks (Mount Everest is in both challenges). There may not be a consensus regarding which mountain is the world's most dangerous but it appears that most of the great climbers consider K-2 to be the most difficult but Ed Viesturs, the first American to become a member of the club, climbing all of them without oxygen, considers Anapurna as the most dangerous, due to treacherous ice conditions.

The "Seven Summits" was first accomplished by Dick Bass, a man known more for his businesses acumen and achievements than his athleticism and certainly not, in any one's estimation, including his own, a world-class climber. In fact, he may have been the first one to do it because he was the first one to conceptualize it. However, it should be noted that Bass had an unusually low heart beat and apparently was not as negatively affected by the high altitude's lack of oxygen as most of us are. He also had a dogged determination, returning to Everest a second time, having failed the first time due to weather and medical problems of a teammate.

The only mountain (other than a few small one's in Utah near the ski resort he owns) of any stature that Bass had climbed was the magnificent Swiss Alp, the 15,000+ foot Matterhorn, a significant challenge for non-rock climbers. In fact, he climbed it twice, the second time wearing a tuxedo under his climbing clothing, as he had originally planned to get married on the summit. The plan was to have his bride flown to the top by helicopter but, later cooler heads prevailed, and Bass got married in a Zermatt church immediately following his Matterhorn climb.

Another, much less significant, mountain "Grand Slam" challenge is to climb all fifty-four 14,000 foot peaks (most often referred to as 14ers) in Colorado, obviously much easier and less dangerous than those mentioned above. There are actually 59-14ers in Colorado but 5 don't count, as they are considered too close to other peaks (sub peaks) and without enough vertical drop or distance between them. There are fifteen 14ers in California (Mt. Whitney being the highest in the 48 states), one in Washington (Rainier) and seven mountains over 16,625 feet in Alaska and no others in any other state. But more about the Colorado Grand Slam later.

Apparently mountain climbing attracts certain types of people, those seeking a physical challenge, often pushing themselves to exhaustion, something considered almost unattainable—the harder the better. Such people are sometimes referred to as "Ascenders," (as though that is a personality trait), people who always want to climb above or away from, or possibly to, something.

I guess I'm one of those people but I think I have the condition, (some might consider it a neurosis), under control. It's a little like one wondering if one's an alcoholic, knowing that if he takes one more drink that he's sick. Sometimes I wonder if I can resist that one more mountain challenge.

Why do some people climb mountains, when the vast majority of people would never even consider it? This is a question posed for years by those who can't imagine why one would intentionally do something so massively exhausting, exposing them to extreme cold, lightning, falling and potentially unstable snow (avalanches), let alone putting themselves in risk of serious injury or death from any of those conditions.

I mean, sure, simplistically, one could say that it's because the mountains are so beautiful—which is very true, as they are absolutely spectacular, incredibly awesome, magnificent and majestic—hey, I'm a mountain lover, much preferring mountain scenery to beach front. For example, I believe the most beautiful place in the U.S. is Telluride, Colorado (surrounded by four classic 14ers), not ocean front property.

But, regarding climbing mountains you can actually see them far better from a distance than you can see them when you are standing on the mountain itself. Tigers are beautiful but do we get in their cage and try to caress them. Others might say it's because mountains represent a challenge, perhaps the ultimate test of one's stamina and intestinal fortitude.

When asked that question, George Mallory, the famous British climber who lost his life trying to be the first to ascend Everest, supposedly replied, "Because it is there." Frankly, I suspect, that explanation falls far short of his real reasons but, most likely, Mallory had never asked himself that same question and his answer was the first thing that came to his mind.

Obviously people relish challenges, feeling a great sense of pride when meeting such extreme challenges, the harder the better, and facing dangers. I'm sure that some psychiatrists today might view this "need" to challenge oneself as an illness, something to be treated, perhaps on the side of a bi-polar illness, falling on the manic side. I can imagine some psychiatrists thinking that I should undergo therapy, understand why I find these mountain challenges so seductive, so powerful, so overwhelmingly rewarding and satisfying.

I'm sure a case could be made that people so compelled to meet challenges, take risks and expend all that energy, are doing it to escape from something; their problems, their doubts, their insecurities—always feeling the need to prove something, if only to one's self, knowing that in the world of sport, climbing most mountains would be considered relatively insignificant, in the sense that climbing mountains doesn't require superb hand eye coordination, speed (quickness), or man to man toughness—it's not a competitive sport, as no one is trying to knock you off the mountain, although Mother Nature sometimes seems to try her best to do so but mountain climbers are very tough, as they must overcome extreme obstacles, exhausting challenges and expose themselves to the very real possibility of dying.

Mountains require enormous stamina and mental toughness to overcome the obstacles—overcoming fear is a huge exhilarator.

Obviously people climb mountains for their own reasons, their inner satisfaction, not for fame or money, in a world today where so often professional sports appear to be just about business.

Some may say they climb to stay in shape, as the mountains require a high degree of physical fitness. Actually, I can relate to that explanation because when I retired from professional football two things were clear to me. One, I knew that I needed to find a "hobby" to replace the excitement of football. Two, I thought it wise to give myself a physical goal that would require me to stay in shape, knowing that my doctor telling me that I should stay fit in order to live a few years longer, or to improve the quality of my life, might not give me the impetus to drive myself to remain fit.

When I was playing football, which was nearly 25 years of being forced to stay in shape for the rigors of training camp and the physical challenge of just surviving the game during the season, I had no trouble finding the motivation to find the time for a work out—it was my job.

As mentioned earlier, Ray Mansfield, my best Steelers buddy, and I decided to retire together after the 1976 season, after fourteen years in the league, and we asked ourselves what could we possibly do to replace football. Our businesses (Ray's Insurance, my Investment Banking) were challenging and fun but there was no way those business efforts would replace the passion, the exhilaration and the physical challenge of playing professional football.

Knowing that a lot of former pro athletes become very sedentary, gaining lots of weight, I just knew we needed something more physical—an activity that would force us to work out regularly and stay in shape. We needed a reason, a goal, and a challenge, planned in the future, to force ourselves to work out much the way we had preparing for training camp. Goal orientation had always worked for us.

At first we chose "Adventure Travel," taking on various physical challenges; such things as a non-stop (well, we did take three 15 minute naps) 63 hours, 42 minute, solo, 48 different lakes, 168 mile canoe race in the wild lake country of Northern Minnesota (the Boundary Waters Wilderness) and Canada, called the "Hunter's Island Route (the hardest thing I have ever done);" climbing up and down four steep, grueling days in the Grand Canyon; hiking the Laurel Ridge Trail's 31 miles between Ohio Pyle and Seven Springs on the hottest day of the year (it took us about 14 hours) which just happened to be the same day the Steelers started training camp (yes, for us very symbolic—a rite of passage); and a 220 mile non stop canoe race called the Texas Water Safari, a race down two rivers with lots of obstacles—rapids, trees, snakes, rocks, culverts and even an occasional dam (we failed—not even reaching the half way point) and never went back—shame on us).

Granted, these weren't hugely competitive challenges against well trained athletes, like the Hawaii Triathlon or the Leadville One Hundred—a one hundred mile non stop running race over mountain passes with the average elevation being near 12,000 feet. Nor were our little challenges wildly dangerous adventures such as going into dangerous jungles, crossing deserts, climbing in the high Himalayan Mountains or exploring the ice packs of our polar regions. Such adventures were only in our dreams.

We began referring to our experiences as "gut-tests," exhausting physical challenges that told us we still had it—we weren't just washed up ex-jocks (actually we were, as our wilderness challenges required little, if any, true athleticism, but they reproduced some of the same feelings we had found exhilarating about our football efforts—like the enormous fatigue after the game, where we found ourselves so mellow, without a hint of animosity or a trace of contentiousness—completely at peace with ourselves and others). When you've done your best, given your all, or nearly so, regardless of whether you've won or lost, you feel tranquil, centered and blissful.

Over time (years away from football) however, our so-called "gut tests" became easier and easier, our last being to play eighteen holes of golf with only one six pack of beer—shame on us, as hard is good, easy is bad.

As a young boy I had always loved to climb, almost anything I could find: jungle gyms, ropes, trees, and roofs—anything that appeared ascendable. In fact my parents often received phone calls from neighbors, concerned about my safety, warning them that I was again up on our third story roof. I don't have a clue what drove me to always want to climb things. I guess it was just part of my nature, an impulsive urge that felt very normal and made me happy.

When my family visited our relatives in Denver, Colorado back in the 1940's, we'd often go into the mountains and camp out. Naturally I wanted to climb everything in sight but my parents weren't really into physical challenges, and would always call me back down. Somehow I intuitively knew, way back then, that climbing mountains was something that would make me very happy, but I never asked myself why.

But football got in the way and I didn't get back to the idea of mountain climbing until 1982, when Sam Zacharias, my great friend and earliest business partner, and I went to the Mt. Rainier (Washington state's only 14er) one-day climbing school where we were taught some of the basics—techniques like "self arrest" using one's ice axe and crampons to stop a fall down an icy slope; roping up, proper climbing and breathing techniques, and equipment use. Many years later, I would learn that Ed Viesturs, arguably America's best climber, was there at Rainier (as a young intern) that same year handing out the equipment.

We found the climb of Rainier totally exhausting (9500 vertical feet in two days—5000 up the first day and 4500 up and 9500 down the second day) and I rediscovered how much I loved the blissful mellowness I felt as we drove back to the Seattle Airport that night—very much like our post game football experience (totally exhausted, achy but exhilarated). Sam took the "red-eye" home and I flew to Montana for more hiking, fishing and climbing (much lower elevations) with my family and friends.

It was a few months later (September) that Ray and I decided to climb four Colorado 14ers in the same day, after participating in the Denver Bronco Alumni Golf Tournament. Despite being relatively easy mountains (Mt Democrat, Lincoln, Bross and Cameron—not far from the town of Breckenridge), with no real exposure to a fall, we faced enough challenges (mostly bad weather—it rained, hailed, snowed and the wind blew with 40 or 50 mile an hour gusts causing us to hunker down in our Gortex bivy sacks during a blizzard for some time; a steep scree gully; and lots of large rocks to maneuver around for us to find the experience exactly the right antidote for our post football blahs.

Later, that same month on a business trip around the world with Sam, we decided to climb Mount Olympus in Greece on one of our days off. We found Olympus to be a glorious mountain, enjoying the experience tremendously—because of our busy business schedule, forced to climb it all in the dark.

Flying back to Pittsburgh a few days later, my adventurous spirit satisfied for the moment, it never occurred to me that someday I would attempt the Colorado "Grand Slam." First of all, living in Pittsburgh it would be very difficult to find the time to climb all those mountains. Secondly, we had young children and I wanted to show them the world (we did find time for the family to visit Africa (twice), New Zealand/ Australia, Europe and the Western United States), never returning to the same place for our annual vacations. Although, I realized that being a partner in our own business (Russell, Rea and Zappala) I could probably take off to Colorado for long weekend climbing trips.

Another reason I didn't consider attempting the Slam was that I thought the concept of "peak bagging," to be too ego driven, as though the achiever was setting himself, or herself, apart, to be special or different, bragging about what was accomplished and, in a way, denigrating the mountain. In fact, you don't slam (or bag) anything, as the mountains and the weather can turn very nasty and you certainly never own or dominate anything of those mountains—climbing Rainier, those four 14ers and Mount Olympus had already taught me that the mountains are in charge—they had all given me another lesson in humility, much like the NFL so often dished out. I had discovered the truth in the saying that "the journey is the destination."

In September of 2004, 23 years later, despite the rhetoric in the above paragraph, I had just been fortunate enough to complete the Colorado's 14er Grand Slam, climbing Culebra Peak, which, as 14ers go, was a fairly easy climb, the most difficult aspect of the climb being the fact that the mountain is privately owned and the owners only allow two "expeditions" a year, of 24 people each, organized and led by the Colorado Mountain Club. It took me three years to get on the list and I climbed with my Mizzou buddy, Jerry Fogel, and his brother Guy.

Culebra was fun because it was by far the largest group I had ever climbed with, made up mostly of people passionate about climbing, most of whom had climbed fifty or more, all highly motivated and fairly knowledgeable climbers, some with technical experience. However, with that many people the "logistics" were somewhat more complicated: arranging to meet at 5:30 am (some people were slightly late) at the Catholic Church's parking lot in San Luis, Colorado, a place you'd never find yourself unless you wanted to climb all 54 peaks; our two guides arranging to meet the ranch manager at the locked gate; handing him everyone's CMC permit and liability waiver; keeping the group together (so no one got lost—virtually herding us up the mountain); and staying out of each others way, as we all have our own pace and climbing style; listening to lectures on being environmentally friendly (like the need to transport one's toilet paper out of the ranch).

As I climbed up the mountain, feeling very fortunate to have been chosen as one of the 48 climbers by the CMC allowed to climb Culebra that year, I reflected back on all the wonderful climbs and experiences with so many special people. Mountain challenges are definitely a bonding experience. It is a simple concept—do something difficult together and you will bond, have respect for one another. Do something easy together and it might be "fun" but it will not bond you.

Why did fraternities (before politically correct, wimpy college administrators bared all hazing, no matter how harmless) ask their pledges to go through difficult physical challenges together, such things as standing at attention all night, doing calisthenics until you drop from exhaustion, running relay races in the dark? I believe that the purpose of these activities would bond that class together forever.

Another concept I subscribe to is the theory that if one is experiencing aching muscles or joints (something I and all my ex-teammates have to deal with because of playing all those years in the NFL) that you need to get out there and exercise, to work an injury—the old "use it or lose it," "motion is lotion" and "pain is good," theories.

Typically, I had climbed only one or two 14ers a year, sometimes alone but in most cases, with a climbing partner, most often with my second wife, Cindy) who also loves to climb, and sometimes with a group. In fact, I have organized two "Steelers" climbs; convincing some former teammates (Rocky Bleier, Mike Wagner, Moon Mullins, Frank Atkinson, Dave Reavis, John Banaszak and, of course, Ray Mansfield) to come along and see what kind of shape they're in (they all did great—all reaching the summits—except Banaszak, who had climbed nearly to the top despite having bad back spasms—yes, a tough ex-Marine). Jim Card, my college roommate, someone who fights vertigo, had acted as "base camp manager" (supplying the post climb beer to "replenish our bodily fluids," a favorite Chuck Noll phrase) on both of those climbs.

Cindy and I organized two "couples" climbs, asking some of our best friends to join us on the next challenge and the ladies did every bit as well as the men. Unfortunately the last one was in a driving rain (in lower elevations) and a blizzard above, causing many to lose much of their enthusiasm for climbing the "14ers." Fortunately, it was one of the easiest mountains, Handies Peak, and we all were able to reach the summit despite the inclement weather.

Fortunately Cindy discovered that she too loved ascending mountains (for her own reasons), climbing 29 of the 54, and loving every minute of it. She is a strong climber, who has the same passion I do for climbing and we look forward to climbing many more mountains before we become too old (hopefully, not until our nineties). We frequently run into climbers in their 80's high in the mountains of Colorado and hope, with a little luck that we will be climbing when we're that age.

This essay is not intended to describe each climb (the best or the most difficult or most dangerous—etc.) but more to try and explain why I, or anyone, would even attempt such an undertaking. I'm sure there are many out there who would think such an activity is patently absurd, giving many potentially valid reasons (too ego driven; too dangerous—you could seriously hurt yourself; a waste of valuable time—you could be playing golf, watching a great movies, reading a classic book; too exhausting, etc., etc.).

But, I have to admit, that as I was ascending this last mountain, Culebra Peak, I found myself feeling very out of sorts, weird, discombobulated and a little sad. It was like finishing a great Reinhold Messner (the world's greatest mountain climber) book. I found myself not wanting to finish, to slow down and savor every word (step), and, worrying, much as I had when I retired from the Steelers, about how I would replace this wonderful challenge, a special, unique activity that had truly become a passion—it had inspired, compelled, exhilarated, thrilled, exhausted, humbled, frightened, satisfied, bonded and challenged me for twenty three years, almost the same number of years football had done the same thing for me. The experience, causing me to feels those emotions listed above, also had forced me to remain focused, diligent, persistent, driven, motivated, determined, hard working and refusing to quit—all words that Chuck Noll stressed that we emphasize in our efforts to win all those Super Bowls.

How could all those adjectives come out of such a fundamentally simple exercise, pushing one's body up a steep slope, trying to enjoy every step (yes, as Reinhold Messner would say, "One step at a time,"), basking in the glorious wilderness of high mountains? The word "frightened" was listed in reference to the danger that always exists in the mountains—the danger of falling (off a cliff or into a ice crevasse), of being struck by lightening, crossing ice slicked rocks (known as verglass), buried by avalanches and many other potential calamities.

Feeling danger, an emotion rarely felt by any us in our daily lives, can be a very frightening but also can generate a high. It is clear that many extreme athletes seek out danger, pushing themselves further in attempting to feel that kind of exhilaration—try and imagine climbing a huge rock wall, parasailing high above the mountains, exposing oneself to avalanche danger, skiing off cliffs or sky-diving and one can understand that the thrill of danger, the very real risk, can be the driver.

At the same time, one must admit that putting one's life in danger just to get a "natural" high is not much different than taking a mood altering drug that also could be life threatening. So my sensible side tells me to avoid danger, to not risk a serious injury, to not always escalate the level of fear but my adventurous side knows the thrill and wants to find it again and again. My mature side says to stay out of harm's way, lead a normal life and play with my grandchildren (I have seven). But the mountains, and yes the risks, keep calling me and I will probably, if I stay lucky, continue to attempt to find "acceptable" levels of adventurous risk to satisfy this graving I have.

Playing professional football for so long satisfied this urge to challenge myself. Arguably there is some level of danger in football at any level. After all, as a linebacker, you have very large men hunting you, trying to take you out, not intentionally trying to hurt you but, if they did, they wouldn't have been too concerned and there goal was to wipe me out. All NFL players face the danger of major concussions, potential damage to one's spinal column causing paralysis, shoulder injuries, torn knees, hips and ankles, broken bones, etc. I believe that the danger of major injury is one reason the game is so exciting.

My whole life I've had to deal with what is now referred to as Attention Deficit Disorder, a major problem in staying focused, becoming distracted very easily. Well, I never once had that problem on a football field, my focus being totally riveted to what I was doing—the same being true while climbing mountains.

So, why are all those adjectives listed above for me impacted positively by climbing? I don't know—they just are. Quite probably other people enjoy climbing for other reasons. In the world of sports, where talented athletes set amazing new world records almost weekly, climbing most mountains would be considered by the major sporting media an insignificant sporting accomplishment—it certainly would never make the ESPN Sports Center. But the wonderful thing about this challenge, Colorado's 54-14ers, is that almost anyone can do it—it doesn't require what most sports require (super coordination, speed, strength, size, technique or ability—for example, the levels of athleticism required in most professional sports, like NBL, NBA, NHL or the NFL).

All it takes, on most mountains, is a certain level of fitness, determination, and commitment—something all of us have the mental capacity to control and generate. Granted, the finest climbers in the world undoubtedly have worked extraordinarily hard to gain their unbelievable level of fitness and skills but probably many of them were born with an unusual lung and heart capabilities. On the other hand, sporting events (football or basketball games) normally only take a few hours, whereas a mountain climb, even in Colorado, may take between 8 and 14 hours (most folks complete a marathon between three to four plus hours).

Granted, to scale the vertical north face of the Eiger will require enormous athleticism and with that in mind, I consider Reinhold

Messner one of the greatest "athletes" ever, as his sport was far more dangerous than anything on a football field—every time he climbed he was facing the possibility that he might die. Try climbing a mountain and maybe you'll find that it can become a passion that will stay with you your entire life as it has for so many of us.

Of course, despite mountaineering not requiring what is considered significant athletic talent, one critical attribute one needs to have is a serious degree of caution. Obviously, professional basketball and football players don't consider their games life threatening events but the climbing major peaks of the world can take your life.

One must plan his or her trip in great detail, have the proper clothing (hypothermia can happen very quickly), climbing gear (layers of clothing, rope, ice axe and crampons—when on steep snow and ice), and, perhaps most importantly, be willing to turn back, to give up (something most of us are not taught to do) when the weather turns bad (heavy snows, high winds and lightning have killed many climbers). On a mountain in bad weather, one needs to control their macho instincts and retreat, trying another year. Ed Viesturs, America's greatest climber, says that the summit is an option, returning to your family is mandatory. Following that program he was still able to climb the 14 eight thousand meter peaks without oxygen.

Despite these dangers, I can honestly say that I have never found an "activity" (including football) quite as exhilarating and rewarding as mountain climbing. I have been blessed to have had the time (understanding business partners), and money to fly out to Colorado (an absolutely fabulous state), "bag" those 54-14ers, and as many of the 13ers (there are over 600) as I can.

Chapter 6

FANTASY CAMP

In July of 2005 the Steelers held their first ever Fantasy Camp and a number of us former players (Tunch Ilkin, Craig Wolfley, Mike Wagner, Louis Lipps, John Kolb, Edmund Nelson and myself) were invited back to St. Vincent's to try and recapture what it was like at training camp and to instruct those crazy enough to sign up. We were aware of the success of these Fantasy Camps in baseball (the Pirates have had them for years, where gung-ho fans show up every spring to try and imagine what it would have been like to be a professional baseball player).

Some might think that people who go to "fantasy" camps are a bit delusional—i.e., they think they might have been able to play at the NFL level but I think they just love the game and want to experience a bit of what every professional player goes through yearly, training camp.

But baseball, unlike football, is a game where one can actually play the game with relatively little danger of being hurt. Football is a contact sport and athletes are hurt every time the players go full speed, referred to as going "live," whether it's touch football or flag, let alone the real game. Without real contact I couldn't imagine how we could make the experience interesting enough for those loyal fans that would show up at St. Vincent's trying to get a feel for how the game is played at the professional level.

Arriving Saturday morning, having not been back to St. Vincent's since my final season (1976) I was amazed at the number of new buildings, both classrooms and dormitories. We had been told that the Steelers no longer have rooms without air conditioning and that the current players show up with 52-inch Television screens (non of us had TVs back in the 70's) and fancy stereo systems. Each room also had its own bathroom. Frankly it was like staying at a Ritz Carlton as compared to what we had experienced but I still felt something within me stir—this was where the great journey had begun, rising from the ashes so to speak, when the Steelers went from a perpetual loser, SOS (Same Old Steelers), to the top of the mountain, the winner of four Super Bowls in six years. It had been a glorious journey. Granted, I was only there for two of those Super Bowls but, remember, as Nike reminds us, the journey is the destination.

Approaching the meeting room, where Coach Tim Lewis (Steelers Defensive Coordinator) was already speaking to the group, I could hear shouting and cheering and feet stomping—these guys were psyched, clearly ready to rumble. Entering the room, feeling the electricity of their unbridled enthusiasm, I was amazed when I was told that there were 150 participants who had arrived from 24 different states—one guy had driven his RV from Oregon. Others had driven in from Vermont, New York, flown in from San Diego and Los Angeles, chasing their dreams, going with their passion and every minute or so they would stand and give Coach Lewis a standing ovation for some clever remark he had made, comments like "the Steelers play smash mouth football."

The group appeared to range in age from 20 to 50 but most of them looked in shape, some ripped from weight training, others with the slight beer bellies, but all ready to show their stuff, clearly former jocks or want-to-be's.

Later that afternoon, after going through various stretching exercises (lying in the mud—it had rained heavily all morning) they were divided up into five groups (kicking, receiving and quarterbacking, running backs, defensive and offensive line play and linebacking). My job, of course, was to teach the linebacking and I wondered what I could teach that would not require their participation—after all, without pads and helmets, we couldn't go live, tackling and blitzing (two of linebacker's biggest task). When the first group arrived I realized that these guys hadn't come from all parts of the country just to hear some old timer like me simply lecture on the intricacies of linebacking—they clearly wanted to hit somebody.

So I ran them through a series of drills and despite their slipping and falling on the wet turf and mud their enthusiasm never waned. This was their fantasy—to go to a professional training camp and test their stuff against whoever showed up. Most of them were former football players, having played at some level, whether it be Pony League, High school, or College and there were two huge, brawny fellows who were currently playing semi-pro football in Staten Island, New York, clearly hoping to get a Steeler tryout.

Soon, however, I realized that there just wasn't any way we could go full speed and actually practice tackling or blitzing, which necessitated me lecturing them on the finer points of such skills. I could quickly see that they were getting antsy, restless, preferring action to listening and I struggled to keep their attention despite giving them what I thought were some good points on linebacking skills/techniques.

When I started talking about my anti violence theories they seemed put off. But when I asked them what attribute was most important for a defensive player between the following: quickness; strength; toughness; agility; or intellect one smart guy raised his hand and said, "all of the above." Admitting that was a clever answer, I asked them to choose only one of the five attributes and they consistently came up with intellect. I was surprised because I thought most people think football players are just rough, tough guys who fly around and try to hit one another.

When I told them that my biggest weaknesses as a player were that I was often too impatient and too aggressive. I could see that they weren't used to the idea that one could be too aggressive when playing the game of football but I didn't give them the opportunity for debate, as, over my career, my aggressiveness and impatience, wanting badly to make a big play, had caused me, and the team, many yards and a few times even worse—touchdowns.

Later that evening each of us ex-player "coaches" got up and told more stories about some incidents in training camps we remembered. The audience was raucous, shouting their own commentary, knowing some of the stories better than we did. I told them that I truly appreciated their love of the game and that their wonderful enthusiasm and great attitudes had, in a way, rekindled, and reminded me, of my own passion for the game. When Franco Harris gave the featured speech they went wild with appreciation.

Later that night I broke curfew (there wasn't any) and sneaked out after bed check (again none) and went to a few pubs that I remembered where we often frequented to "replenish our bodily fluids," as

Coach Noll used to urge us to do (not with beer, of course). Deciding to turn in early I drove back to the campus to spend one more night in the dormitory, basking in my own memories of such a wonderful time in my life.

Perhaps there is another reason the Steelers and their fans have had such a strong bond. I believe that the Steelers became a sort of symbol of the city's resurrection. Pittsburgh's economy, based on Steel, had fallen on very hard times during the 60's and through the great work of guys like Jay Aldridge of Penn Southwest (a group put together to entice foreign companies to Pittsburgh), Dave Roderick and Tom Usher (U.S. Steel Chairmen), Tom O'Brien (PNC's Chairman), Tony O'Reilly (H.J. Heinz Chairman), the Hillmans (Elsie and Henry) and Chuck Queenan (a top partner at Kirkpatrick Lockhart) and the leaders of Mellon Bank, Alcoa, PPG, and too many other visionaries to mention, and, of course, all those hard working employees of those companies, the city, in the early 70's, was starting to fight back, much like the Steelers were starting to become a good team and then a great team.

The team, I believe, became an unconscious symbol of City pride. No one was going to kick us around any more, no more ugly smokestacks, lost jobs, failed businesses—look out we're coming back. We've got a beautiful city, with a lot of vibrant businesses and, by the way, the best damn pro football team in history.

Chapter 7

JOHNNY, "THE JUNGLE BOY"

A few years ago Cindy and I went on our first ever trip to Costa Rica and went to the beautiful Pacific Ocean beach town named Jaco where we had enjoyed staying at Ed Podolak's (yes, the former Kansas City Chief running back who now is a successful real estate developer) Club Del Mar. On our way to the San Jose Airport, hating to leave, we met the Club's van driver, Johnny, and after some encouragement and our constant questioning he told us about his life and for almost two hours no one said a word as Johnny told us his story.

When we had first met Johnny the night before, being introduced by Ed, he appeared to be somewhat disheveled, long haired, handsome, slightly charismatic but somehow insecure, showing a lack of confidence, perhaps worrying about his lack of social graces. But he was definitely cute and friendly, the kind of man the ladies like. The next day, on the long drive to San Jose, we would discover that Johnny had good reason to distrust people.

Johnny was born to his mother, Flora, who gave birth to him at age 14, two years after she had been abducted by his "Dad," who had been 18 at the time of his birth. Their father had ridden up to their mother on his horse, hoisted her up and rode off into the jungle. Johnny's narrative made it unclear whether she went with him voluntarily or not—but his description sounded like a kidnapping. Flora gave birth to Johnny in their jungle shack because had she gone to the hospital the authorities would have arrested Johnny's Dad for abducting his mom, and given Flora and Johnny back to her parents.

Johnny lived with his family (Mom, Dad and younger brother, born one year later) in a one room shack, with walls, floors and the ceiling made of all natural jungle materials such as bamboo and leaves (the leaves turned into a plastic like material if heated by the sun, that would be waterproof for three years).

64

They were deep in the rain forest, next to a river full of crocodiles, and a rain forest full of monkeys, jaguars, deadly frogs and poisonous snakes. Their jungle home was a three day walk from the nearest village, located on the Pacific Ocean, near the border to Panama— wild country in those days, even today.

To appreciate how wild the country was back in those early years, Johnny explained, one has to understand that the government was very understaffed and inefficient—even more so than most governments. For example, the penitentiary was so poorly policed that criminals frequently escaped and migrated to the wild southern shores of the Pacific coast. In fact, so many criminals, all males, took up residence in one spot along the coast that it actually became a sort of town. It wasn't long afterwards, that prostitutes, under the guidance of a powerful lady named Rita, occasionally visited the new town and they were so successful the men, (the former criminals who had been starving for women until Rita's team moved there), eventually named the town Conrita in her honor.

Rita would go on to become a legendary figure in Costa Rica and lived in her town to the ripe age of 108. Johnny's dad was not only from Conrita; he knew Rita personally and he interacted with her large family but, because of his lawlessness (i.e., abducting Johnny's mother), he visited only at night, hidden by the darkness.

Since Johnny's Dad was wanted for kidnapping their underage mother he could not return to Flora's hometown, at least during the day, as the police would put him in jail. The family would have to live in the jungle until their mother reached age eighteen and they could then return to living in the town (apparently the authorities would then ignore their dad's kidnapping).

So Johnny's early years were all spent in the rain forest. He and his brother had no toys or neighboring kids to play with. Instead they would capture baby crocs and tape their jaws shut and pull them around the clearing near their tree house. The winner was judged as the croc that made the greatest swath, clearing the opening of debris, as they fought furiously to grab onto anything to prevent from being pulled forward.

Later the boys would take the exhausted baby crocs and place them in a basket and put them in their shack (presumably to pull around another day). Apparently, the young crocs would make an almost inaudible sound that could only be heard by their giant parent's lurking outside the shack at night (clearly looking for their children). When Johnny's father figured this out he banned baby crocs from the household.

Actually, they did have one toy—well, sort of. They were given a couple of old rusty ball bearings that they used to play marbles with but, unfortunately, Johnny's brother, Grabien, accidentally swallowed one (nearly 3/4 inch wide ball) and nearly suffocated before he was able to swallow it down.

Johnny instructed Grabien to always analyze his stool to see if the ball had come out. Of course this meant that he could not take a dump in the family outhouse because his stool would be lost down below. Consequently, Grabien began sneaking out and depositing his number 2s in the jungle near their shack. Unfortunately, he made the mistake of doing his number on the trail used by his dad. The dad was outraged, (stepping barefoot on someone's stool) but the boys blamed other jungle folk who occasionally visited.

Grabien had become somewhat obsessed with finding his ball bearing, so much so that he once decided to climb up into a tree so that Johnny could clearly see (from below) whether the ball dropped out. Unfortunately they heard their father coming along the path below the tree and Johnny, fearing another beating, ran, leaving Grabien, bare-assed up in the tree, right above their dad.

The dad stopped, cussing as he discovered more poop on the trail as Grabien held his breath above, scared to death he might unloose another projectile right on his dad's head and knowing that if that happened he would die, or at best receive a severe beating. The father looked around, trying to see the culprit, never suspecting that he was high above him in the tree. So, Grabien survived that little episode.

Their father frequently came home drunk in such a foul mood that he would threaten the boys with his knife. When this happened the boys would choose to sleep outside in the jungle, despite the snakes and crocs, fearing their dad's knife threats, anger and beatings much more.

One morning they awoke to hear their father fighting outside their cabin with their mother (not an unusual event, as apparently it happened often). Upon arriving at the scene they found that their father was trying to convince their mother to climb down into a new outhouse pit he had recently dug (about 3 meters deep and 4 long) asking her to attach a rope to a large adult croc that had fallen into the pit so it could be removed.

Their dad was claiming that the croc was dead but the mom wasn't convinced. Finally, after much arguing, the father grabbed a long pole (about 3 meters), saying he would prove the croc was dead, but when he poked the croc in his groin area (Johnny claimed crocs are quite sensitive in this area and recommended that if we were ever in the jaws of a croc that we should tickle that spot, joking that would be the only way to get away from a crocodile). Unfortunately, or fortunately (as the boys were terrified of their father and might not have minded if he was accidentally killed) the very live croc grabbed the pole, instantly snapping it in half, causing their dad to be pulled off balance and fall into the hole.

The boys, "happily" watching from a distance, could only see their father desperately trying to get out, shoulders above the hole, and elbows on the edge, yelling for their mother's assistance, who refused, probably fearing that he'd pull her in also. First the croc pulled his left rubber boot right off but then it went for the other boot, biting deep into their dad's ankle and removing a sizeable chunk of it. Dad would limp for the rest of his life from this bizarre accident. Apparently, their Dad got out when the croc's tail inadvertently flipped him up and out of the hole.

Dad was also bitten three times by vipers, very poisonous snakes, causing on one occasion to be hospitalized for 27 days. Snake bites (7 kinds of poisonous snakes) are a very serious issue in Costa Rica and people often die or lose limbs from such bites. We had earlier learned that crocodiles in Costa Rica kill about 150 people a year and snakes even more.

Dad's primary occupation at that time, other than giving Johnny and Grabien lots of beatings, (for trivial mistakes) was to train roosters for late night fighting, a practice illegal in most of Costa Rica but not in Conrita.

Apparently, their father was very successful because he nearly always won. His secret was threefold: (1) building the strength of the birds by making them climb up and down a steep ladder up into the jungle canopy to build up their leg muscles; (2) forcing them to eat scorpions and (3) stuffing them with red hot peppers (this last move would make them very "pissed off"). Of course, the boys did all the work and dad took all the glory.

Apparently, the primary prize (at least as far as the boys were concerned) for winning a cockfight was that their Dad got to keep the other competitor's dead rooster and they would take it home for dinner. Unfortunately, on some occasions, the boys, carrying the dead cocks over their shoulder in a bag, would discover that the cocks were not dead, moving as they recovered slightly from their wounds.

Their Dad would then decide whether or not to kill the cock or help it heal to fight again. The boys just hated when their dad decided to keep the delicious bird because they went hungry again—their entire diet was food from the jungle and sometimes it was scarce.

To help the cock recover from its' wounds, they would find a special sap from a tree and apply it to the cock. Amazingly most of these cocks rebounded and with the help of the muscle building ladders, scorpion food and the peppers became better fighters than they had ever been. Sometimes his fellow competitors would be suspicious, accusing their dad of keeping one of their fighter cocks (unfairly because they weren't dead), but once they saw them fight, juiced up by scorpion piss and red hot peppers, they agreed that it couldn't possibly be the same sluggish bird that had fought so badly for them.

But when the cocks were nearly dead and their father deemed them unfit for future fighting, Johnny was given the responsibility of killing them. Grabien would grab the wounded cock's feet and below the head and stretch the neck across a tree trunk and Johnny, wielding a large machete, would slice off the bird's head.

Unfortunately, there were a few times when Johnny's aim was slightly off where his stroke cut the neck but not all the way through. On these occasions, Grabien would release his grip on the bird and the cock might run off with blood spurting everywhere, even on their mother's wash hanging outside to dry. This mistake made their mother wildly angry and they would receive a spanking from her, which was not nearly as scary a thing as a beating from their old man.

One time Johnny thought that Grabien should learn how to cut off the cock's head and he held the bird down. Johnny admitted being nervous about Grabien's aim, particularly when he looked up and noticed that Grabien had closed his eyes in the middle of taking the machete back. As one might guess—this was a bad idea and when

Grabien made his stroke, Johnny saw no wound on the neck of the bird but lots of blood. He soon realized that it was his own blood as Grabien had missed so badly that he sliced Johnny's arm near the elbow and to today he has a huge scar.

An interesting sidebar to this story is that Johnny had grown up wanting to be a pilot, perhaps because he occasionally saw a plane fly overhead. Since Johnny's wound was severe the local hospital (apparently this incident occurred after their mom turned 18) was understaffed and he had to be flown to a larger facility north. Unfortunately there were four other badly wounded people who needed immediate help or they would die.

The pilot, who had indicated they could not fly with more than four passengers, decided to take all the injured making the plane very overweight. On takeoff the plane barely cleared the trees and the pilot decided to not fly out over the ocean, nor would he fly over the mountain pass (for obvious reasons). Deciding to fly instead directly over the abundant banana tree orchards (bananas are one of Costa Rica's major products), the plane barely cleared the top of the trees and even, on occasion, dipped down, clipping the trees and leaving bananas in the wheel wells.

This single flight experience was so frightening to Johnny that he made the choice to not be a pilot after all. Many years later, he would decide to study resort and tourist management and is licensed to guide people in the rain forest, something he obviously grew up knowing a lot about.

The only other thing the boys liked about the cockfights (other than the food provided by dead cocks) is that they got to go into town every Saturday night and were allowed to take a sip of their dad's coke. Before he knew it, they were taking huge sips that took the entire coke. They lived for those trips to the town where they could enjoy a coke. Today, Johnny never drinks a coke, preferring to drink fruit juices and water and, not wanting to be like their father, thus no alcohol.

Their dad's best fighter was called "Rey," or King in English. Rey won 75 fights, (27 when he was blind) after which their dad decided to let him retire and built him a special cage. One morning they heard their dad outside crying and cussing, agonizing over something. They rushed outside to find him stabbing a large (3 meter) boa constrictor that had eaten King. It was the only time they ever saw their dad cry.

The boa had not been able to escape the cage because after eating the bird he was too fat to get through the hole he had entered. Their dad finally cut the boa's head off and removed Rey, telling the boys to bury him formally in the clearing around their shack. They then ate the boa and learned that the meat was "excellent," tasting much like shrimp.

Eventually, when their mom hit 18 (now he could claim they were a legitimate family and not have to worry about having kidnapped her) they moved closer to town, living about three miles up the river. The boys and dad would frequently take a small dug out canoe down the river, through frequent and some severe rapids returning the canoe to their home tied to the back of their horse. Those rapids were especially bad in the winter and their dad forbid them from using the river.

Their mother never went on these trips because she didn't know how to swim and was very afraid of the crocodiles. However, one winter morning, with the water very high, their dad announced that he and their mom would be taking a river trip to town and the boys were suspicious. They knew it was very dangerous and their mom couldn't swim. Why would dad take their mom on such a dangerous trip? It even occurred to them that he was trying to get rid of her, as they fought constantly and obviously their "marriage" wasn't a happy one.

With great trepidation, at their Dad's command, they pushed their mom and dad's canoe into the river and watched them fly around the first bend, barely under control—the water was extremely high and the dangers would be numerous—rapids, logs, rocks and, even possibly, a murderous father.

The boys worried all day and later that night they saw a single figure walking back towards their shack—it was their father, alone. They asked their father where their mother was but he only replied "she won't be coming back here tonight—go to sleep."

The next day and night—no mom and their father's only comment was that she would not be returning. But, on the night of the third day, they saw another single figure walking up the path towards their home. It was their mother, cut, bruised and bright red from sunburn. She explained that she, sitting in the front of the canoe, not even having a paddle, had turned around to find that their father had disappeared. Had he fallen out of the canoe? She had heard nothing—

surely he would have cried for help, or yelled to alert her of the danger, if he had accidentally fallen out.

All of a sudden, she found herself alone, flying down the wild river, sitting in front of a small canoe with no paddle. Soon it had capsized and she, unable to swim, was, by the grace of God, tossed up onto a small sandbar ("about the size of this van," said Johnny). She couldn't leave the sandbar and, still in the wilderness, she couldn't cry out for help, as there was no one out there, except hungry Jaguars and Crocodiles.

For three days, without food or shelter from the sun, she survived on that small sandbar, worrying constantly about the crocodiles, which could have made an easy meal out of her. Finally, late in the third day, she heard voices and was discovered by men from town, searching for some lost cows.

They shouted to her, "Hey, what you doing out there—that's no place to sun bath!"

"Yah, right—please get me off here," Flora coolly replied.

They helped her off the sandbar and she had limped back home along the river's edge.

Later, the family had moved further north, up the coast to Capos, where they lived a more normal existence. Johnny went to school, but worked afterwards, carrying 45 to 50 sharks off boats for fifteen cents per day (which bought him a coke and a cracker). Later, he and his brother would walk one hour up into the hills where his dad was working in a production plant of some kind. They would carry him a bottle of hot coffee but if the coffee was not hot enough their father would beat them.

The most frightening thing in their life was these beatings. It wasn't the challenges of their school, or hoisting heavy sharks or even the crocodiles they passed on the way there, nor was it avoiding the poisonous snakes lurking along the path—it was the five seconds it took for their father to figure out whether the coffee was hot or cold.

Since it was too often cold, Johnny asked his mother what could be done because these beatings were so painful. Not wanting her boys to be beaten, she did everything she could, wrapping the glass bottle in papers (this was before thermos bottles), pouring the coffee into the bottle piping hot. The boys tried walking faster but it was a good one-hour hike up into the hills to their dad's workplace.

Finally, Johnny observed his brother opening the cap and putting his finger into the bottle, testing its warmth. When asked how often he did that, Johnny's brother told him three or four times on the hike up. Johnny realized that that was the cause of the cold coffee and they finally solved that problem as the brother was not allowed to test its' warmth—another beating avoided.

Their father had said nothing about their mother's strange boat accident and had almost seemed unhappy about her return. The boys were not allowed to question him about this incident until they had reached the age of 18—before that, the Costa Rican custom was that they would be punished (beaten) for insubordination. Johnny waited, wanting badly to question his dad about this incident. But his father died, age 37, when Johnny was seventeen, so he will never know what really happened but it is clear that Johnny believed that his dad was trying to "get rid" of his mother.

Today Johnny's mother lives ten miles south of San Jose and he and his brother take care of her. She is "still young, less than fifty, a beautiful woman," who somehow survived her abduction into the jungle, giving birth at age 14 and 15 to her two sons, and surviving her husband's apparent planned murder attempt.

Despite such a bizarre upraising, Johnny appears very well adjusted, even happy. He's married (to a woman who also works at Podolak's club in the back office), with two kids, a son 9 and a daughter 7 and he gets to tell wild stories to naïve, but often cynical, tourists, just maybe to enhance his tip—actually, in my opinion, these stories were too bizarre to be made up for entertainment purposes.

Oh yes, life is good for Johnny, despite his strange childhood. When asked if he would ever beat his children he replied, "Never. I do not want to repeat the same mistakes of my father. My brother and I do not drink a drop of alcohol and we are very gentle with our children."

Of course, now his life is less challenging, not having to worry about receiving beatings from his employer, Ed Podolak, one of the NFL's nicest and most considerate running backs—he always apologized when his elusiveness made me miss tackling him.

Sitting on the airplane, flying home, I realized what a striking contrast there was between how Johnny was raised and how I was raised. Here he lived in a jungle with a wacko Dad, no schooling and no friends (except his brother and baby crocs) where I had lived in nice suburban communities in Detroit, Chicago, New York and St. Louis, going to good schools, playing organized sports and having very supportive parents.

I also realized that where I found myself always seeking adventure, risk and danger (very modest stuff compared to Johnny's experiences), Johnny had all that right in his back yard (the jungle and a sick father).

Despite those differences Johnny has not only survived but come out of those experiences with an amazingly good attitude, approaching his life intelligently and seems very happy.

Isn't it an amazing world!

Chapter 8

THE STEEL CURTAIN

With some of the latest Super Bowls won by teams, (Baltimore, New England, Tampa Bay and Pittsburgh), known more for their defense than their offense, announcers seem to constantly compare those defenses to the Steelers defense of the 70's. Statistical comparisons are often unfair because strategies change as the rules change—the style of play today is dramatically different than it was back in the 70's.

Defense today is arguably more difficult to play as there is no jamming and rerouting receivers (except for one jam in the first five yards), making it much more difficult to play pass defense, and offensive lineman are now allowed to push out with their arms and even hold jerseys inside the shoulders making it harder to rush the passer.

We must also not forget when comparing defenses to compare their offenses. How much time did the offense run off the clock? How often did they turn the ball over in bad field position? Were the opponents forced to play catch up because the offense had built up such a big lead? Did their special teams leave them with good field position?

Obviously offenses impact the defensive performance and we had a very efficient, ball control offense that rarely turned the ball over which, of course, might work against us when comparisons are made. But we certainly would not have had those five shut outs in 1975 if our offense was turning the ball over inside our own twenty, something they rarely did.

What made that Steeler defense so special? Who were the unsung heroes? How did we get along? These are questions we are asked frequently and it might be fun to explore those questions.

It is often stated that any unit is only as strong as its' weakest link, as offenses would unerringly attack that player or strategy viewed as

74

the least effective. The problem teams had with that Steeler defense of the 70's was that there were very few weaknesses, if any.

When discussing our defense one usually begins by talking about our magnificent front four ("Mean" Joe Greene, L.C. "Hollywood Bags" Greenwood, Ernie "Fats" Holmes and Dwight "Mad Dog" White), the so called, "Steel Curtain," four players who could cause offenses serious problems whether they tried to run it or pass it. This outstanding group is often compared to other outstanding defensive lines, such as the Viking's "Purple People Eaters," or the L.A. Ram's "Fearsome Foursome." Frankly, I'd take our guys every time.

It is extraordinarily sad that two of that vaulted defensive line, Dwight and Ernie, have passed away in their 50's, way too early. Both of them played with incredible effort and skill, with concentration, intensity, focus and passion. Having played on the right side immediately behind them I can vouch for their greatness and professionalism—it was an honor to play with them both.

If they chose to run away from Joe Greene, arguably our best lineman (*to me Joe is clearly the Player of the Decade as no player ever did more for his team—offense or defense in the 70's), they might attack Ernie, our only 300+ pounder, who, when focused, could be devastatingly destructive to an offense. Ernie's only problem was that he would often concentrate all his attention on destroying the offensive lineman across from him, almost ignoring the running back. But choosing to run at Ernie was often a mistake, as Oakland found out in the AFC championship game in 1974. Ernie and Dwight stuffed the vaunted Oakland running game, limiting them to only small gains.

L.C. Greenwood, a six time Pro Bowler, was a phenomenal pass rusher, ending up the top sack getter of the Steel Curtain. If they had chosen a "Defensive Player of the Game" in our first Super Bowl against the Vikings, I'm sure that L.C. would have won that honor, as he continually pressured Fran Tarkenton into bad throws and had a number of passed ball knock downs.

Dwight White, known as "Mad Dog," unrelenting in his commitment to excellence, drove himself hard to become one of the greats. Dwight loved to carry on a conversation, seldom amiable, with the offensive tackle across from him. Dwight, a very tough character, full of vim and vigor, just had to make it personal and played the game with a total passion, as though he was fighting for his life. Since he played on my side I was often left with little to do but help the other team's players up off the ground. Sometimes, when opponents ran our side, coming in behind Dwight and Fats, it was like arriving at the scene of an accident. Hammer often had the same experience on the left side with Mean Joe and L.C. frequently causing equal havoc.

Our front four was so good, particularly at putting pressure on the quarterback, that we rarely blitzed, relying instead on them to hurry the opponent's quarterback. I can remember, more times than I'd like to admit, where my man had me slightly beat, knowing he was open, praying the QB wouldn't notice him but then being saved by one of our front four making the big sack or forcing an errant throw.

Of course, there were times when our great secondary (Mel Blount, J.T. Thomas, Mike Wagner and Pine Edwards—all All-Pros in their own right) would have all the receivers covered forcing the QB to wait, giving the front four that extra second to make the sack.

Wagner always seemed to make the key interception with the game on the line. He was clearly "Mr. Clutch," giving us the ball back in critical situations. I knew from the first day at training camp that Wagner was going to be the All Pro he became. Mike was smart, tough (a great tackler) and very opportunistic.

J.T. and Pine were consummate All Pros, always in the right place, rarely gambling to make the big play, trying to stay within the confines of the defensive strategy—they defined team players.

In fact, I would say that Glen Edwards was the toughest guy, pound for pound, on that Steel Curtain defense, a great open field tackler and a player who seldom gets his due. Don't forget that Glen caused the key interception (made by Mel Blount) in our first Super Bowl denying the Vikings a score near the end of the first half.

J.T. could cover or support the run with equal strength and seldom got fooled, always opting to do the things that would help the team instead of worrying about his own stats or ego.

Last, but certainly not least, was Mel Blount, a Hall of Fame player, who typically took on the opponent's best receivers and overwhelmed them, stuffing them at the line of scrimmage. Mel, 225 pounds and 4.4 speed, was probably the reason the NFL decided to go with the one jam in five yards rule. Too often, Mel would just take the receiver and destroy him at the line of scrimmage or just throw him out of bounds.

76

The NFL, believing that fan's want offensive scoring, have made the game easier for offenses and harder for defenses and, yet, defensive teams not only keep up but seem to dominate. How do they do that? —I'm certainly impressed.

The linebackers (Ham, Lambert, both Hall of Famers, and some guy named Russell) weren't bad coverage guys either but that will be discussed in greater detail in the Ham Lambert chapter.

It is also important to note that the Steel Curtain wasn't just eleven guys as we were backed up by a number of outstandingly good reserves. Loren Toews was a terrific young outside linebacker who did a great job filling in for me when I got hurt late in the third quarter in Super Bowl IX—the Vikings definitely went after him and he responded with some great stops. In the same game, Ed Bradley, replacing injured Jack Lambert in the first quarter, played an outstanding game. We also shouldn't forget our quality backups of the front four, John Banaszak and Steve Furness, who filled in admirably for injured Joe Greene in Super Bowl X. Without quality reserves we'd have been in big trouble, as no defense can make it through the year without injuries. Most of those guys went on to be starters later in their career.

I had played on defenses in the 60's when we just didn't have the ability to stop the opponent at the most critical times in the game. We'd often play well for three quarters only to lose in the final minutes because of a slip, a mistake, a freak bounce of the ball, missed tackle or just flat getting beat deep by a faster, better player where we had given the QB all day to throw the ball. That didn't happen very often to that 70's defense.

I can remember Coach Don Shula, the great Miami Dolphin coach, saying that he hated to play the Steelers, complaining, "We can't even make a first down." Oh, that was sweet music to our ears after so many years of frustrating losses—truly it was going from the agony to the ecstasy.

Granted, against the run our front four carried the burden of taking on the opponent's offensive line, often the largest players on the field. This frequently allowed us linebackers to slip into the hole and stop the running back for no gain. Obviously taking on a giant blocker and defeating him is frequently a lot more difficult a task than stopping the typically smaller running backs, especially when they are confined, forced to run through a small gap/hole (not in open field). When they did bounce outside, because the hole was closed, our secondary was very good at open field tackling—resisting the "devil ego, trying to be on "Sports Center" with the devastating hit, but just getting the job done by hitting them low and hanging on.

The Steel Curtain had shown teams in the league that it was going to be a force as early as 1972, when we beat two big league teams in Three Rivers, the Kansas City Chiefs, winners of the Super Bowl (1969) and the Minnesota Vikings (K.C. and the Vikings were former NFC conference champions). Neither of those teams was able to move the ball late in the game and our offense was able to dominate the line of scrimmage with Franco moving the sticks on third and long.

But it was 1974 when the "Curtain" closed, demonstrating to the League that times had changed; the Steelers had arrived and would not be denied. Perhaps the most meaningful change we made that year was Joe Greene's new alignment. Joe, frustrated by people trying to run away from him, denying him the action he craved, decided to jump into the gap (between center and guard), turn his shoulders sideways to the line of scrimmage and, on the snap of the ball, to use his amazing quickness to jump into the gap and pursue the action. This simple little stunt, all Joe's idea but immediately approved by the coaches, caused offenses serious problems, not allowing them to pull the guard opposite Joe, forcing the center to "attempt" to cut Joe off which, of course, (1) they rarely accomplished and, (2) freed up our new super star middle linebacker, Jack Lambert. Frankly, that move turned out to be devastating for offenses as Joe was spending a lot of time in their backfield, getting cozy with their running backs—certainly not good for the opponent's offense.

Another tactic that significantly helped our defense was a new technique we called the "hug-em-up," that allowed Jack Ham and me to cover the quicker halfbacks from running what was referred to as an "option route," where they could go either way, coming out of the backfield, a play that offenses in those days used often to move the sticks on third and short. In the past we often gave up those first downs, as we cautiously kept the receiver in front of us, fearing his ability to take off up field for potentially a touchdown.

It was with great satisfaction that Jack and I took something that used to be a weakness and with lots of effort, made it into a strength. I knew we had discovered something important when, acting as a "color commentator" for NBC the year after I retired (1977), the opposing coaches would ask me how to teach the "hug-em-up." Clearly the technique was appreciated in the League.

Frankly, the Steel Curtain had melded together, in a totally harmonious fashion, working together, never pointing the finger, or accusing teammates of not getting the job done. We were a loyal, dedicated, intense but confident group that would not hesitate to sacrifice for our teammates—all of us playing hurt, most of the time. To this day we are forever bonded, a band of brothers, as close as family, appreciating each other's meaningful contributions to that very special defensive unit.

Having started in the early 60's I was the old guy, (my teammates, good naturedly, joked that I was a "dinosaur"), hanging on for a few more years (the NFL has a way of beating up your body) and I have to say, that through that experience, struggling together to turn the franchise around, watching my teammates work together, I learned to love every player on that defense.

As to the comparisons between the 70's Steeler Defense and the top defenses of today, I suggest that until any of those teams win four Super Bowls, in six years, that any comparison be postponed. But I have to admit that our Steelers defense playing now, earning number one status is truly extraordinary!

Chapter 9

A WAKE UP CALL

It was April 1st, 2004 and, despite all the Fools Day jokes, Sam Zacharias and I were off to China to see if we could find a way to cash in on the current China boom. Granted, neither of us were completely naïve, understanding that all our prospects (three) were long shots at best. Maybe, we figured it would be just another chapter in our long over due book about our business career that we had already agreed to entitle, *Addicted to Stupidity*, listing all our failed deals. But our gut was telling us that there were deals to be made, to keep the bat off our shoulders and keep swinging and something good would happen—even as far away as China.

We were certainly aware of the enormous number of jobs China was "stealing" from the U.S., all impacted by the globalization of the world's economy which, of course, saw U.S. companies "outsourcing" jobs to China because of its hugely reduced labor costs. We understood that the U.S. had a negative trade balance with China as our spenders were buying far more Chinese goods than Chinese were buying from us. But what surprised us was that China's huge need for basic commodities, such as steel and oil, were driving those prices up and benefiting U.S. companies that served those markets. As the economy of China had become extraordinarily robust many companies around the world were attempting to see if they could make a profit utilizing China's cheap labor and relaxed laws.

The Chinese immigrants in other parts of Southeast Asia had always been known for their business acumen, sometimes referred to as the "Jews of the Orient," (a compliment to the Jewish intelligence, business sense and work ethic) and now that the Chinese government had loosened their restrictions on businesses (all government owned but allowing individuals to own a significant share but never more than 49%), the entrepreneurs within China had succeeded beyond anyone's wildest forecast.

However, most investment advisors were cautioning their clients to be careful in China, identifying a "bubble" that was soon to pop. It seemed as though there was no way that China could continue growing at its current pace and even the Chinese government had backed off, predicting a carefully orchestrated slow down. Analysts worried that Chinese banks would soon be in trouble as many of their loans went unpaid.

Our interest had been piqued from having spent a dinner with our Dutch friend, Joep van den Neuven Hausen, one of Holland's legendary entrepreneurs. Joep, whose wife and family live in Amsterdam, resides part time in Aruba where he built his own golf course (recently voted one of the top five in the world) and every two weeks he travels around the world, visiting his 50 private businesses: i.e., M.D. (that's McDonald Douglas) Helicopters in Tempe, Arizona and the Port of Rotterdam in Holland where he owns at least 51% of the company.

We had dinner with Joep at the Palm Steak house in Manhattan, after trying to help Joep raise some money (not that he needed our help) for MD Helicopters. We had spent the day at the Chart Group offices run by our friend Chris Brady, son of Reagan's former Secretary of the Treasury, Nicholas Brady (remember the Brady Bonds?). Chris had started Chart, a boutique investment bank, after many successful years in the investment banking business and we had made a modest contribution to its initial capitalization. Unlike us, Chart has powerful investors located all over the world, obviously one of the things that had attracted us to Chart in the first place.

Chris had worked hard with a number of venture capital groups to provide MD Helicopters with the capital they needed to take the company to the next level. Unfortunately, Joep had borrowed a lot of money from his Dutch friends and wasn't in a position to write off this debt and the equity Chris was proposing was too dilutive—leaving Joep with so little of the company he couldn't begin to pay back his friends.

Despite what had been a disappointing day, Joep had seemed upbeat, telling us not to worry about MD Helicopter, confident that new orders and powerful partners would appear—the kind of confidence critical to entrepreneurial success. Joep decided to tell us about one of his successful ventures—his most recent activity in China where he had agreed to build a golf course, and develop the lots around it, in one of China's less well known provinces, Jaingxi.

Joep had sold the lots around the course the first day he put them on the market and was in the process of developing homes on those lots. He had confided in us that it was a pretty good deal since he was able to build the homes for one hundred dollars a square foot and then sell them for seven or eight times that cost. Fortunately, the local bank was willing to finance 75% of the purchase price and Joep took a second mortgage on the rest. Since he made a huge profit on his initial sale (collecting the mortgage amount) he was happy to carry the homeowner's equity. He reasoned that if the person failed to pay off his second mortgage he could just foreclose and own the home himself. Of course, he would still have to pay off the first mortgage an amount that might still be way above its' value, and since these homes were sold on the low side for $2,000,000 and on the high $10,000,000 I thought that might be a serious problem, one that Joep seemed to ignore.

Joep had regaled us with more stories about the wild Chinese economy. Apparently, they had built more miles of highways in the past eleven years than we Americans had built in the past seventy (the period of time it took to develop our interstate highway system). Of course, building highways in China was not as difficult as in the U.S. because when they ran into a cluster of homes smack in front of their route, the authorities just told the home owners to get out within the next thirty days as they were coming through—if the homes were not vacated within the time limit they were just mowed down with huge bulldozers as their owners hurriedly evacuated.

Apparently the city of Nanchang, where Joep had built his golf course and homes, had torn down a recently built row of town homes, 800 meters long, that blocked the view from his golf course lots and the city authorities had just decided to remove those homes to improve the view from Joep's golf course—talk about having some clout with the local authorities.

A few years earlier we had heard, at a New York luncheon, a Deutche Bank economist state, rather forebodingly, that we should "all enjoy ourselves over the next ten years because in the future nothing will be manufactured in the U.S. because it would all be done in China.

We had figured, incorrectly, that our economy would be OK, as it would concentrate on controlling the high-tech world and leave the difficult world of manufacturing to the Chinese. Unfortunately, over the past few years we all had seen huge billion dollar contracts for software creation, from mega companies like Microsoft and IBM, go to India, where one could hire a Ph.D. in I.T. for $6,000 per year. Americans were starting to seriously wonder if this globalization was really such a good thing, since it appeared that everything was happening outside our country. After all, we have to do something—just can't be the world's biggest consumers without revenue coming in.

Other reports claimed this wasn't such a problem because many foreign companies (mostly European) were building factories in the U.S., creating as many jobs as were being lost. Somehow, that intuitively didn't make sense since our unions so often demanded high pay and lots of time off—the Chinese work twelve hour days seven days a week.

Anyway, Sam and I had figured that maybe we better get involved in investing some of our money in China and get in the game. After our dinner with Joep we figured that we had just had a wake up call,— get in the game or perish.

So, there we were on April Fools Day, (how appropriate) flying over to China, on a thirteen hour flight to Beijing, hoping to push forward a number of possible China initiatives: (1) the possibility of obtaining a license to put together a municipal solid waste disposal plan for the city of Nanchang; (2) trying to forge a relationship between China Power and Amperion, a company we have a small interest in and could facilitate the availability of the wireless internet over power lines; (3) obtaining a license to run a leasing company and (4) to investigate opportunities with our only China contact, Jack Perkowski, a former Pittsburgher who had moved there and bought an auto parts business. Mr. Perkowski has been referred to as "Mr. China," in a book by that name recently published whether it would make sense to merge his auto parts business in China with one of Eagle Picher's divisions in the U.S.

Granted none of these were easy deals and all would take some serious effort and luck. Fortunately, we were headed over to meet some of Joep's partners; Chinese people who had helped him get started in China. Also, there were a number of Dutchmen, working for Joep and living in Nanchang, who had offered to help. So, we weren't going over just totally blind, without connections—always important when dealing in third world countries.

The first thing that struck me on the first day of this strange journey happened in Pittsburgh, as I boarded the United flight to Chicago I was excited because our layover in Beijing for a few hours would allow us to meet with the aforementioned, Jack Perkowski.

As I waited to board the flight I noticed an older, well-dressed (coat and tie—so unusual these days) gentleman standing next to me, waiting also to board. They were boarding by numbered zones and apparently the gentleman didn't understand how it worked (or he couldn't see the numbers) so I explained it to him and he boarded correctly in front of me. He smiled as I walked down the aisle, moving toward my seat, and I was struck by the number of people (all saying hello to me) who recognized me as a former Steeler (something that will mean nothing in China)—it was almost as though I was on a flight to the Super Bowl.

The guy next to me, however, was not from Pittsburgh but we started to talk and I discovered that both of us were going a long way that day, as he was traveling to the island of Fiji with his family to celebrate his Dad's birthday, his 80th, (his Dad had fought in WWII in the Pacific and wanted to revisit some of the places he had fought). During the course of this conversation he mentioned that his brother would also be joining him in Fiji. As we were about to land, he asked me what I do and when I told him investment banking he said his brother also was "in investments," now working with a V.C. firm in California and that he'd formerly worked for Sisco, which just happened to be one of Amperion's key investors. I told the Fiji traveler to mention Amperion and tell him we were going to China to see if we can create some opportunities for Amperion. As we got off the plane I was struck by how small the world is—how often Sam and I have met someone on the other side of the world who has some amazing connection with us—out of the blue so to speak.

Walking down the terminal in Chicago I noticed the older gentleman, whom I had spoken with getting on the plane, and asked him where he was going. He said Las Vegas, for some kind of seminar and asked where I was going. When I replied China, he stopped dead, and said "there's no one in Pittsburgh who knows more about China than me," and he proceeded to tell me that he had worked for U.S. Steel for most of his career and had lived in China. He quickly gave me two cards, one of which I noted introduced him as a Robert P. Little-field, former chairman of something called the "China-America Trade Society and Co-Founder and Executive Manager of the Pittsburgh-Wuhan Friendship Committee, Inc. and the other card introduced Mr. Littlefield as President, CEO of something called, Amerasia Trade and Technology, Inc.

After saying goodbye (and wishing them well in Vegas) I walked down the concourse even more amazed at how serendipitous life can be. Here in the space of thirty minutes (on my first trip back to China since the 80's) I had met two gentlemen with truly amazing connections. The old story that there are just six degrees of separation (that you could get to anyone in the world through no more than six personal connections) seemed to be more real every day but now it seems more like two degrees of separation.

So, now we get on the flight to Beijing, where you might expect to meet someone with a China connection, and the American guy sitting right next to us turns out to know Jack Perkowski—again, only two degrees. So, I sit here, on this forever flight, and just know that something very interesting is going to come out of this journey. It may not make us any money but it will be fascinating and fun—I can feel it in my gut. Sammy and I have traveled all over this world and always something good has happened.

So, we arrived in Beijing, after a 13 hour flight, and were met by Jack Perkowski, a former Pittsburgh North Hill's High School Grad, Yale undergrad, Harvard Business School, and former head of Paine Webber's Investment Banking Dept on Wall Street. Jack had left Wall Street twelve years ago to find the new world economy that would emulate the U.S. economy back in the early 1800's and had finally (after spending time in Singapore and Hong Kong) decided to move to Beijing.

Jack had contacted me (on a trip home to Pittsburgh to see his Mom) and invited me to lunch, suggesting we had a number of similarities in our backgrounds (Jack had played football at Yale and we were both investment bankers—but clearly I was not in his investment's league).

At our luncheon, Jack had described to me his belief that China was the world's next big economic boom area and that he intended to participate. Later I would learn that Jack had executed a consolidation play, wrapping up many of China's top auto parts companies (I never knew China even had an auto parts industry).

Jack met us outside the luggage claim and took us, by private limo, on a wonderful tour of Beijing, enabling Sam to see the Tiananmen Square where the soldiers, years before, had killed a number of protesting students. We then drove back to his office and talked about what is happening in China, one of the world's fastest growing economies.

Jack warned us that "in China everything is possible" but then, pausing for effects, said, "nothing is easy." With that advice, he drove us back to the airport, despite our protestations that we could take a cab—Jack wanted to help, even coming into the airport with us, where we were told at the airline check in counter that the flight was full and, since we had not confirmed our flight within 72 hours that we would have to fly out the next day. Since we had only purchased our tickets 48 hours ago we protested vigorously and they sent us over to a counter full of tough looking Chinese officials who immediately told us that we would have to fly out the next day, if we were lucky.

Jack, observing our problem, had taken his cell phone out and called somebody. After a short conversation he gave his phone to one of the officials who listened politely and then told us we were upgraded to first class and could fly out on our original flight. We realized, from this example, that it is important to know the right folks in China. Moments later we flew away to Nanchang, two hours to the south, a city, supposedly, many years behind Beijing in terms of economic growth.

Arriving in Nanchang, (around 10:00 pm) as we left the baggage claim, we were amazed to see a huge banner (four feet wide and ten feet across) welcoming Sam and me to Nanchang (as though we were special guests). Driven to a very nice hotel (the Gloria Plaza Hotel) in a private Limo, we were even more surprised to see an even larger banner (spanning 20 feet across and 5 feet deep) hanging from the Hotel's inner balcony, "Welcome Sam and Andy," being escorted to our very nice rooms and told to be ready to meet with the Mayor of Nanchang the next morning.

The next morning, after a nice breakfast in the hotel's premium room, we met our host Chen, and he explained the plans for the day. We were taken by limo across the river to the new city of Honggutan, a city consisting of beautiful office buildings and 20 story apartment buildings and we were told that by December of 2005 the population of the new city would be 500,000 people. There we met with the mayor of Honggutan, a truly incredible new city where we pitched the head of the Communist party. Afterwards we had a lunch at a fine hotel restaurant with representatives of the Communist party and, as the custom is, they encouraged us to drink many toasts of their 140 proof liquor—all and all a very interesting day.

We then went out to Joep's new resort and toured the golf course, actually hitting a shot on one of the par threes (miraculously, as I'm not that good, I hit it on the green—about a 180 meter shot into the wind).

Later that evening we were escorted to the City's old castle where we were scheduled to give our formal presentation, regarding our ability to handle the City's trash problems, to the Mayor of Nanchang. The ancient castle was stunning, surrounded by high walls and a moat and we were taken up to a large room (90 feet long by 30 feet wide with high ceilings) with two throne chairs facing down the room and a row of chairs against the wall for the Communist party along one side, facing out, and another row of chairs for Joep's team (both Dutchies and Chinese teammates) along the other side facing the government officials.

I was escorted to one of the throne chairs and seated next to me was the Mayor and behind us were two interpreters (mine, one of Joeps Chinese team who spoke excellent English and the mayor's) and I was told to begin my presentation.

As I began speaking, I noticed a television camera man walk to the middle of the room and focusing directly on me and the presentation (apparently broadcasting the presentation live, as there was a red light on the camera). Struggling to balance my presentation book on my knees and turn awkwardly towards the Mayor, sitting within two feet of me (both throne chairs beside each other facing out) distracted by this incredible scene, I struggled to make the presentation which I had practiced only once on the long flight over.

About half way through the presentation, distracted by the camera man, the Communist party officials disapproving looks, listening to the interpreters repeating what I had said, I was amazed when the two interpreters started arguing over how to interpret what I had said and I realized that there was a high probability that the details of my presentation might be seriously changed, depending upon what my interpreters decided the Mayor wanted to hear—who knew what they were saying.

Later, being told by our Dutch friends that every thing had gone very well and that the Mayor was very impressed with our Liberty Waste capabilities, we drove away, with me wondering what had really happened and what the City of Nanchang was really going to offer.

On the third day we visited the existing Nanchang landfill and then made a presentation to the landfill's top executives, with lunch afterwards, again with many "white lightenings," (their very potent liquor—a 40% alcohol rice wine), with again many toasts. At the same time Sam and I both had a heated reaction to some very hot sauce and went out into a beautiful garden sweating profusely. However, there we were approached by a camera man and were both interviewed (presumably on tape) about our reaction to their fine city. Later we took a tour of a number of their city's fairly mediocre waste transfer stations.

That night, after another sumptuous meal at a local restaurant, we were taken to have our feet massaged (with full toe nail treatment) and back, shoulder and thigh massage—another very interesting day. The following day we traveled to Juijang (north of Nanchange on the Yangtze River) and pitched the Vice Mayor on our interest in handling his city's waste problems. Apparently, Joep, had been selected to manage the Juijang harbor, as he had the Rotterdam harbor in Holland. Afterwards, we had another fine luncheon and hiked up onto the beautiful Lushan mountain, a famous mountain where both Chiang Kai Shek and Mao Tse Sung had had summer homes.

On the way to the mountain, switch backing our way up, we were stopped by an accident (two buses had collided with little damage). Chen, one of Joep's top guys, jumped out and started yelling orders to the police and bus drivers, demanding that they back up one bus to allow a single line of traffic to advance between the buses. As soon as the bus moved, an auto heading down the mountain tried to sneak down through the gap first but Chen jumped in front of it and stopped it, yelling and waving his arms. Apparently, Chen thought it was the turn of those heading up the mountain to pass and he demanded the driver back up.

The police uniformed driver jumped out of the car and shook his fist at Chen and told him he was a police official, transporting Police monetary funds. Seeing his boss being threatened, David Pu, another Joep worker, jumped out of our car and sprinted up to help Chen, who was yelling back that he should either back up or he, the police-man, would be transporting garbage in the future—the guy backed up and we drove on through.

That night driving back, we decided we did not need to eat, and the next day we were taken to the airport by David Pu and off we went back to Pittsburgh, via Hong Kong and Chicago—very long flights.

Sitting on those flights, Sam and I had plenty of hours to discuss our whirlwind tour of Nanchang, and concluded that we smelled a rat—the Chinese officials we had met never once committed to pay for our services. Clearly they wanted us to bring in $20,000,000 of waste disposal infrastructure (compactors, containers, trucks, hauling stations and landfills) without ever committing to what they were willing to pay for the service, assuming that we would be able to recycle most of the waste and potentially make money that way.

We had also learned that a Swiss Disposal Company had come into Nanchang a few years before but had "mysteriously" withdrawn their operation, retreating back to Switzerland. I would ask for contact information, assuming that the Swiss would tell us how terrible their experience had been. The Chinese officials refused to ever send me the names and phone numbers.

Upon returning to Pittsburgh I sent an e-mail to our Dutch friends who had tried to help, essentially showing them that we, with all due respect, would not be sending millions of dollars worth of equipment to their city. After a month or so we received a response from them that gave us little optimism, nor did it change our opinion. Obviously, we needed firm commitments, contracts, and we could see that they had no intention of providing those. They had basically just "given" us the right to conduct a due diligence, promising to give us in depth data with regard to the amount of waste but little with regard to what they would pay us for disposing of it.

When they realized our interest in waste disposal had waned for their city, they focused on something we had almost forgotten to mention—Broad Band over the Power Lines. We would go on to form a new company, called BPL Global, Inc. with the idea that we would roll out the new wireless internet technology throughout Asia in high density buildings where there was no competition from cable or DSL. We had no idea what we were getting into and that new company would become one of our most interesting chapters of our business careers.

Today BPL Global has over a dozen major business opportunities from Brazil to China and the company has raised many millions of dollars, some from the Chart Group's (thanks to the help of Chris Brady) investors in Kuwait. Along the way, as Duquesne Light is one of our investors, we discovered that this wireless technology and our software could help Power Companies have a more efficient system (the Smart Grid) and the company has completely morphed it's business plan focusing primarily on helping power companies save power all over the world with wireless internet being relegated to a secondary position. Recently BPL Global won an award for the fasting growing company in Pittsburgh in the energy category.

Chapter 10

THREE RIVERS STADIUM

What does a stadium mean to a team? Can an inanimate object take on a life of its own? Was Three Rivers Stadium a major contributor to the success of the Steelers in the 70's? Did the fans and the team come together with a passion and determination that made it very difficult for opponents to prevail?

All these questions and more were asked, ad nausea, when we came together on December 16th, 2001 to celebrate the good things that happened in Three Rivers Stadium, remember the bad (humility is good) and come together one more time as former players from three or four different generations.

The Steelers invited 50 players back from the three decades of football and I was one of those players lucky enough to be included. However, standing in the end-zone, staring at all the players from later generations, prior to our introduction to a stadium full of our so wonderful fans, many of whom, I'm sure, feeling much the same way we did—(is it really necessary to tear this stadium down?), I felt out of sorts, as though something was missing, my equilibrium off center, somewhat discombobulated, wondering what was wrong.

But then I realized what it was—I was the oldest player by at least five years. There was nobody from my generation there. Ray Mansfield, the team's most beloved player, and I had played in the '60s with a great group of guys who had played their guts out, during one losing season after another, being booed by some of the fans, having snow balls thrown at us, hearing Johnny Carson tell Steeler jokes, setting new levels of inadequacy and humorous incompetence. Funny unless you were there, player or fan, and having to endure one humiliating defeat after another.

Some of us had played at Forbes Field and others at Pitt Stadium. We practiced at South Park, a place that didn't even have a football field, just a grassy area (with lots of rocks) inside a horse track.

For our locker room we used the basement of the park's medical infirmary, a clap board, two story, old wooden house with our training room and meeting rooms all crammed in on the first and second floors. The basement locker room was by far the worst locker room I had ever seen, even at the high school level, and one winter morning we showed up to find snow drift all over our pads, having come in through the cracks in the walls. That was the NFL in the 50's and 60's. But, hey, I loved every minute of it—well, almost.

Other than Rocky Bleier and Terry Hanratty, (two old Notre Dame buddies) none of the players invited back had any perspective—contrast makes things so much more meaningful. Except for Dick Hoak, a great Steeler player, was the Steelers backfield coach and not part of the 50 odd players, although he was there working for the team, coaching the running backs. Most had arrived following the 70's teams that had won 4 out of 6 Super Bowls, a feat never before accomplished or since. I stood there thinking that these guys can't really have a true appreciation for what this stadium really meant to those of us who came before, traveling such a very long, difficult, often humiliating, embarrassing road but one that finally ending with the exhilaration of being a part of those Super Bowl championship teams.

Of course, I could remember the old guys, who came way before me, telling us the same thing—"you rookies don't have a clue." They knew we couldn't appreciate what this game used to be like—taking the train and buses to away games; staying in fleabag hotels; eating in old diners; using equipment that was falling apart and barely getting paid enough to exist on. But all those old guys loved it, just like we did.

Our predecessors, great players and colorful characters like Bobby Layne, Ernie Stautner, Tom the Bomb Tracy, Myron Pottios, Clendon Thomas, Buddy Dial, Brady Keys, and too many more to mention, told great stories though, of drinking and playing poker with the Chief on all night train rides to Chicago, of walking to the stadium because they didn't have enough money for a taxi and many other stories showing just how good we had it in the sixties. They were right. I couldn't imagine but I tried to respect what they had gone through and understood that without them our day never would have come. They, the owners and the loyal fans had built the NFL.

So, I stood there thinking about my old teammates and knew that the younger players standing there, waiting to be announced, really had no true appreciate for those who came before, they just weren't there during all those bad seasons, losing game after game, being labeled the "SOS-Same Old Steelers." We had struggled valiantly but vainly, just not having the talent—as Chuck Noll had let us know, we couldn't run fast enough, jump high enough, nor were we strong enough and not nearly good enough but we had given it everything, fighting until the last minute.

But believe me, we lived and died with every loss in all those years prior to moving into Three Rivers Stadium. We didn't understand that it had nothing to do with our mental attitude, our courage, our heart, or our lack of commitment—we tried so hard. In fact, I'd say we tried as hard or harder than any of those teams representing the three decades of play in the stadium. We just weren't good enough.

Nevertheless, I realized, standing one last time on Three River's turf, that I was missing all my teammates from those bad days—it would have been great if all of them could have also been there—celebrating not a place, but instead an experience, that has bonded us all together forever. But, as Pat Conroy stated in his so special sports book, *My Losing Season*, where he describes the agony of a failed team, "There are no reunions for losing teams."

Despite our losing seasons we had many good players who were terrific guys, all trying their best. If they were so good, why didn't we win? Good question and the answer, of course, is that we didn't have enough such players to be a winner but all the players from those days were good people—in those years, coaches didn't put up with players who had bad attitudes—"prima donnas" need not apply. But that's another story and I'm getting away from talking about Three Rivers Stadium, a place that few of those former great Steelers were able to make it all the way to.

Ray Mansfield, my best Steeler buddy, who had won the prestigious NFL Blocker of the Year Award in 1970, was also missing, having died tragically while hiking with his son, Jimmy, in the Grand Canyon in 1996. But Ray had played 7 years in Three Rivers, started in two

Super Bowl wins, truly going with his bliss, and I strongly felt that I could sense his presence, hovering above us, enjoying the scene.

The new stadium's locker room was a huge improvement over South Park's, big enough so as not to feel cramped, actually permitting us to play various games to break the tension (like throwing a Frisbee into a towel bin 30 feet away), and certainly there was no snow coming through cracks in the walls.

I felt like I had a special relationship with Three Rivers, one that went back to its origins. Working in my office in the off-season selling Wall Street syndications, I had received a rare phone call from Art Rooney, known as the Chief, back in 1968.

"Russell, I want you to come over to the North side for a 'photo-op.'"

"What's a 'photo op'"?

"Just come on over as soon as you can."

Standing in a barren field on the North Side, with a couple of reporters and probably no more than a dozen Steeler friends in attendance, I helped put the shovel in the ground for that "Photo Op" with the Chief and his son Dan (now the Steeler's Chairman) back in 1968, the year they started construction. Months later Ray and I, and our partners Sam Zacharias and Chuck Puskar walked the rafters with Dahl Ritchey, the stadium's architect, before it was completed and were there opening day in 1970 when we lost to the Oilers, a huge disappointment, especially after having won all of our preseason games that year.

One of the important benefits of Three Rivers was that it had artificial turf, called Tartan Turf. At first all of us found that our legs hurt from running on the new field but as the first season progressed we discovered that our legs didn't hurt on this artificial turf but only when we were required to practice on real grass (i.e., when preparing for a Cleveland game by practicing on the real grass field of Carnegie Mellon. Practicing on the tartan turf every day we learned what shoes to wear, how to make cuts and eventually liked the turf so much we started calling it the "God Tartan," in the sense that other teams had hard time playing on it, where we knew where the treacherous spots were.

I was also the first player, and the only one for a number of years, to use the stadium as a work out facility. I developed a running routine that took me up and down the four ramps, running four laps around the stadium and then hit the stairs in the steep upper sections, where I'd run half way around the stadium, doing every other stairwell—up one and down the other.

Mike Webster, our HOF, super conditioned center, (who won the NFL Strongman contest a number of times) would later take that workout to a new level, running around the entire stadium, going up one upper stairwell and down the next.

I remember one year, returning to these stadium workouts in the late spring, after months of traveling on business overseas, badly out of shape and running into Coach Noll, who suggested that he join me for my workout. Not wanting him to know how badly out of shape I was, I nearly killed myself trying to keep up with him. Chuck, in good shape himself, barely breathed going up and down the ramps, talking to me the entire time—I was impressed how strong he was although I'm sure he wasn't thrilled with the state of my conditioning.

Sometimes I would run the lower steps (easier), the ones that moved out for baseball, while the Pirates were going through batting practice. I would go up one aisle and then down the other and do both sides and then back again, four times. The Pirates who barely worked out (one Steeler practice would require more energy than ten Pirate games) would wave and shake their heads as though I had lost mine.

Once, I remember working out after work on a hot summer day down on the field, just before training camp. I could see that the stadium was set up for some kind of concert but I didn't know who the entertainer was.

I was doing a progression work out where you did eight different exercises (i.e., jumping jacks, pushups, sit ups, etc. and finally 20 yard sprints) and you'd do them eight times and then seven times and then six times and so forth—down to one time. If done quickly it was a difficult workout and I was breathing hard.

About halfway through the progression, I noticed that a person was being led out onto the stage and taken over to a large, raised piano and I realized that it was the great entertainer Stevie Wonder. He sat down and his assistant who had escorted him left the stage, apparently leaving him alone to practice his songs. I looked around and noticed that no one but the two of us were in the stadium—all the workers apparently taking a break.

There we were, two artists, (yah, right!) working to improve our skills. I noticed him stop and listen and, as I was only 20 or so yards away from him, and I figured that he probably heard me gasping for air. He might have wondered what was making that strange noise. He could have imagined it being Franco or Swann, instead of some beat up old linebacker.

Being a big Stevie Wonder fan, always enjoying his music, I had one of my all time favorite workouts, listening to his sweet rhythms as I ran through the progressions. The music made the workout seem so much more enjoyable (this was before Ipods) and I was thrilled to have this private performance—just me and Stevie, hanging out together—well, sort of. When I was through I wanted to go up on the stage and tell him how much I loved his music, but then he seemed really into it and, not wanting to interrupt his concentration, I left him alone.

Chuck Noll always had us trying the latest in-vogue training strategy. One year he would take something from the training program of our astronauts (i.e., running a mile, keeping our heart rate at 180 beats per minute—if it was lower than that we were told to speed up, if higher to slow down) and the next year, trying something our Olympic sprinters do, (running down hill), a practice that is supposed to stretch out your leg muscles, allowing for greater speed. Unfortunately, for most of us, it only caused us to have pulled hamstrings.

One year Chuck hired our own stretch (flexibility) coach, Paul Uram. Always too stiff, I worked diligently with Paul all summer, significantly improving my flexibility to where I could easily touch my toes without bending my legs—granted, that's not much but it was a great improvement for me. That training camp, after being hit awkwardly, pulling a muscle in my lower back in our first scrimmage, forced to sit out a week, I met with Dr. John Best, our crusty old Steeler Doc.

"So, Russell, what's wrong with you?

"My back went out."

"Did you do anything different in your preparation this year?
"I worked on becoming more flexible."

"There you have it—don't do any of those exercises anymore—your back should improve over time. You are hereby excused from any stretching exercises for the rest of the season." My back got better within a week.

There was a time when the stadium was having problems with a growing pigeon population that had made Three Rivers its home, apparently finding plenty of food, spilled by the fans. But the cleanup crew was finding that it was easier to clean up spilled popcorn than it was dried pigeon poop.

Hearing of this problem (we were close to the crew) a number of the players who were hunters came up with a solution. Arriving early before an early fall practice with their shotguns ready to send those pigeons on their way, they planned to kill a few of them, figuring that most of them would fly away, unharmed, and not return.

So three or four of our finest hunters, early one fall morning, walked out into the middle of the field, armed with plenty of shells, ready to solve the problem. But nothing happened—the birds just ignored them and continued to peck away at the trash thrown in amongst the seats at the previous night's Pirate game. So one of our guys had the idea of just shooting right into the seats, assuming that that would startle the pigeons and get them airborne. Ok, it might mar the seats a little but hey, we had a problem here and it had to be solved.

Well, that tactic worked beautifully and all the pigeons immediately went up into the air and shots rang out in all directions. Suddenly, these brave hunters realized that the birds had to circle before gaining enough elevation and it would take them some time to get high enough to exit Three Rivers. Before anyone, like an environmentalist, or tree hugger, could intercede, they had shot over a dozen birds. After that Three Rivers was no longer bothered by a bird problem. Pigeons apparently have very good memories.

Mike Wagner, an avid golfer, wondered if it would be possible to hit a ball out of the stadium from anywhere on the field. Trying a number of different clubs, the best he could do was to leave a dozen balls up in the upper tier. Hearing the balls smashing against the upper seats, Mike finally stopped when he realized that he was undoubtedly chipping the paint off of the seats.

Of course, the real excitement and meaning of the stadium is all those wonderful experiences we, and the fans, had from participating in some of the most amazing games ever played. For me, the most exciting year, the Steelers quintessential year, the turn around year, was 1972, a year when we went from the perennial loser to our first division championship and that amazing playoff victory against the

Raiders—with Franco's incredible "Immaculate Reception." But despite feeling the pain of losing the AFC Championship Game to the 17-0 Dolphins there a few weeks later, it did not ruin that great year.

There is another aspect to why Three Rivers Stadium had been such a meaningful landmark for the teams and the fans. I believe it was a symbol of the city's resurrection. Pittsburgh's economy, based on Steel, had fallen on very hard times during the 60's and through the great work of guys like Jay Aldridge of Penn Southwest (a group put together to entice foreign companies to Pittsburgh), Dave Roderick, Tom O'Brien (PNC's Chairman), Tony O'Reilly (H.J. Heinz Chairman), Prosser and Sandy Mellon, the Hillmans (Elsie and Henry) and Chuck Queenan (a top partner at Kirkpatrick Lockhart) and the leaders of Mellon Bank, Alcoa, PPG, and too many others visionaries to mention, and, of course, all those hard working employees of those companies, the city, in the early 70's, was starting to fight back, much like the Steelers were.

The team, and the stadium, became, I believe, an unconscious symbol of City pride. No one was going to kick us around any more, no more ugly smokestacks, no loser companies—look out we're coming back. We've got a beautiful city, with lot of vibrant businesses and, by the way, the best damn pro football team in history—stick that in your ear America.

Long after I retired, needing a good workout to deal with the always-present hassles of business, I would still occasionally go over to the stadium and walk in and run the steps. It was nice—no one would bother me, the ground crew would wave me on in, like in the old days. The stadium was a place of refuge, like spending time with an old friend not seen for a while.

So, I must admit that watching the implosion of Three Rivers was a painful experience. I'm going to miss that great stadium, home of so many championship teams (Steelers and Pirates), Three Rivers. I know logically that the new stadium will be better, have more luxury boxes that will enable the team to stay competitive in the ever-escalating salary wars, but I'm still going to miss it—a lot. It does feel good that the new Heinz Field is basically in the same place, only yards away from our old friend, Three Rivers

Chapter 11

THE NEEDLES

Back in the early 90's, Ray Mansfield and I, out of the game for over fifteen years, still continued to seek new adventures that we hoped would wash away our post football lethargy. We figured that we needed physical challenges that would test us: our level of conditioning; our intestinal fortitude, our ability to push forward despite the pain, just as we had when playing all those years with the Steelers—that need was in our blood and we needed to reach down, to find out if we still had our Mojo, and to prove to ourselves that it hadn't been diluted. Of course it had been, as we weren't getting any younger, but we still felt the need to challenge ourselves—you can never over-exaggerate the ego of a former jock.

So, we looked for another test, one that would have most of the ingredients we were seeking: a physical challenge, overcoming fears, bonding with our team, and the bliss that comes from pushing oneself near to one's physical limits. After much discussion and analysis we decided to go to a mountain range in Southwestern Colorado's San Juan Mountains, down near Durango, called the "Needles." It has a high basin, named Chicago, with two lakes surrounded by three fourteen thousand foot mountains; all considered relatively (not in the top five most difficult) hard climbs—not technical but difficult with some modest exposure to a fall.

One might wonder why I would write about a trip that happened so many years ago and not focus on an adventure more recently tackled. But just recently (April, 2005) I read an article in Backpacker Magazine about the ten toughest hikes in America and was surprised to find the hike up to Windom Peak (one of the 14ers surrounding Chicago Basin) listed as number seven. Of course, the article was referring to a marathon hike up and back the same day—granted that would be an exhausting hike—well over twenty miles with lots of vertical feet (4200+) to climb.

One of the things that appealed to us was that the best way to get to the trail head was to take the old narrow gauge railroad from Durango, Colorado, going through a beautiful gorge before finally getting off the train at a wilderness depot, the start of the climb up to the Chicago Basin.

Our team consisted of a group of aging ex-jocks, much like ourselves, old buddies, who had participated in previous hikes, climbs or other challenges, but, this time, two of our party decided to bring their daughters (a new experience for the group). The participants were: my business partner, Sam Zacharias; my brother, Will; then brother-in-law, Bill Comfort; Ray Mansfield and his daughter, Kathleen and my old Mizzou buddy, Jack Musgrave and his daughter, Hilary. All the guys were in their mid to late 40s and both young ladies were in the early 20's.

Sam, a driven businessman, the only non-athlete (well, I guess he does play tennis once a week with his buddies), and partner of mine in various international business ventures we had pursued over the years, is primarily a very successful insurance salesman for his own company, Gateway Financial Group. Sam, a veteran of many of our Grand Canyon hikes, had proven his ability, never giving up, regardless of how tired he was—Sam had also learned how to play hurt.

Jack, a former All State football player in St. Louis and University of Missouri teammate, too consumed by the demands of his law practice to work out very often, was just coming off a major trial where he had represented Monsanto in a record setting class action lawsuit (the longest jury trial in the history of U.S. jurisprudence—8 years).

Bill Comfort, an all around good guy, insurance salesman, runner of major marathons, a track star in high school, was always in shape and ready for any tough hike/climb.

Actually, Ray, Sam, Jack and Bill were all veterans of many difficult, 3-night, 4 day, Grand Canyon hikes on wilderness trails that challenged all of our conditioning and sometimes having to deal with some exposure to serious falls.

My older brother, Will, ski instructor, avid pilot (ex FAA), was usually in shape, as he was a stickler for eating the right foods and always exercising—basically your driven, perfect older brother. It had been difficult to live up to his level of perfection (grades, work ethic, etc.) as a kid growing up.

The two daughters, both smart, athletic and very pretty, were in their early twenties and would definitely have the advantage of youth. They would soon both discover that one needs, regardless of age, to take their time in the mountains.

We had all arrived in Durango on the same day, planning to spend the night at an old hotel in the center of the town, almost across the street from the train station. Before turning in we decided to treat ourselves to a great dinner of Mexican food, drinking far too many margaritas that we viewed as OK since it was only a short walk from the restaurant to the hotel (no need for a designated driver) and we knew we'd sweat it all out the next day.

Arriving early the next morning at the train station, loaded down with our heavy backpacks (50 pounds each or more), I worried about the possibility of a screw up with the railroad tickets, as we had been forced to make the reservations months in advance due to the fact that the railroad was nearly sold out the entire summer—after weeks of trying we had finally been able to confirm dates compatible with all parties to reserve those eight tickets.

Fortunately, they had our reservation and we had boarded the train in plenty of time and found ourselves in awe at the beautiful terrain, as the train wound it's way out of the city and up into the gorge, on it's way to the famous mining town, Silverton, at the top of the track.

About an hour and a half up through and out of the gorge, and about three fourths of the way to Silverton, the train stopped along the river, in the middle of the woods, with no apparent depot, a truly wilderness stopover, and we were surprised to find that nearly two dozen people got off, (including ourselves), some apparently (they had huge backpacks) going to be out for a couple of weeks of hiking and camping.

Our group was the last to get all its' gear off the train, around 11:30 am, and the last to start up a nice trail that would wind up a valley, next to a rushing creek, for the next eight miles before hitting a head wall up into the Chicago Basin. Leading the way, going slowly and methodically (I'd learned long ago that you don't want to hurry up mountains), I was soon passed by an impatient Kathleen Mansfield, who charged up the trail.

It was a beautiful trail, with lots of huge fir trees along the creek, deep in the steep valley. Soon it started to rain lightly and we all stopped to put on our rain gear, enjoying the coolness and light breezes. It truly was a great trail with new and different scenery every hundred meters, as the trail wound its' way up the valley.

Coming around a corner we found Kathleen, sitting by the edge of the trail, feeling ill—probably from a combination of having gone too fast, the elevation (about 10,500 feet) and the margarita consumption the night before. Taking a break next to her we cautioned her not to go too fast, explaining that the need for a proper pace was critical.

It's not uncommon for anyone challenging the high country to experience some level of altitude sickness, its' most common symptoms being headaches, slight nausea, shortness of breath and sleeplessness. We would all experience some of those conditions during the trip.

As the day wore on we started to feel the natural fatigue despite stopping for a ten minute rest every hour and drinking as much fluid as we could. There were good reasons for the energy drop: the trail was consistently steep with few level spots; we had not acclimated, having arrived the night before; we weren't in all that good shape and the excitement of the climb had probably caused all of us to climb slightly too fast. Fortunately the rain stopped and a bright sun appeared just as we stopped for a lunch of peanut butter sandwiches.

After lunch our group, which had stayed together pretty well during the morning, became spread out on the trail, with Bill Comfort, up in front, followed by me, with Sam and Will not far behind. Bringing up the rear were Ray, Jack and the two young ladies. Ray had mentioned to me after lunch that he thought the four of them might have to stop early, avoiding the head wall, because of Kathleen's nausea and the fact that he was feeling very tired, not having been able to work out much before the trip.

Around 5:30 pm the front four found ourselves nearing the steep headwall that was at the end of the valley and Ray and Jack, at least a quarter mile behind us across an open area, waved us on ahead, as they apparently had decided to stay at one of the beautiful campsites along the river with the idea that they would complete the climb to the basin in the morning, not concerned whether they would be able to climb all the mountains.

Excited about getting to our base camp in the Chicago Basin where we would be in a great position to bag all three of the 14ers, mountains called Windom, Sunlight and Eolus, we charged forward. We planned to do Windom and Sunlight the next day and Eolus the following day. In all we had planned to spend three nights, four days, climbing the three mountains, before meeting the train on its' way down from Silverton in mid afternoon the fourth day.

Approaching the head wall we were somewhat awed by its' height and wondered how the trail could wind its' way up such a steep wall— our guide books told us that the wall would be about a one thousand foot climb, getting us to the campsite around 6:30 pm, leaving, since it was summer, plenty of time before dark to cook our dinner of chicken soup with lots of noodles and fried spam (which really is pretty good inside pita bread).

Bill and I took turns winding up the very steep and rocky slope, with Sam and Will falling a little behind. It was definitely a test of our conditioning after the long hike in from the train drop off point. My legs ached but I kept on making that one lock step at a time, finally finding a rhythm that felt somewhat comfortable.

After what seemed like an eternity, we topped out onto the basin, slightly over 12,000 feet, which consisted of two small lakes and relatively flat areas surrounding them, probably no more than two or three acres in total, making for good tent areas. Surprisingly there were no other campers/climbers there.

Since Bill was teamed up with Sam, both carrying part of their tent, and the same with Will and I, we had started dinner by the time Will and Sam appeared at the top of the head wall—we were all definitely fatigued and needing a good nights rest before tackling the 14ers rising above us.

After dinner, full of energy giving calories, we sat with our backs against our backpacks and watched a beautiful sunset as it slowly disappeared to the west but our fatigue almost overcame our awe at such a beautiful place. I say "almost" because even with our extreme fatigue (I felt like I was near exhaustion but probably wasn't) we still loved that campsite, sitting comfortably, talking about our hike that day, and appreciating such an incredibly beautiful place.

"I sure hope the Old Ranger and Jack and the girls are OK—they obviously don't have a vista like this. I wonder what time they'll get up that headwall tomorrow morning." I said.

"Sure wouldn't count on that group very early tomorrow—we'll probably be half way up the mountain before they arrive." Sam said.

As soon as the darkness came, so did the cold and we quickly crawled into our tents and sleeping bags, with the promise that we'd get up early the next morning at the break of dawn, getting the necessary early start to hopefully, depending on good weather, bag both mountains slightly past noon, (the normal deadline to be off 14ers because the high likelihood of afternoon rains and the dread lightnings).

Awaking early, with it still quite cold despite it being in the middle of August, the four of us ate a quick breakfast and started up a short (maybe 100 yards) but steep slope from the lake that appeared to point towards a large canyon/gully/drainage running down between Sunlight on the left and Windom on the right. I glanced down to my right toward the top of yesterday's headwall, hoping to see Ray, Jack and their girls but saw no movement.

"I thought it possible that the four down below might have gotten up early enough to join us," I said.

"No chance—I'm sure they're still deep in their cozy sleeping bags waiting for the sun to warm things up," Sam said.

"Knowing Mansfield, he probably had a bottle of Scotch deep in his pack and they were up late sipping it and telling old war stories," Bill said.

We had already topped the small rocky slope above the campsite and we paused to see if we could see a trail. Unfortunately, because of the numerous animals up in the basin area (mule deer, Big Horn Sheep, Mountain Goats, Elk & others), there were just small animal trails heading off in all directions. So we chose the most promising looking one that headed off to our right (west), appearing as though it would be a good way to access Windom Peak's north facing ridge, our line of attack.

However, within a half an hour, after climbing up and over some steep rocks, often being forced to use our arms to assist the effort, Bill Comfort and I found ourselves separated from Sam and Will, as they had fallen back behind us. Despite our view being blocked by steep boulder fields above us (not being able to see Windom), we intuitively sensed that we had angled too far west and turned back slightly east (left), finally gaining the beginning of the ridge.

Shortly thereafter, Bill and I, sitting on some rocks, feeling the need to already drink some of our fluids (Gatorade), waited for a short rest for Sam and Will to catch up but there was no sight of them. Both of us being somewhat impatient by nature, quickly jumped up and began the long and sometimes steep climb up Windom Peak's northern ridge.

We were fortunate in that there was very little wind, the sun was already up high enough where we could feel it and we could see no clouds in the distance, a rare occurrence in Colorado. We were buoyed by the good weather and picked up our pace slightly, knowing that we had two mountains to climb before noon. Heavy clouds and rain can appear quickly, usually in the afternoon, and one must avoid the resulting lightening strikes that can hit the upper crests.

We tried to get into a comfortable climbing pace, working our way up through the rocks and large boulders of the ridge but I felt awkward and out of synch. I remember being irritated that the climb was causing me to breath so hard—I guess my training program had just not been tough enough to get me ready for taking these giant steps, some waist high. Bill, having again completed the Boston Marathon in April, seemed to be having no problem. Wondering if I could continue, I found myself pausing frequently, gasping for breath, breathing in deep gulps of air, as I had been trained to do on the Mount Rainer climbing school.

Finally, after a tough couple of hours of steep climbing on the nasty rock ridge (really more like a steep boulder field) we could sense that we were nearing the top but I forced myself to not get excited, to maintain my slow, methodical pace because it might have just been a "false summit," a point that you think is the top but, upon reaching it, you find that there is another higher peak looming in front of you, still left to climb.

But, in this case, the summit we could see turned out to be the real thing and after some point to point climbing over some gnarly rocks, with some exposures to falls, we found ourselves on the summit. After a quick high five, a sip of water, congratulating ourselves for having finally found the correct route, we started back down the ridge we had come up, looking for a very steep gully (the guidebook's route) off to our right, facing down, (East) off the ridge we had come up.

That gully would take us directly down to near the top (a saddle between Windom and an unknown 13er) of the large drainage that runs down between the two mountains. We would then be able to angle over (northeast) towards Sunlight without losing too many precious vertical feet before starting to climb back up. We appreciated that we didn't have to climb all the way back down to our campsite before starting back up Sunlight. We were quite happy with the success of the Windom climb and the weather still seemed excellent, so we realized that there was a good chance that we could summit Sunlight by noon before starting down.

Nearing the top of the gully we were searching for, still on the north ridge, only a few 100 yards from the summit of Windom, we ran into Sam, who was just sitting there, on a rock, looking very exhausted. We explained that he was close to the summit, telling him what to expect at the top but Sam, who doesn't like heights, appeared disinterested, as though he had already decided that he had reached a high enough point on the mountain to make himself happy.

After negotiating our way down the very steep gully (probably no more than 300 vertical feet), we angled left (north) toward the Sunlight Peak which was easily visible and not that far away, and scrambled over rough terrain beneath the unknown 13,000 footer to our right.

Within a half an hour of struggling to make our way (again no trail), around numerous precarious obstacles (mainly steep drop offs to our left and cliff ledges), we circled left around behind the summit tower, towards the north side of Sunlight Peak where our guide book promised a "natural arch" of sorts that we could climb through and gain the summit boulder, made famous by some lunatic who had done a hand stand on it, despite the 1000 foot drop right behind him.

Feeling the void to our left we angled up towards the summit massive, only 20 yards away. Glancing upwards on the 70 degree slope we could see what appeared to be almost a cave, because of the shadows caused by the huge summit boulders. Scampering up into it we realized that it really isn't a natural arch but just two or three huge rock slabs lying against one another, causing the tunnel through which we climbed. Climbing out of the six foot "cavern" we came out on a relatively flat boulder which angled up to the left only 15 yards or so to the summit boulder.

Sitting on the top, Bill and I again congratulated each other, the first time we had climbed two 14ers together in the same day and it was a great feeling. We had avoided many potential pitfalls and we could feel the effort it had taken. I was again struck by how much I love to climb. It is truly a passion. Bill and I would sit on that summit for probably no more than fifteen minutes, but I can still see it in my mind's eye now like it happened yesterday.

We also discovered, as we seldom looked at our watches, that it was right at twelve noon. In the distance, north of us, we could see Mount Eolus, our objective the next day, and from that distance (probably about two or three miles as the crow flies) its' slopes seemed almost vertical, unclimbable for non rock climbers like ourselves.

As we started down, heading back down the big gully between the two mountains towards our campsite where we planned to have some lunch (more chicken noodle soup) I realized that I didn't want the day to be over. I could feel the pride of succeeding, the joy of being up so high, away from all my problems, real or imagined.

Bill and I inched down the very steep and rocky slope into the drainage angling down to our campsite. Within an hour we had returned to the Chicago Basin only to find an empty campsite. We wondered where Will and Sam were—had they summited Windom and on their way down the ridge? Knowing they were not planning on climbing Sunlight we assumed they would return soon. We were also surprised not to find Ray and Jack's heavy gear laying near ours— surely they had started up Windom by then.

After a good lunch we sat back and waited for our comrades to appear. It was after 1:30 pm and we were surprised, but not worried, about the no show of our teammates—they were all taking their own good time, apparently taking my advice the previous day, which was "go as slow as you can go and then go a little slower."

Soon both Sam and Will appeared, climbing carefully down the steep headwall from the gully. When they arrived we learned that Sam had gone no farther than where we had seen him, close to the summit but that Will, having gotten even further lost, going too far west before angling back to the north ridge, despite having a pretty good sense of direction (a Russell trait), had summited soon after.

Apparently Sam had felt his fear of heights starting to dominate his attention and had wisely refused to go any further. Will, an accomplished pilot, presumably not overly afraid of heights, had been able to handle the upper exposed section.

Bill and I realized that it was a good thing that they hadn't attempted to climb Sunlight, as it was a great deal steeper and more exposed. About that time, nearly 2:00 pm we heard a shout from below and there were Ray and Jack and their daughters just climbing out of the lower headwall. When they arrived at our campsite they explained that they had been up late, enjoying their beautiful campsite, telling their daughters their favorite stories, sipping some good whiskey, and that they had all slept in and taken their time coming up the headwall. They were quite content to just take photos of Windom and Sunlight and attempt Eolus the next day.

That afternoon we would enjoy sitting around the campsite, observing the unbelievably beautiful views and talking about our lives and families. I missed having my two kids there. My son, Andy, and daughter, Amy, had accompanied me and their Mom on my first mountain climb, Mount Kenya in Africa.

Amy would have especially loved being in such a wild place, having spent one month in Alaska, climbing and trekking through wild and gnarly places. She was a strong hiker, climber, having been the first to the top of our climb of Kilimanjaro. Andy would have brought his fly rod and would be trout fishing through that afternoon. As I got older I realized that I would have a tough time of even keeping up with either one of them, as both of them stayed in very good shape.

That leisurely afternoon, we also enjoyed observing a pack of Mountain Goats who congregated very near our campsite, obviously having no fear of hikers, probably because campers had fed them. That night we enjoyed sitting around our candles (campfires were not allowed in the wilderness) and telling more good stories (challenges we had all faced in sports, school or business—life in particular).

Soon, we all hit the sack early, promising to get up at the crack of dawn, hoping to get an early start of our climb of Eolus so we could get down below the headwall and half way down the trail to the railroad pickup point before dark.

Unfortunately the next morning it was pouring rain at 6 am and we all stayed in our tents until nearly 8:00 am when the weather

Andy with Colorado mine ruin in background.

Andy and his guide, Fernando, after climbing mountain in background above Machu Picchu, Peru.

With
Pittsburgher
and famous
actor Michael
Keaton at the
Taste of the
NFL event at
Super Bowl
XLI.

Our dog Woody
and me at
Bridal Veil
Falls, Telluride,
Colorado.

Our two children, Amy and Andy, skiing at Snowmass, Colorado.

Wife Cindy and me with Andy, his wife Brigitte and their two boys, Carsten (left) and Finn (right).

Me rowing a
raft in Alaska
with friend
Gary Zenter
laughing at my
bad rowing.

Cindy and I in
Beijing, China's
"Forbidden City."

Pirate game with grandchildren Brody, Kim and Cindy

Two old buddies, Jack Musgrave and me, in Moscow's Kremlin.

Proud dad with daughter Amy.

Elated to arrive at the summit of Pyramid Peak, Colorado.

Riding a zipline/cable in Costa Rica's mountainous jungle.

Standing in front of Prayer Flags and the Tiger's Nest Temple, Bhutan.

Cindy and I at a charitable wine party.

With my brother Will (center) and brother-in-law, Allan.

In the Dolomites
of Italy with friend
John Ball.

With dear friend,
Jim Card, who
survived our
adventures in
Close to the Edge
chapter.

Me, almost to the top of Capital Peak, one of Colorado's toughest.

With fund raiser "extraordinaire," EconomicsPA President Fritz Heinemann, with his daughter Karen.

To Andy and family — may God be with you at all times. your friend always "Chuhi"

With my son, Andy, ex-wife, Nancy, and Chi Chi Rodriquex.

Son Andy and daughter Amy on Tasmin Glacier, New Zealand ski adventure.

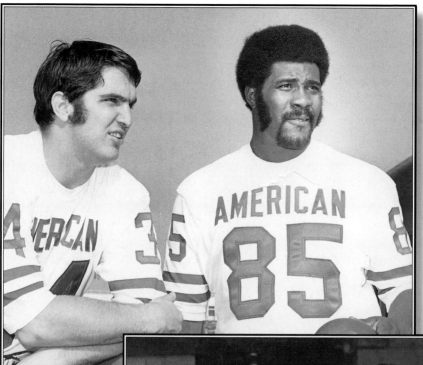

With Joe
Greene at
1971 ProBowl.

Giving game ball
to defensive MVP
after every game.

With good friends Carl Dozzi, Marc Mondair, and Sam Zacharias

Grandkids love their Steelers—from left to right, Jackie, Derek, Cindy, Finn, me, Carsten, and Molly.

Having fun with Bill Cowher, Mario, and Rick Sharp at a charitable golf outing.

Three Rivers Stadium, a place of Joy!

With Dick Hoak, an outstanding Steeler running back and Coach.

Six former Steelers on top of Mt. Princeton, Colorado. Front row, left to right, Frank Atkinson, Moon Mullins, Rocky Bleier. Back row, left to right, Dave Reavis, Andy, and Ray Mansfield.

Andy with partners Don Rea and Jeff Kendall.

Family at our Colorado home.
From front to back and left to right, Carsten, Finn, Jackie, Derek, son Andy, Brigitte, me, Cindy, Amy, Dave, and Molly.

miraculously cleared with bright sunshine. After a quick breakfast, we were all trudging up another steep slope, opposite the Windom ridge, angling towards the saddle between Eolus and it's sub peak, North Eolus, also a 14er (although not one that counts on the 54 challenge because it was too close to the main summit and the saddle between didn't fall enough vertical feet—it is considered a sub peak). Soon we had separated with our group of eight strewn a couple of hundred meters apart, stopping only once (after an hours climb) to replenish our bodily fluids and have an energy snack.

Approaching the saddle (nearly 2000 feet above our campsite) we angled right, away from the saddle, up a wide but steep rocky ledge, which put us in a slightly flat area, east (or right) of the saddle (the ridge between Eolus and North Eolus). Turning back left towards the ridge we climbed up its' rather steep face which often required the use of our hands, pulling ourselves up large boulders. Scampering up this little challenge, Bill and I again distanced ourselves from the others and gaining the ridge we could see that it was going to take some time for the others to join us.

So we pushed on towards the "crux" of the Eolus climb (the climb's most exposed challenge), known as the "Sidewalk in the Sky," a place where the Col between the two summits narrowed to about two feet wide with major drop offs (i.e. 500 feet or more) to either side. Climbing down onto the "Sidewalk" we observed that it was about thirty yards across with most of it substantially wider than two feet, only narrowing down to that width near the far side and only for about ten feet.

Nevertheless, both Bill and I hesitated before crossing the Sidewalk's narrowest point, trying to decide whether it was safe to just walk across or whether we should drop down and straddle it and inch our way across on our bottoms. Eventually, as there was no wind, nor were the rocks slick (vergloss) from the earlier rain, we decided to be bold and just walk across, which obviously took no talent as anyone could easily walk across a two foot wide floor section if the voids weren't looming below both right and left.

Arriving at the other side, without even glancing back (we'd forgotten about the others) Bill and I charged up the south facing headwall which appeared very steep despite it having some grass growing between various rock ledges. Soon we topped out onto the small summit ridge and we angled right, slightly up 30 yards or so to the area of the craggy peak (probably ten feet by five feet). Only then did we look for our comrades, observing them all sitting at where they had summited the lower ridge, probably 80 or so yards from the sidewalk in the sky. Apparently, they had opted to go no further, deciding that even from a distance that the sidewalk was not something they cared to challenge.

After a short time on the summit, taking the obligatory photos of each other standing on the highest point, signing the register (that was kept safe by an aluminum tube), smiling ear to ear, drinking some water, we started down the steep headwall, discovering that it was much worse to descend than to climb because while descending one was forced to observe the huge void at the bottom of the slope (at least a 500 foot vertical fall). If we slipped there would be nothing to grab onto and we might easily tumble down the slope and be launched off the cliff. Making it worse we were forced a number of times to turn our stomachs to the steep slope (probably around 70 degrees, whereas double black ski slopes are rarely over 45 degrees), reaching down with our toes to grasp the next ledge. Being un-roped and exposed on such a steep slope is truly an exhilarating experience.

Arriving at the bottom we discovered a smiling Hilary as she had just come by herself across the sidewalk. Realizing that it wouldn't be safe for her to tackle the headwall alone, knowing I was already feeling the fatigue of the previous day's climbs, unwilling to accompany her, I decided to try and talk her out of it.

Despite knowing that she had had some rock climbing training at her University of Colorado, I said, "Hilary, I really think you should return with us—it's not safe to go up any further by yourself."

"I'm quite capable of climbing up that grassy slope, thank you," she replied.

Appreciating her spunk, knowing her Mom, Susan (who loves to climb) would have said the same thing, I said, "Look, it's too dangerous to go by yourself, and Bill and I are too exhausted to accompany you and, besides, you're only 20 years old and you and your pals can come back here sometime in the future and bag this sucker." Fortunately she bought that argument and she agreed to come back with us.

After crossing the "Sidewalk," and retracing our steps back up to the group, it took us what seemed like an eternity to get down the slope to our camp site at the top of the head wall and another hour to pack up all our gear and get down that. Eventually, we found ourselves, late afternoon, choosing a nice campsite along the creek only about half of the way to where we would meet the train.

That night we would again sit and bond, enjoying immensely each others company, realizing once again that doing something relatively difficult together is a bonding experience.

The final day of our trek we got up late and took our time returning to the pick up point at the required 2:00 pm time, feeling the euphoria of physical accomplishment as the train wound it's way down through the gorge, eventually arriving at the Durango station.

That night we would stay at the fabulous resort Tamarron, eating a luxurious dinner at their finest restaurant (pampering ourselves after being in the wilderness, eating freeze dried foods, sleeping on the ground), listen to some good jazz in their disco bar, and fall into a blissful sleep that night.

The next day, despite our sore muscles, we would play golf and for the first and only time in my life, I shot eleven straight pars in a row. I contribute that lucky streak to being so blissful after the climbing of those three such beautiful and challenging mountains with great friends.

Chapter 12

THE STEELER FANS

In order to give the reader some perspective with regard to how much the Steelers love their fans, and why, I need to go back in time. In 1967 we had just completed another embarrassingly bad season, losing 9 games, winning 4 and tying 1. Things couldn't have been much worse for the Steelers franchise: we were totally incompetent and the fans and players were in a deep funk.

But in January of '68 I was on a USO tour to Saigon during that war's worst TET offensive, where the Viet Cong had attacked all over the country. We were in shock, just coming from a bunker near the U.S. Embassy where we had seen at least 20 dead U.S. soldiers stuffed in body bags. We were about to visit a military hospital to speak with our wounded, and hopefully give them some solace.

Walking into the hospital, seeing their horrible injuries, hearing their moans, feeling the humid 100 degree heat, smelling the disinfectants and blood, I was immediately struck by what an enormous price our soldiers pay. We are the only nation in the world that asks its young men and women to go across the world and risk their lives to protect other peoples' lives and rights, to stop ethnic cleansing, to take out tyrannical rulers, basically helping others to experience the advantages of a free society.

The hospital was a small, one story, temporary wooden building, with only three wards of any size, holding about one hundred soldiers, whose injuries were mostly large gaping, gruesome wounds, amputations and worse.

I felt totally out of sorts, feeling like an intruder, being where we had no right to be. What could we possibly say to those soldiers that might help them feel even slightly better? I thought that we NFLers should get down on our knees and thank the wounded for their efforts, and their sacrifices, on our behalf (and all the people back home).

Feeling as though it was totally inappropriate to interrupt them at all, we nevertheless, began by introducing our group, stumbling to find the right words to explain our presence. How could we even begin to lessen their suffering?

But before beginning our speech, a young soldier, covered in bandages, half way down the room raised his hand and said, "Hey Russell, what's wrong with our Stillers?" I couldn't believe my ears. Here was a soldier, with devastating injuries, that would undoubtedly impact him for the rest of his life and he wanted to know why his team was still so bad.

I walked over to him having no idea what to say but he shook my hand, smiled and then carried the conversation, "I'm from Braddock. My old man and me used to go to every game at Forbes Field—we luv our Stillers. What do you think—can we turn it around?"

I was totally surprised that he was so upbeat and seemingly so interested in the team. I didn't want to talk about the Steelers, I wanted to comfort him but all he wanted to talk about was the team and its future.

This strange experience gave me just a glimmer of understanding of what our team meant to our fans and I started to truly appreciate how much they cared. I hope that young man survived his wounds and came back to witness the amazing Chuck Noll turnaround and enjoy those championship years. I hope he is sitting every week in Heinz Field pulling for our current team, urging them on for the seventh Super Bowl.

* * *

Steeler fans, our hugely enthusiastic supporters, waving their "Terrible Towels" are in a league by themselves. During our run for those first four Super Bowls we truly had a mutual love affair with our fans. For the first two of those wins I was a player but for the second two I was one of those rabid fans. The Steeler players appreciated our fans as much as they appreciated us. But it was in the '60's that the true Steeler fans would show me their dogged loyalty and would refuse to accept that their team would continue to be SOS (Same Old Steelers).

On Mondays, after our latest loss, I would travel all over Western Pennsylvania visiting local watering holes, being paid by Iron City Beer to say hello to their customers. At every stop I would always be astounded at the enthusiasm and undying support our fans would demonstrate.

"What's wrong wid yuns?—you're playing like bums," someone might yell, but those loyal fans, granted not afraid to voice their opinions, would always have smiles on their faces. I would stand there making the 'excuse de jour' and could still feel the fan's conviction that somehow we would turn it around and become winners. Our fans had put up with year after year of incompetence and yet they continued to yell their support, with only an occasional boo-bird (not that we didn't deserve it).

Granted, we might have to dodge a few snowballs on the way out onto the field and deal with the occasional heckler but the overwhelming majority of them were classy folks who enjoyed their home team.

I can remember being out for dinner with my family and being approached by fans asking for autographs or, sometimes, just stopping to chat. They were always respectful of our privacy, leaving after a short conversation.

One of my fondest memories of fan interaction came when we returned from Oakland after beating a very good Raider team to get into our first Super Bowl. In my opinion that victory was the single most important game the Steelers ever won. After all those years of struggling we had finally made it to the top of the mountain—getting to the Super Bowl. We were on such a natural high we could have flown back under our own power.

On the flight back I remember giving Mr. Rooney (the "Chief") the game ball as he basked in the warmth of our first AFC Championship. Arriving in the middle of the night (2:30 am), expecting a totally vacant airport, we were completely awestruck to find hundreds of our loyal fans, lining the Airport corridor, shouting their support, reaching out to shake our hands and pat our backs. Having played on so many horrible teams, seen our fans humiliated (as we were) and continually disappointed, I was overwhelmed with emotion—it had been a difficult but worthwhile journey.

Now, so many years later, the Steelers of the 70s, the winners of four out of the six Super Bowls (we should have won more) are constantly amazed at and appreciative of the continued respect we receive from the Steeler fans. Just a few months ago seven of us (Greene, Bradshaw, Lambert, Harris, Bleier, Fuqua, and myself) found ourselves signing memorabilia (everything from a Three Rivers seats to terrible towels) at a Washington, D.C. mall—can you imagine seven Redskins sitting in the South Hills Village Mall—they'd be booed, or at least ignored. Most of us today because of the NFLs increased popularity get far more mail asking for autographs and such then we did back when we played.

Enthusiastic fans are obviously a good thing but I think it's important for our fans to remember that it is only a game—the ball can take an unlucky bounce, deflections can go into the hands of an opponent, games are won and lost—it is not the end of the world. Professional sports are not as important as our national issues: economy, war/peace, law and jobs or family issues. As our great commentator, Myron Cope, used to say, "Sports are not important enough to merit true indignation!" Let's all keep things in perspective.

I sometimes feel sorry for our current players, having to always hear about the good old days. It's almost as though despite the current team's excellence, (winning two of the past three Super Bowls), the better the teams and players of the 70's get, the legends and myths growing bigger with the years.

Over the past few years I have enjoyed writing two books, *A Steeler Odyssey* and *An Odd Steelers Journey*, books that contain observations about my teammates (what a glorious bunch) and some post football adventures. Asked by the publisher to help market the book by going to book signings I have again been struck by the bond between we players and the fans. I loved every minute of those book signings because the people in Pittsburgh not only love their team but they're also good people, who are interesting and fun to talk to.

Don't get me wrong. It's not like every time I go out that I'm overwhelmed by huge numbers of Steelers fans wanting to talk. In fact, book signings can be a humbling experience. At one such signing, being a born salesman, I was trying hard to make eye contact with all the masses of people, busy shopping away, walking happily down the mall, totally disinterested in some ex-jock trying to hustle his stories about how it "used to be."

Sitting there I would hear bits of conversation like this.

One guy to his young son, "Hey, that's Andy Russell sitting there."

"Who's Andy Russell?" the youngster replies, looking for the nearest candy store.

"I have no idea but the sign says he's some ex-Steeler—trying to hustle a book."

Moments later, a fellow walked up looking very agitated and asks, "Where's the men's room?"

Later, a youngish, rather attractive woman, a "babe" actually, walked up.

"Hi Mr. Russell."

The Mr. is always a tip off—that you're just an old fart.

"You were my grandmother's favorite."

Noting her cute smile, I smiled back at her, suddenly feeling very old.

"Would you like to buy a book? Make a terrific Grandmother's Day gift."

"She died ten years ago but I do need to buy a book for my son."

"How old is your son? Maybe he'd be interested in A *Steeler Odyssey*."

I picked up the book, turning it over to show her the photo of me standing with Ham and Lambert 22 years ago in the locker room.

She stood there, studying the book.

"He's twelve and just hates sports."

Minutes later I noticed a guy standing across the mall glaring at me. I motioned for him to come on over. As he approached I noticed that he was very short, maybe 5′3″ tall, dressed nattily, hair dyed black and nearly my age. He kind of reminded me of Danny DeVito.

He stopped, stared down at the books, picked one up and read the comments by Shula, Noll, Madden, Ditka and Myron on the back cover, threw it back on the table.

"I'm Tony from Youngstown—how ya doin?" He did not offer to shake hands.

"Hi, I'm Andy from Malls-ville—I'm fine, how are you feeling?"

Tony stared at me for some time, without smiling.

"You know, I've hated you for a long time."

I looked up at Tony, somewhat apprehensively, wondering if he was a nut case, trying to remember him but realized I've never seen him before in my life.

"So, Tony, what's the problem?"

"You cost me a thousand bucks—when you picked up that damn fumble against Baltimore in the playoff and ran it back 90 yards for a touchdown. It covered the spread."

"It was 93 yards—anyway, bad idea to bet against us. We were a better team than the Colts."

With that he turned around and walked away, as though he was afraid his temper would get the best of him.

Moments later Tony returned and appeared to be in a better mood. Apparently he has just thought about it and figured out how I could make things OK with him for losing him his "thou" so many years ago.

"I'm gonna buy two of your books and you'll sign the first one to 'to Tony, Sorry I cost you the thou' and then sign the other one to my pal, Sal and write, 'Tony wants to know if you paid your taxes on that thou I won for you'."

Just at that time, a guy wearing scruffy jeans and a dirty t-shirt, picked up another book.

"I'd sure like to buy a copy of your book but I don't know."

He shook his head, looking doubtful.

"Twenty bucks is a lot of money for a sports book—when's it coming out in paperback?"

"Look, here's twenty five bucks—go buy the damn book and keep the change," Tony said.

The guy stared at the money in his hand as though he couldn't believe someone had just given him $25 to buy a book and smiled, winked at me, and then walked slowly into the store. I couldn't help wondering if he would really buy the book. Maybe, he needed the money for food for his family.

Tony stood there staring at me with a real proud look on his face, motioning for me to begin signing his two books as directed.

"So Tony, what do you do for a living in Youngstown? Must do all right if you can afford to buy a perfect stranger a book!"

"I brokered stocks for a lot of years and did real good. I just bet big time on some Dot Com stocks, cashed out and now I'm retired."

"So, that $1000 is no big deal now."

"You know you're right—Sal needed it more than me anyway."

With that we shook hands, I signed the books and he strutted away, nodding happily to his fellow shoppers.

I sat there thinking about Tony and how interesting people are when the guy who Tony's gave the 25 bucks to, came back holding a book.

"I want you to sign this to 'George' and say 'thanks for giving Fred all that good advice'."

"Who's George and who's Fred and what was the good advice?"

"I'm Fred and George is my financial advisor."

With that he smiled at me and picked up his book and walked slowly down the Mall.

I sat there, appreciating how wonderful life is, contemplating the humor in Tony getting ripped off by a guy who has enough money for a financial advisor when a middle aged guy walked up.

"Is there anything in this book about Ray Mansfield?"

"Of course, he was my best Steeler buddy and he's in almost every chapter. .This book is dedicated to Ray Mansfield. In many ways it's really a tribute to what a wonderful person he was." I replied.

As I picked up a book and offered to sign if for him he says, "Just say 'To Jack, Ray Mansfield's biggest fan."

As I gladly signed his request, Jack explained.

"I grew up in Washington State and watched the Washington University Huskies when Ray was All American there his final two years. He was the best. I'm a lawyer now, out in North Dakota, and I had a deposition here Friday and another one on Monday so I thought instead of flying home over the weekend and billing my clients the cost, I figured I'd just stay the weekend. I've discovered that Pittsburgh's a great city with real nice people."

Jack was right about a lot of things. About saving his client money. About Ray Mansfield. And about Pittsburgh being a wonderful city filled with great people. We former and active Steelers are blessed to have fans that have always supported their team through the good and the bad.

Chapter 13

A LETTER TO PAT CONROY

Dear Mr. Conroy,

I just finished your salutary, sensational saga, *MY LOSING SEASON*, and, as a former athlete, I found it absolutely riveting, resonating with wisdom, pain, misery, anger, humiliation, and finally understanding, forgiveness and redemption—feelings that most of us experience sometime during our journey, although in substantially different doses. Your book just blew me away.

Having been lucky enough to get two books published, I have some sense, granted minimal compared to yours, of how difficult it is to write a book. I'm sure you get a lot of stuff that ends up in the waste basket, or never gets past your agent, and, yes, as suggested in your book, my books may be instances of bad books that get published only because of winning programs.

Nevertheless, I'm still trying and just got my second book, *An Odd Steelers Journey*, (copy enclosed) published, where I tried to write about the game of football, touching on some of the same issues you wrote about regarding the challenges of basketball. I was fascinated by the way you described your experiences in the world of sport, often harsh but so often sublime.

At first I thought that me talking to you as though I'm a writer is something akin to you telling Michael Jordan that you have also played basketball. But actually, your basketball accomplishments (Captain & MVP at the Citadel) are significantly superior to my writing credits and your writing is certainly comparable to Michael Jordan's brilliance on a basketball court.

I also realized, reading your book, how our lives have been in some ways, almost mirror opposites—you the brilliant and hugely successful writer but athletically, at least in your mind, coming up short of your goals and me, a reasonably successful professional athlete (granted, not in your league—I was definitely not one of the top five athletes in the country, a position you surely hold in the world of writing) who had almost everything go his way in the world of sports but coming up woefully short of being a quality writer, a goal of mine since childhood.

Much the way you described feeling as an overachieving athlete, your book made me realize just how much of a loser I am when it comes to writing. I know well that I am a rookie writer, just trying to tell some good stories and make sense out of too many athletic failures. But, I not only can't carry your jock, (excuse me, your pen), I feel that in the analogy of sport, that I would not have even made your team, let alone be a bench warmer, who your teammates referred to as the "Green Weenies."

Reading your latest book was a truly humbling experience much the way you must have felt when you watched Jerry West play at the basketball summer camp. Surprisingly, I felt this more deeply than when I read your classics, *Prince Of Tides* and *Beach Music*—perhaps because I had just finished attempting to put in words the challenges of sport but also because I could never even imagine myself writing the Great American Novel as those books truly are—but, having spent so much of my life participating in organized sports (nearly 25 years), I understand athletics very well and yet could never come close to your ability to put in words what it is that makes sports so challenging, seductive, and exhilarating.

Reading your book, I related to many of the issues you spoke about. For example, my coach, Dan Devine, rarely spoke directly to me, most often speaking through emissaries, his assistant coaches or trainers, in my four years at the University of Missouri. Like your coach he was a tough guy with little time for dealing with player's psyches.

Having played for some truly awful Steeler teams and some tough, demanding, seemingly unfeeling and somewhat eccentric coaches (Buddy Parker and Bill Austin), in the sixties, where over a four year stretch we won 12, lost 41 and tied 3 (21.43%), making your 7-17 (29.17%) look pretty good, struggling with my own game (or lack there of), and falling woefully short of my personal goals in college, I could totally relate to your feelings. I realized, as I sat there reading your book, feeling thoroughly inadequate and dazzled by your prose, that we have had some similarities in our histories but also some strikingly opposite experiences.

You were obviously a much better player than you gave your self-credit for. Your story tells us that you were relegated to the bench, your senior year but that you were soon named captain and a starter and that you played with a ferocious energy, diving for balls, skinning your shins, playing defense with passion, running until you'd drop from exhaustion, and ultimately winning the MVP award—chosen the best player on your team, although you believe, undeservedly. Possibly, your unwillingness to recognize the value of your contribution was due to how you grew up, having a father who never praised you, always being critical, not to mention the horrors of his physical and mental abuse.

I thought I had a tough father until reading your book. Mine was an immigrant from Scotland, coming over on the boat when he was 12, leaving school in the eighth grade to work on a farm in Upper Michigan to send money home to help support his father and mother. My Grandfather, who defined toughness, having been the open hearth furnace operator for the Glasgow steel mill, took pride in making me cry every time we were together. He strongly believed it was his duty to toughen me up so that I could survive in the jungle that is life— perhaps your father had some of those same old school ideas and maybe they were right.

But my father was on the road most of the time, not particularly interested in his kids' activities, but allowing me to find my own path with only occasional criticism. When I scored five touchdowns and one extra point in my last game in high school to win the St. Louis scoring championship (1958) by that single point, and as my teammates were hoisting my jersey up the school's flagpole, with it flapping in the wind next to the flag of the United States of America, he pulled me aside and said, "You missed a block in the third quarter," but I could see the pride in his eyes and, for the first time understanding that he was bluffing, I almost cried with joy.

When I was in college, starting all three years (in those days you couldn't play varsity as a freshman), my Dad only saw three games, since he lived and worked in Europe. When I intercepted two passes in the Orange Bowl helping Mizzou win over Joe Bellino's Navy he said, "You missed a tackle on the punt team."

My father used a belt but only on occasion, when I probably deserved it—like when I stole coins from his dresser to buy candy. Your Dad used his fists to pummel you when you hadn't done anything wrong. At the risk of playing amateur psychologist (forgive me if I say something inappropriate), your father was obviously an unhappy, angry and some times violent man, often treating you in a brutal fashion and yet, he seemed to care, he was there, watching you perform, and in the end, you still loved him and forgave him. I loved and forgave mine too.

Our lives were also similar in the fact that we both moved often, jumping from city to city, always forced to make new friends, deal with new environments. You were a military brat. I was a corporate brat, living in Detroit, Chicago, New York, St. Louis, Brussels, and Geneva.

Knowing something about how sports teams destroy themselves, imploding when the pressure mounts, unable to deal with the competition's superiority (hey, been there done that), I think what impressed me the most was the way you write.

For example, when you compared your team's lack of cohesiveness with a geographic reference, describing the incongruity between the bays, coves, rivers, and islands of an archipelago, I sat there stunned, as every bit humiliated as I had been by missing a tackle of Jim Brown, Gale Sayers or O.J. Simpson. I realized that I would never, in my wildest imagination, have ever thought to compare our lack of teamwork with an archipelago. I thought about it and realized that you're a seasoned pro and I'm a raw rookie. As I think about it more, our sixties team's dreadful, discombobulated disharmony was more like a swamp, moving very slowly, weaving in strange directions, stagnating in various positions.

There were many other analogies that you blew over my head and metaphors that made me hesitant and caused me to lose confidence, something that rarely happened on the playing fields. For example, I marveled at the one comparing your psyche to a cavern, with poison tipped stalactites, sick bats and pools of fetid water.

The other thing you do, and this is more important I think than brilliant wordsmithing, clever analogies or unique metaphors, is that you are devastatingly honest, telling your story without a hint of ego preservation, telling your truth, whether it be about a contriving, former wife or a father, ill from his overwhelming insecurities, or a bunch of overzealous, diabolical cadets wanting to destroy a plebe's psyche, you tell it the way it was, sparing no one, including yourself. You are my hero.

Your point that everyone in life is struck by the quicksilver nature of life, how our lives blow by us with such astounding speed, particularly struck me. Here I'm 68 and can't believe it—where did all that time go? I thought it might slow down as I'd get older but it seems to have speeded up. I recently read about a woman who turned age 124, a former slave, and she said that her longevity was due to the fact that she just kept working. Use it or lose it, I guess.

When I sent my first book's manuscript to my writer friend, Roy Blount (who had written an earlier book about the 70's Steelers, called *About Three Bricks Shy of Load*), his reaction was "Russell, I liked some of your stories but I wouldn't give up your day job just yet." How true—I would starve. So, I haven't, still doing deals, buying and selling companies and trying not to screw them up. We do investment banking, private equity, and venture capital—stuff like that.

You stating that one learns more from losing than one ever learns from winning struck me as absolutely true. Yes, there are no reunions of losing teams. While writing my second book I continually found myself returning to the sixties, when we were terrible and the laughing stock of the NFL. Johnny Carson told Steeler jokes, ridiculing our dismal incompetence. Our coaches even found our failures humorous, often berating us about our laughable inadequacies.

We fought hard, giving what we thought was every ounce of our strength, trying our best, but always ended up in defeat—somehow, in those losing years, it felt as though the effort had been more poignant, the loss more devastating, the serendipitous nature of life more unfair as the ball always bounced into the hands of the opponent in the most inopportune moments, always finding a way to lose and feeling inadequate, shamed by our inability to win, blaming our failures on our lack of commitment, our flawed personalities, our loser mentalities, never ever thinking that it also might have to do with our physical, genetic inferiority—we just weren't talented enough, couldn't execute the quality techniques required or run fast enough, jump high enough, or be strong enough to defeat our opponents.

We would be told later by Chuck Noll, the great coach who won four out of six Super Bowls, that our incompetence had little to do with our lack of effort, intensity, or mental toughness. We just weren't physically talented enough (not fast enough or strong enough) and our techniques were flawed and clearly this is how you felt about yourself and your fellow Citadel warriors, who all, incidentally, seemed like terrific guys—much the way my teammates were in those losing seasons of the '60s.

Another significant difference in this mirroring of our lives, is that when it came to your favorite game, basketball, you practiced by going to a summer camp where you learned to handle the ball despite flying at full speed and penetrating amongst the giants and to play stifling defense, smothering your opponent. You were paying the price to be the kind of athlete you wanted to be—hardworking, daring, bold, fearless and competent.

But, where you practiced your writing, I have never really worked at being a good writer, never paying the price, working doggedly to learn the skills as you did, writing poetry or articles, sometimes even offending your coach, for your college paper. My favorite course in college was composition and I actually lived for a short period in the house my writing professor and some of his friends had rented, sleeping in their foyer in a bunk bed. My interest was listening to them talk about books and writers, whereas they, being sports fans, just wanted to hear me talk about football experiences. To this day I'm still in contact with my writing mentor, Professor Paul Doherty, who currently teaches writing at Boston College. Paul was nice enough to critique a few chapters of the *Odd Steelers Journey*.

I did read Stephen King's effort to explain his thoughts on your trade in his book, *On Writing*, where he basically said that the three most important aspects to being a good writer is practice, practice and more practice, reciting the huge number of rejection slips he received as a youngster trying to get something, anything, published. Didn't we hear the same thing from numerous coaches?

I did go to a summer sports camp, a football camp up in Minnesota, where I was coached by Bud Wilkinson, Murray Warmath and the Elliot brothers, Pete and Bump, (as well as my high school coach, Bob Davis) a place where I tried to learn the techniques required of a good football player.

Actually, my favorite sport was also basketball. Not being a very naturally violent person, football came to me slowly, finally learning how to play (it had little to do with violence) in my thirties after many years in the pros. I much preferred basketball and, having played decently in high school, averaging slightly over 20 points a game, I had a scholarship to play at Missouri. Unfortunately (perhaps I should say thank goodness), my freshman year Missouri went to the Orange Bowl and Coach Dan Devine wanted a freshman running back for cannon fodder for his practices so I was busy with football until the end of December. Freshman basketball had already started and I needed to focus on my grades. I figured I'd play the following year but my sophomore year we went to the Orange Bowl again.

So, I ended up playing fraternity basketball, woefully short of quality stuff (no coaches) but still a lot of fun. In fact, they picked a fraternity all-star team, and, despite my protestations, the organizers, thinking that the varsity team wasn't any good (having a bad won/loss percentage in the Big Eight), challenged the Varsity to a game—how arrogant. School officials decided we could play the freshman team, (as a prelim game prior to the varsity game) and they beat us by 45 points—very humbling.

While serving in the army (I was a Lieutenant in Germany for two years—1964 and 1965), our football team won the United States Military Europe Championship. Our Seventh Corp General, Truman, a 4 star, asked me if I knew anything about basketball. Not wanting to return to my unit (an 8" self propelled howitzer unit that was in the field for over 200 days a year) I fibbed, stating, "I know more about basketball than football." So, he made me the head coach of the Seventh Corp team.

Having over 20,000 men to select my team, we had decent athletes. I read every book I could find on basketball coaching tactics and put together a solid team that won about half its games. I was a player coach and remember guarding a soldier who had played for the Knicks (granted, probably for only a few weeks) and shutting him down by denying him the ball—what a thrill. We were in a small gym, in some obscure town in Germany, with a crowd of less than a hundred, in a game that meant absolutely nothing to the sporting world, and, despite losing the game, I was totally psyched and thrilled to hold the former pro to only twelve points when he was averaging over thirty. From reading your book I know that you would have made the same effort and felt the same thrill of the challenge—it could have been in somebody's backyard.

Well, sorry to bore you with all this but I just couldn't help but be struck by how some of our experiences and feelings were both so similar but, in other cases, such mirror opposites.

Please accept this tribute to your fine book. It moved me as no other sports book has ever.

I know I have no right to do this, that it is somewhat arrogant of me to ask (over the top), but, since we were always taught to be bold, to risk rejection and face humiliation, would you be willing to come to Pittsburgh this spring (invitation enclosed) to play in our Celebrity Classic Golf Tournament as one of our celebrity athletes—hey, MVP at the Citadel is big here in the Burgh.

I don't know if you play golf but, being the athlete you were, I'm sure you could if you chose to. Frankly, I find the game hugely frustrating but the tournament is for a worthy cause (the University of Pittsburgh Medical Center's Cancer Research efforts) and it would be a huge benefit for our tournament to have you in attendance. You could play with one of my ex-Steeler teammates—guys like, Franco Harris, Rocky Bleier, Lynn Swann, Jack Ham or Joe Greene. I'm sure you would not want to play with me (see chapter 4 of my book). The format is a five person scramble and we will play on a Jack Nicklaus designed golf course, Nevillewood.

Also, please don't think that the heart felt praise written above about your book has anything to do with this golf invitation, buttering you up so to speak. I meant everything I said above about your amazing ability to write your feelings and describe your actions. Please forgive my occasional alliteration silliness. I thought that it might make you smile—"look at this rookie—he doesn't have a clue, trying to impress me with his sophomoric, almost pitiful, literary efforts."

I read where Elmore Leonard often takes a full day to work on one page of his novels. I'm sorry; I just don't have the patience, or the dedication to do that.

Incidentally, have you ever read James Lee Burke or Robert Parker or Scot Turow? I think they are terrific—not in your league but really good.

Best regards,
Andy Russell

Chapter 14

THE VALUE OF TEAMWORK

I am sometimes asked to assess the importance of teamwork on our Steelers teams of the '70s. Were we just a bunch of good players running around doing their own thing or were we collectively better because of our commitment to the team and what does that mean? Our coaches would always remind us that "there is no letter I in the word TEAM."

Since most people have been part of a team at some time in their lives (sports teams, debate teams, business teams, family teams, etc.) we all think we know something about teamwork but I think it is a far more complicated subject than most people give it credit for. Many people would sum up teamwork by just saying it is simple—"Just work together, support each other and try hard and do good." Nevertheless, since almost all of us have been taught, at some point in our lives to appreciate the power of good teamwork, we all are interested in what makes some teams perform better than others.

Obviously there are some basic factors involved. Good teams must prepare, practice, communicate well, work hard, care about each other and take care of the details. Good players (team members) must be a lot of things: hard working, disciplined, totally concentrated (focused), intense, committed, responsible, accountable, determined, having fortitude and positive attitudes, smart, unselfish, trusting, willing to play hurt, and, oh yes, have a certain level of physical/intellectual talent. Obviously, good teams must have good players and therefore the teams will demonstrate the same qualities. Note that the following adjectives or thoughts are not included: selfish, impatient, full of excuses, trying too hard to be the hero, too aggressive, etc.

Teamwork is something that sports teams and business teams are constantly trying to improve. What are the most significant ingredients of quality teamwork? What causes some teams to play better than their level of talent? Naturally, I will focus on what factors influence quality teamwork in sports but I do believe that these same attributes can very positively influence business teams.

I always thought that my college teams at University of Missouri, coached by the great Dan Devine played better than our player's collective level of talent. Why, because Devine demanded that we pursue excellence and that we give every ounce of our strength to work together as a cohesive unit. By having survived Devine's exhausting and often brutal practice sessions those Missouri teams were emotionally bonded, willing to give it our all to help each other win.

Later, Chuck Noll would take us to a new level of superior quality teamwork. Chuck wasn't into Rah Rah. He didn't want us to waste our energy with unrestrained, unfocused, gung ho emotion. At one of our first meetings on the field, his first year as coach in 1969, when we were all making noise, thinking that he would want us to show our un-bridled enthusiasm, he said "I want you to be quiet," explaining that he wanted total concentration, and that he didn't want to hear any of that "pseudo-chatter." "You don't win games with noise," he said.

I remember being shocked by his honesty but also agreeing that emotional stuff had very little to do with success on the field. Every time I got too excited, too emotional, too aggressive or just too impatient I would make mistakes and play badly. Yes, I was trying too hard and that often led to reacting too quickly and making critical mistakes— quality judgments and intelligent thinking is critical. Chuck would go on to explain that noise, false enthusiasm meant nothing, that the only thing that mattered on the football field was quality thought processes, proper techniques and superior execution—if every one would do his job to the best of his ability and, better than the person across from him, the team would succeed.

Once he went so far as to say, "I will never give you a motivational speech—if I have to motivate you I will fire you." He wanted totally committed athletes who would give their all on every play. In fact, he believed that one of his biggest challenges would be to channel all that gung-ho enthusiasm and to teach us to play smart and be patient. Sometimes a player can exert his maximum effort in the wrong fashion or direction, as the opponent wants you to react too quickly.

It was also important to understand that success was in the details, the execution, the performance, not the emotion. You could passionately want to be successful but, if you didn't do the right things, execute the correct techniques, anticipate the opponent's next move, and ultimately take care of your own responsibility, you would still be beaten, regardless of the amount of passion or effort you committed.

Psyched up players, anxious to make a big play, impatient to make tackles or blocks will often make mistakes, reacting too quickly, too aggressively, wanting to be the hero, not waiting that micro second before acting, a moment of recognition that can make all the difference between success and failure.

That's not to say that great teams aren't made up of passionate, enthusiastic, highly motivated players. Those Steelers teams of the 70's consisted of extraordinarily motivated players—players who gave it their all to defeat the opponent, players who absolutely hated to make physical or mental mistakes, being out played by their opponents, and loathed losing. But that motivation did not come from our leader, Coach Noll, or the many great assistants we had at that time (George Perles, Bud Carson, Woody Widenhoefer, Dan Radakovich) but instead came from within, which is where those great coaches wanted it to come from.

Somewhere along our journey, from the grade school play grounds to the NFL stadiums we had learned to expect, no demand of ourselves, perfection. Of course, along the way I'm sure most of us did have quality mentors who taught us what to expect of ourselves. We were very proud players who expected to play well and when we didn't it was very frustrating and it hurt.

Coach Noll also explained that you couldn't really try and help out a teammate, doing his job, because such a maneuver would make us vulnerable to some other tactic used by the opponent—each player, (worker), had to do his own job, recognizing that you'd get in trouble trying to help out a teammate because it might cause you to fail to properly execute your own responsibility. The best way to help the team was to do your own job correctly and trust that the rest of your teammates will also be successful in doing their job, executing their responsibility.

There is that old analysis that every team is only as good as its weakest link. But, if you try to cover up for, or help out a teammate, to do his job, you aren't doing your own job, essentially making the team more vulnerable. I discovered the truth in his theory early when trying to help out my teammates on the other side of the line, leaving my own line of responsibility and we were beaten by a reverse to my side. The opponent had taken advantage of my over zealousness and irresponsible behavior.

On the other hand, I'm sure that one can make the point in business, where goals/missions often take months to accomplish, that one who has finished his work for the day could help his fellow employees to do their job better. The willingness to expend extra effort, helping others, can be a good thing, whereas in football it can sometimes be a liability.

As you can see, teamwork is a very complicated subject and lots of quality coaches, leaders, managing directors, etc, have struggled with getting a group to perform better than the aggregate of their individual talents. In my opinion it is often because they spend way too much time trying to motivate, believing that the failure lies in a lack of effort, while, in reality, it has much more to do with a failure to execute specific techniques or strategies—success is definitely in the details.

Essentially, Noll believed it was his job to draft enough quality players so that we wouldn't have any meaningful weaknesses and that's exactly what he did. But, perhaps as important, he thought of himself as a teacher and he taught us how to think and how to execute the techniques that would enable us to succeed—physical talent alone will not get the job done and I'm sure in business that intellectual talent still needs to be focused on the details.

Coach Noll would explain in minute detail what he expected from every player but there were times when he asked for our input. Real leaders are not afraid to get advice from their team—quality communication between leaders and their teams is essential. For example, after explaining the current week's game plan (how we might attack the next foe's tendencies) we would go out onto the practice field and attempt to execute that plan.

Sometimes we would collectively discover that something the coaches had thought would work (on the black board) didn't work so well on the field. We would then improvise and come up with new ideas (schemes), sometimes suggested by a player, as to how best to stop the opponent (the defense) or how to attack them (the offense). Coach would say, "I don't want you to surprise me on Sunday. Don't do it my way all week and then do it your way in the game." I wonder how many businesses make this same mistake.

Teams need to have everyone committed to the game plan. Of course, the game or business is very complicated and we were often forced to change our mutually agreed to plan after the first quarter, realizing that the opponent was doing something better or different than we had anticipated. Teams have to be fluid and have to be able to quickly react to change—flexibility is critical; being wiling to try new ideas, seek previously unused strategies and techniques is very important.

So, it's critical that leaders listen to their team's input. For example, in one game, against the Oakland Raiders, Coach wanted me to stop the block of their giant, All Pro tackle, Art Shell, by giving him a hand shiver, grabbing his jersey below his pads (legal if the player remains in front of you) and then "shucking" him (disengagement is critical) inside or outside to make the tackle. I had argued all week that Shell was just too big (320 lbs+) for my 215 lbs to handle in that fashion, preferring to give him a fake and jump around him. But Coach was stubborn and he urged me to try his technique which, granted, was the traditional strategy but, in this case, just, at least in my mind, unrealistic.

Well, during the game, the first time they tried that play (called a U block, where the tight end blocks down on Dwight White and Art loops around to get me, committed to trying it Chuck's way, I jumped across into Art's face, jammed him as hard as I could under his shoulder pads and he didn't even break stride, burying me in the turf—quite embarrassing. Later, as I was exiting the field, after we had made them punt, walking past Coach, with my head down but steaming, he whispered, "OK, try it your way." I did and was able to stop, for the most part, that play by confusing or avoiding Mr. Shell—so, it's important for leaders to show flexibility.

On the other hand, there were, embarrassing moments, times when my way, which I had sold all week to the coaches, absolutely convinced that I was right, also didn't work and we quickly decided to do it the coach's way, discarding mine. It wasn't about ego (who was right)—it was about getting the job done the best way possible.

Coach Noll also didn't exhaust us during the week, allowing us to recharge our batteries so to speak so that we would be physically rejuvenated by the following weekend. We would also stay late after practice to help our teammates, or to be helped, in perfecting our techniques. I believe it is very unique for professional football players to voluntarily stay out after practice to help their teammates get better. We truly cared about each other and when teammates care they encourage, teach, listen, and give quality feedback—trust is something that has to be developed over time.

For example, on a number of occasions, Rocky Bleier and Preston Pearson would stay out after practice to run running back receiving routes, particularly the halfback option, against Jack Ham and me to help us develop a better coverage technique, Often they would beat us by making different types of unexpected moves but eventually, with the extra practice, we were able to perfect the technique to where we could cover the best running back receivers at least most of the time.

In quality teamwork there can be no room for petty jealousies, office politics, or bad relationships—all must be eliminated. This does not mean that the participants aren't competitive between each other but, if so, only in a positive way. For example, the Steelers linebackers would have small wagers (i.e., $5.00) given for outstanding play, determined by the bettors themselves. In other words, if Jack Ham made an outstanding play (an interception, for example) all the other linebackers (4 of us) would have to contribute 5 bucks each to our Linebacker Christmas Party kitty. If, on the other hand, Jack made a mistake (granted, this rarely happened) he would have to contribute the $5.00 himself—true for all of us. Such competition included the backups who would make their contributions to the kitty for either making great plays on the special teams or not.

We had lots of fun with this, sometimes noticing mistakes that the coaches had either not seen or ignored. Frankly, I hated to be docked for making a mistake (paying the five dollars), more than I enjoyed having the other guys chip in when I made a good play. I'm certain that these fun challenges had something to do with the excellent chemistry we had in our Linebacker Corp.

Another thing that's important in the formation and continuance of a superb team is that the leaders, and the team members, must always tell the truth. One of the great things about Chuck Noll is that he always told us his truth, never candy coating things, eliminating meaningless rhetoric—he always spoke what he truly believed—not that he was always right, no one is, but he certainly was right most of the time. For example, in his first year with the team, when we went 1-13, (yes that's an unbelievable 1 win and 13 losses), he never lost us, and the reason he never did was that he always spoke his truth and it always made sense. His criticisms were honest and we could understand and appreciate their validity—i.e., we hadn't lost because of a lack of effort but because of flawed thinking and careless techniques.

One of his truisms that year was stated simply and straight for-wardly. He said, "We will get worse before we get better because I am going to require that you play the game as it's meant to be played—no guessing, no playing your hunches, no wild blitzes, and no trying to cover up our weaknesses with gimmicks or poorly conceived stunts. I am going to require you to play your position the right way, executing the correct techniques and it will be difficult for you but, in the long run, we will be a better team for it." Unspoken, was the understand-ing that if we did not learn to execute those techniques that we would be set free (cut from the team) to "seek our life's work," one of Coach Noll's favorite sayings.

I also believe that those players with a passion for the game are not doing it for the money. It's not that money isn't important—obviously one must support his family to the best of his ability but it is not the money that should be the motivating force—it should be one's love of the game, the challenge, and the fascination with those many details. Football is the chess of major sports, but in this case all twenty two pieces (players), unlike Chess where you move only one piece, move at the same time, and some go where they are not suppose to.

Since I was making more money in my off season business (actu-ally I was involved with it all year around, going to business meetings before and after practice) than the Steelers were paying me it was extremely important to have that passion for the game—obviously it wasn't about making money. I can remember one time asking Dan Rooney (when negotiating one of my early contracts) how I could justify to my family that I was playing football for less money than I earned in my off season business. Appearing slightly miffed, he replied "you don't have to justify anything, if you want to retire, go ahead and do it." But then he smiled at me and said, "But Russell, we both know that you'd pay me to play this game," and, you know what—he was right, I would have. Fortunately Dan didn't ask me to do so.

It's also clear that a great team's players must have great respect and confidence in each other, always having the defensive players encouraging the offense and vice versa. I always tried to have a positive attitude about our offense, believing that they would make something happen, thinking that our support was critical to their success—the power of positive thinking can be awesome.

Once, for example, in our last series in what could have been our final game (our playoff win against the Raiders in 1972) Glen "Pine" Edwards, who was standing next to me on the sideline was muttering to himself about how bad our offense had played against a very good Raider defense. Glen was upset with their inability to score, essentially blaming our offense for what was appearing to be, or what was about to become, our first playoff loss. I urged him to be positive and pull for them and that maybe something good would happen. Moments later, Franco made his famous "Immaculate Reception." I'm sure it had nothing to do with my little comment but maybe, just maybe, it had to do with all our teammates yelling encouragement onto the field, our offense never giving up and, of course, Terry (and all those blockers) and Franco making an absolutely brilliant play.

Now, so many years later, I find myself on another excellent team, our business team, Laurel Mountain Partners. Like my Steelers teammates, Mansfield, Ham, Lambert, Blount, White, Wagner, L.C. Greenwood, Bleier, Franco, Greene and so many others, my business partners, Don Rea and Jeff Kendall, Sam Zacharias, Keith Schaefer, Ron Carlson, Dale Van Steenberg, Steve Callahan and Jon Stein, and far too many others to mention here, are not only All Pros in the business world, not only smart and committed but also passionate about our team achieving excellence, to be the best that we can be.

Chapter 15

THE UNI-BOMBER

S ometimes I am accused of being too compulsive, or too driven to achieve certain things, like when I compile lists of things to do, or lists of places to go. One of those places has always been Alaska and in July 2005 we were fortunate enough to get invited by good friends to go on an Alaskan journey. I knew very little about Alaska but, like most of us, had read about its territory being purchased from Russia for $7,000,000 or about 8 cents per acre and eventually becoming our 49th state in 1959. If the Russians had known how much oil existed below those acres, I'm sure they would have upped that price significantly. Naturally, as kids, we were all taught about Eskimos (seal hunting, kayaks and Igloos) and the abundant wildlife.

Our itinerary would take us from Pittsburgh to Chicago to Anchorage where we would spend an evening before moving on via railroad to Mount McKinley Lodge where we hoped to be a part of the ten percent of tourists lucky enough to actually get to see the mountain which is most frequently obscured by clouds. From there we would move on via motor coach to the Denali Park Lodge where we would be lectured about the history of this 324,000 acre park. Basically it is all about "Preservation." We would then be transported (a 9 hour train ride) back to the coastal city/town of Whittier where we would board our cruise boat, Princess Coral. The boat would then sail south, along the coast, stopping at other points of interest, Skagway, Ketchikan and Juneau.

Arriving in Anchorage, after a day of dodging Murphy's Law (we were delayed out of Pittsburgh, causing us to miss our flight out of Chicago, but, with some luck, we got another flight and made it to Alaska's largest city with a population of 250,000). The whole state only has 650,000 people but it comprises over 20% of the United States land mass.

Boarding a motor coach at the Anchorage Airport, I stared out at this coastal city, with few tall buildings, ringed by a mountain chain rising up on both sides from the floor of the valley. The strong wind, blowing in from the sea, was pushing wispy clouds across those mountain peaks and the trees were bent over. The city appeared sparse and small townish, as though the real world hadn't discovered it yet. For some reason it reminded me of a military base, with its' functional, Spartan abodes with small lots and modest landscaping. I tried to imagine what this relatively modest city would be like in the winter.

After checking in to a very average Hilton Hotel we joined up with our group (Gary and Robin Zentner, Jerry and Judy Prado, Jeff and Sandy Merten, Rich and Judy Pegher, and Don and Marilyn Jenkins and walked down the street to a tented outdoor café serving mostly seafood, specializing in King Crabs.

The next day we arose to a rare Alaskan sunny day, boarded the train and rode up to the beautiful Lodge where we had an absolutely clear and stunning view of Mount McKinley in all its' glory. We were about to discover that Alaska has many young people, from all over the world, working as tour guides, bus drivers, lecturers, entertainers and hotel and cruise staff. Most of the young people we would meet were intelligent, comfortable speaking in front of large groups and very well informed about Alaskan history, legends, Native Americans, terrain and animals. Almost all of them seemed to genuinely enjoy their jobs which they performed with great enthusiasm. They also all seemed to have a very good sense of humor.

After getting off the train we boarded a large motor coach to take us another hour drive to the lodge. Our driver/guide was a young man named Brian who proceeded to tell us about the landscape and the wildlife of his new home—Brian had grown up in Salt Lake City, Utah and, after earning a college degree in microbiology, he came to Alaska for its' outstanding fishing.

He also explained that Mount McKinley is actually the largest (not highest) mountain in the world (except for the Hawaiian volcanoes if one considers the base of the mountain on the ocean floor) because of the relatively low level of its' base—elevation 2500 feet.

He also spent quite some time talking about bears, especially grizzlies who had recently attacked and eaten some very unlucky human beings. We were about to learn, however, that the Alaskans have a sense of humor about bear attacks. For example, while pass-ing a bicyclist, Brian informed us that cyclists in Alaska are known as "meals on wheels." Pedestrians are "lunch," and runners are "fast food." He also explained that it was not wise to put a bell on your pack (to alert bears of your presence) because, in reality, it could quickly become a "dinner bell."

On a serious note Brian explained that Bears are territorial and it's not a good idea to get too close to them—duh! He claimed that Bears typically avoid humans, apparently fearing them—well, after all we are the most dangerous of all God's species. Brian avoids fishing the smaller clear streams because of the danger of getting too close to bears.

Along the way we would learn that his father had served three tours of duty in Vietnam and that he (Brian) was going to boot camp to be-come a Navy Seal Officer at the end of the summer season (August). He proudly stated that "I'm planning on 30 years as a career soldier." I guessed that most of the people on the bus couldn't help but think about the recent disaster in Afghanistan where 19 Navy Seals were killed in the mountains by the Taliban and hoped that Brian would be able to avoid the horrors of war.

We'd also learn that Brian had recently gotten married and that he had a child on the way. As the bus pulled up to the Lodge he told us to be nice to the lady who was about to get on to the bus to tell us how to check in and receive our additional instructions about various tours we had signed up for on the train. He said, "Because she's my wife."

The tour we'd all signed up for was a rafting trip down a large gray (caused by minerals from the glacier runoff) river running fast down below the Lodge. We were bused down to the river where we put on rubber suits (the water is very cold—35 degrees) and heavy rubber boots over our sneakers and heavy life jackets. The first guide we met was a pretty little young lady (no more than 80 pounds) who introduced herself as Lee Anne who was proud to have been born in Alaska. She looked like a tomboy until studying her further.

Later as we approached the rafts we notice Lee Anne coming out of the woods, buckling up her pants, clearly having just gone to the bathroom in the woods, something most of the ladies on our trip weren't thrilled to do. You could just tell that she was a tough kid and had spent lots of time in the wilderness. We would learn later that Lee Anne was a bush pilot, landing small pontoon planes on wilderness lakes. She also was a mountain climber, having climbed on Mount McKinley three times, summiting once. When we talked to her about her Denali adventures she was shy and modest but animated and quite attractive.

Our group of 12 was split up 8 and 4 (8 per raft) and we were directed to the last raft where a thin, appearing slightly nervous, young man with a long braided ponytail stood waiting for us. He told us his name, Todd, and gave us a safety talk, before pulling the raft off the beach into the shallow water and allowing us to board. He explained that we would be the last raft because we had the repair kits and a pump on board our raft.

Todd at first seemed like a shy, introverted type (some might call him a nerd) who was short and skinny—no body fat on this kid. As we pushed off into the strong current, Todd sat in the middle seat and steered us out into the middle of the river with two large oars. I couldn't help but wonder how good this young man could be because he didn't look very strong. Fortunately, we were told that we would not be facing any strong rapids, despite the fact that the river current was flowing powerfully, powered by the melting ice above.

Soon, as we familiarized ourselves with our seats and position in the river, our group of 4 in the front of the raft began asking Todd some questions and we soon learned that he had four Alaskan Malamute dogs. This, I knew instantly was going to intrigue my wife, Cindy, who is an almost fanatical dog lover.

Before we knew it (or wanted to) we learned Todd's dogs' names (one was Winter, who got his name from being born on the day of the winter solstice) and his love of dog sledding in the winter. Apparently, Todd made enough money in the summer, both working as a farm hand and river guide, to not have to work in the winter, spending that time dog sledding up into the wilderness.

"Are dogs ever attacked by Moose?" Cindy asked, having read numerous books about the Iditarod.

"Usually it's not a problem but, well, one time a Moose did charge us and knocked the sled over," Todd said.

"Were any of your dogs hurt?" Cindy asked, apparently unconcerned about Todd's health.

"No, fortunately the Moose veered off, avoiding us," Todd explained. "If he had gone after my dogs it could have been real trouble because they were all tangled up in the harnesses—be much easier for me to avoid him." Todd added.

He would further explain that in the future he'd probably have to take a gun because as much as he'd hate to kill a moose he'd have to if the moose threatened his dogs.

Cindy began asking Todd more dog questions than any of us thought possible—their breed; their size; their age; their color; whether they had to get shots for heart worms, etc.

At one point, Jerry said, "I'm betting one buck that Cindy can't possibly ask one more dog question."

"You're on," I said, knowing that it was an endless subject when it came to Cindy's passion for dogs.

"What do your dogs like to eat?" Cindy said, as Jerry moaned.

When one of our group asked Todd where he lived and he explained that he had bought his own property and constructed a crude cabin that had no water, no electric power, no telephone, no computer, no washing/drying machines, no television, no furnace but it did have wood burning stove, for warmth. The cabin did have a generator that powered lights and a few appliances. He had an outhouse and we figured he cooked with a hot plate.

When our group tried to imagine how horrible it would be to have to use an outhouse, outside in the middle of the night in the winter, Todd offered that, "Well, I do use a jar in the middle of the night in the winter—call it my "honey pot." He then went farther than any of really wanted to go, explaining that the secret to having a good smelling outhouse is not to ever put any toilet paper down into the pit. We assumed that he used paper but that he burned it rather than putting it down the hole. He also explained that he would occasionally put rotten strawberries down into the pit to help the biodegradation of his waste, also helping to avoid a bad smelling latrine.

Speaking of bad smells, he said he never took showers at his cabin—just occasionally jumped in the lake and went swimming. Sometimes, if he had a big night, however, he would use the shower at the laundromat. Robin would mention later that she could definitely smell him as the 3 hour river trip progressed.

Meanwhile, Todd was maneuvering us down the river, staying about a couple of hundred yards behind the next raft. At one point, getting bored, I asked him if he'd allow me to row the raft and he relented. I climbed into his seat and began pulling on the oars—frankly, any exercise felt good after sitting for so long—on train, bus and now a raft. He would explain that he had a few offers in the past to spell him but no one had ever really meant it. Sometimes he had allowed children to take a few swipes at it. I noticed that Lee Anne was rowing the boat in front of us and I found it irritating that I was having trouble keeping up with her.

After fifteen minutes my arms were getting tired and I tried to remember how it was possible for Ray Mansfield and me to have rowed our canoe for 63 hours and 42 minutes (virtually non stop—we did take 3-fifteen minute rests) in our Hunter's Island Canoe Race in Upper Minnesota's Boundary Waters Canoe Area and Canada's Quetico National Park. We had canoed in a solo race (only our canoe), against the clock, on a 168 mile journey with 48 lakes and portages. After finishing, despite being on an absolute high for having done something so difficult, we had been exhausted for weeks.

When asked about food, Todd explained that he mainly just ate "canned" foods, supplemented by veggies and potatoes he'd bring from the farm he worked on. Since he had no refrigerator he was unable to keep foods (fish, chicken and meats) in the summer, because the smell might "bring the bears."

"If I catch any fish I've got to eat it that day—can't have it lying around." He did pick berries and mushrooms on occasion but not that often.

Naturally we asked about where he was from and if he had any family. Todd had matriculated from Washington State and his Mom and Dad would occasionally visit but that Todd seldom went there because he was afraid of flying. He also had a brother. As a teenager he had often camped out alone in the Cascades in the winter—his Mom thought he was "nuts."

"Don't you ever get lonely?" asked Robin.

"Not really—I've got a single neighbor not far away and he and I get together every so often and I've always got my dogs," Todd answered happily. He said he likes his dogs more than most people. He also explained that he writes songs and plays the fiddle and guitar and that he and his buddies sometimes get together for jam sessions.

We sat there listening to this young man whose experience was so dramatically different than ours, or, for that matter, probably any of his passengers. We having all graduated from various colleges, collecting both under grad and some of us graduate degrees, having worked our entire life in large cities just couldn't quite imagine the wild life of this young man.

I stared up at the wilderness boarding both sides of the river—steep slopes, some with rock outcroppings, the rest covered with large pines. I was struck by the wildness of it all, the desolate nature of this countryside and realized that if we had raft trouble we would not be hiking out—the only rescue would have to come down the river or by helicopter. The sun was out and it was amazingly warm despite the cold glacial water we were traveling down. A slight breeze wafted down the river and, over dressed in our rain gear, we enjoyed its' cooling effect.

I recalled reading John Krakauer's book *Into the Wild* and hoped that Todd was being careful about what he was eating, remembering how that young man, turning his back on the civilized world, moved to Alaska, found an old dilapidated deserted school bus to live in and tried to live off the land. He made the mistake of eating a berry that prevented his stomach from processing food and he died—alone, miserable, totally disenfranchised from the world of people.

When asked if he planned on returning to "civilization," Todd answered that "I love this life of solitude with my dogs and this beautiful wilderness and I plan on living here the rest of my life."

As we drove away from this powerful experience, learning about the life of a strange young man (at least from our standpoint), Jerry jokingly remarked that "that boy is on a path to be our next Unibomber." Cindy, who had truly appreciated Todd's love for his dogs, said, "No way—Todd is a gentle soul."

That night, after another too robust dinner, we sat on the Lodge's deck staring out at Denali Peak (Mt. McKinley—the highest mountain in North America) and I realized that one of the climbing goals that I had contemplated doing was the so-called "Seven Summits"—climbing to the highest points on each continent. I sadly realized that it just wasn't going to happen.

I had completed the 54-14ers (Colorado's 54 mountains higher than 14,000 feet) and that goal seemed to have satisfied my lust for climbing mountains. The problem with the Seven Summits is that four of the seven (Everest, Aconcagua, Vinson and McKinley) have a serious level of risk attached to them—people die on those mountains every year and it was often due to circumstances not in their control—such as bad weather, avalanches, or crevices. The only one of the seven I had climbed was Kilimanjaro in Tanzania, Africa—basically a 3½ day walk up to its 19,000 foot summit. Because of the altitude I had dry heaved all the way up the final day.

Sitting there, staring up at McKinley, I realize that there was a time in my life where the mountain I was looking at had possibly saved my life. I had convinced my fellow climber, Ray Mansfield, that we should climb Elbrus, the highest mountain in Europe. Actually it's in the Urals in what was then one of Russia's USSRs. I read an ad in one of my adventure magazines and called a company in Seattle, Washington called "Mountain Madness," and the phone was answered by its' owner, its enthusiastic owner, named Scott Fisher.

Scott asked me to describe my climbing experiences to that date and I did—about half the Colorado 14ers, Kilimanjaro (Africa's highest), Mount Kenya, the Wetterhorn in the Alps, Ranier, Whitney and Mount Olympus in Greece, telling him I had taken the one day Ranier climbing school, realizing as I spoke that my climbing resume was not particularly impressive. But Scott seemed (or feinted) impressed and he told me that the September trip up Elbrus would be lots of fun and he encouraged me to send in my down payment.

But then Scott surprised me. He asked, "Why don't you join my group going up Everest this spring?

"Everest—you think I'm ready for Everest?" I said, somewhat amazed!

"It's no problem—we'll have it roped all the way to the top. It'll be a piece of cake for you—nothing very technical," he replied.

"How much does that cost? the Scot in me asked.

"$65,000 but remember we're on the mountain for nearly a month and we'll supply everything—food, tents, climbing gear, special clothing—you'll love it," he said.

I paused, clearly excited but still skeptical and said, "Don't you think I ought to climb McKinley first?"

142

There was a long pause at the other end of the phone and then, in a clearly disappointed voice, he said, "Yes, you're probably right. Got to go now but I'll see you in September on Elbrus." As I hung up the cynic in me thought that he probably had a McKinley climb scheduled soon and that I would be hearing from him. Well, we never saw each other on Elbrus because Scott died on that somewhat famous disaster on Everest, detailed in Krakauer's great book, *Into Thin Air*, where the guide services are criticized for taking rookies (like me) up such a dangerous mountain. Scott had apparently died of exhaustion from trying to help all his "clients" up the mountain and not taking care of himself. I tell myself, had I gone on that fateful Everest climb that I would have stayed very close to Krakauer, although realistically I might not have been able to keep up with him.

We would sit there that night staring at McKinley until the sun went down and its' reflection on its' steep slopes disappeared. Walking to our plush little cabin suite, I tried to imagine the climbers up on the mountain, spending many nights (the average climb is over 20 days) in their tents, trying to survive the cold and reach the summit. I wondered why I didn't really want to do it. Was I getting old? Was I afraid?—turning gutless in my old age or did I really prefer spending time with my grandchildren, climbing 13,000 footers in Colorado—probably a combination of all three.

The next day we got on another motor coach to the Denali Park Lodge. Our driver's name was George and informed us that he had made a living as a butcher in previous times. George was older Gentleman than any of our guides, (early 50s), and he had lived in Alaska since the 70s. As soon as he explained that he was a hunter, I knew right away that Cindy, a true animal lover, would not like this gentleman.

But before explaining his love of hunting he spent a great deal of time pointing out the steel reinforcement girders that most of the semi's passing the other way had attached to their front bumpers, asking us if we could imagine what they were for. It turns out that these buttresses were called "Moose Catchers," to protect the driver from running into Moose crossing the highway. Apparently, already in 2005, some 278 Moose had caused accidents on the very highway we were on—the only one between Anchorage and Fairbanks. He claimed that even these huge semis would stop dead if they ran into a Moose. "They're very large animals and humans don't do well in car crashes with them," George said.

He informed us that there are so many Moose killed in car accidents that the State Police have a long list of people interested in butchering the dead moose for their meat. The Police, who rotate the calls sequentially, give each interested party only five minutes to call back and then they move on to the next caller.

George admitted to being called frequently and often responding to the scene where his butchering training came in very handy.

He said, "The typical bull moose will produce nearly 500-700 pounds of good meat. Unlike Todd, presumably George had a freezer.

He then told what he thought was a cute story about taking his son and some friends hunting for deer on an island and they were allowed four deer per person, regardless of sex or age. Before he knew it the kids had killed nearly there limit and some were Does, or as Bruce called them, "Bambis."

He had urged his son and friends to be more selective, picking large bucks instead of the Bambis. I thought Cindy was going to get up out of her seat and go punch the guy. In defense of the hunters, George explained that there are so many deer on this island that they had determined that a number of the deer had actually swam across a 20 mile stretch of sea, luckily avoiding the Orcas, to reach the mainland, where there are no deer—why he didn't explain.

After checking in and having a quick lunch we took an old school bus on the "Denali Park History Tour." But this trip we had a new driver/lecturer, named Doug. Doug, a jolly character, around 40 years of age, from St. Louis, Missouri, had gone to college and received a degree in business from some school in Arkansas, worked a year in Arkansas for an insurance company, moved back to St. Louis, taking a similar job, before finally dropping out of the "rat race" and moving to Alaska. Doug would inform us of things one might not ordinarily expect to be told, like, for example that his Mom and Father are still married, that he has two siblings (a brother and a sister) and eight grandchildren but that he is single and does not anticipate having any children.

In Alaska Doug is a carpenter in the winter and a driver in the summer. We would learn the following trivia from Doug: most of the people who have migrated to Alaska are good with their hands, able to build their own homes and furniture; there were still around 150 climbers on Mt. McKinley hoping to summit (unfortunately, the warmer weather is not good for climbers as the ice tends to break loose causing avalanches and deadly crevices); it took 15 years to build the road into Denali Park because of such harsh winters; Doug recited from memory a poem about Sam Magee and all his adventures; and, he would introduce us to two more slightly strange young people working for a summer wage as lecturers.

The first was a young man who was acting as though he was a settler in 1930 pretending that he had come out to find a long lost uncle and finding him in his grave, behind the cottage he had built with his own hands. This young man claimed to be living as they had in the past, fetching his own water, chopping his wood and picking berries, etc. This kid was not nearly as cute as he perceived himself. Doug also introduced us to a young lady, standing on a hill with the famous mountain behind her, who talked about the amazing "Diversity" of the Native Americans in Alaska, listing at least seven different tribes. Despite having an English name (Brett Featherstone), showing none of the facial characteristics of the Inuit, she still asked us if we thought she was a "Native," and, when no one reacted, she explained that she was from California. I figured she was from Berkley.

I could remember being on Cal's campus, back in my Steeler days, and the long haired, hippy students called us Narcs because of we were wearing sport coats and ties. One of our group (Robin) thought Miss Featherstone would have been far more interesting if she had suggested we sit down, instead of giving her "Diversity" speech while a group of 40 mingled around. Here we had only been in Alaska for 48 hours and we were already becoming somewhat jaded and cynical about our beautiful 49th State.

Doug clearly had a passion for the wilderness and it was clear from his dialogue that he was a "tree hugger," desperately wanting to "preserve" this beautiful Denali National Park/Preserve. He told us about the Park's first Director, a former policeman, who had serious problems stopping the numerous "poachers" that roamed the park, killing some of its' prime wildlife (goats, moose and bears). Apparently the authorities ignored his accusations. The director would send these "criminals" up to Fairbanks accusing them of committing a serious crime—poaching, but the authorities would only charge them a small fine, slap them with a misdemeanor and then send them back.

The poachers began to figure out that the best way to get to Fairbanks on the cheap was to get caught poaching, pay the small fine and come back with new ammo and supplies. Finally, the director, apparently a well trained fist fighter, tired of the authorities ignoring his citations, began beating up the poachers he caught with his fists. Soon the poaching stopped in the park.

For example, as part of his narrative Doug urged us, whenever we could, to "recycle." He finished his speech by imploring us to make a contribution to our planet, giving money to the Agencies that protect our wilderness. He assured us that we could all "make a difference in this beautiful world of ours." Back at the Lodge, exiting the motor coach and despite being somewhat cynical of his plea for recycling (I'm in the waste disposal business) I gave Doug a tip—probably because we had both gone to high school in St. Louis.

The next day we were urged to be up in the Lodge's expansive lobby by 7:30 am and, of course, still functioning on "Lombardi" time (you're fined in the NFL if your even 1 minute late to a meeting) I was there at 7:25. But, as so much is in life, it was again the "Hurry Up and Wait" philosophy—much like my military experience. We finally boarded our bus at 8:15 and were driven over to the railroad depot to board our train for a 9 hour ride to the town of Whittier on the coast, where we would board our cruise ship, the Coral Princess which would take us down to Vancouver.

On the train we met our new "lecturer," Jon, who was a native Alaskan—that he explained was with a small "n" because a large N stood for Native Americans, the Indian tribes. Asked about the fact the we had heard Alaskans referring to themselves as "Sourdoughs" he gave us a long winded explanation that was basically that Sourdoughs were "old timers," or "veterans," which were judged by the number of winters they had spent in Alaska. If it was less than ten winters you were a "Chicawgan," (because, in the old days, many of the people moving to Alaska were from Chicago but the Native American's couldn't pronounce it correctly, let alone spell it), basically a "Rookie." He said the old Sourdoughs were mostly miners who were real tough dudes who somehow survived the winters in the wilderness, "eating shoe leather." Sourdough bread we learned does last longer than most bread. We had already heard about the unbelievable winters in Alaska, as they had had a ten foot dump in one day early this year.

Another thing we learned about Alaska is that the abundant animals (Moose, bears, whales, sea lions, etc.) were not easily seen. Regardless of what mode of transportation (motor coach, school bus, raft, bike, train or ship) we would be told that we should view from the vehicle as a clock—the front of the vehicle being 12:00; our immediate right, 3:00; behind us 6:00 and to our left 9:00.

If we saw an animal we were asked to yell, STOP—bear at 9:00, for example. Unfortunately there were so few animals that people began joking by saying things like "Road kill at 3:00," as we passed a highway. Some of the tours took so long (4 to 5 hours) that people (i.e., two older men from Waco Texas) were whispering things like, "whatever you do, don't say Stop if you see an animal. Just keep your mouth shut. I need my cocktail."

Jon frequently let us down by yelling "Swans," or "Ptarmigans," or some kind of squirrel at 9:00. We hadn't come all the way to Alaska to see animals that were easily seen in our home states. But it did become kind of humorous to hear someone sarcastically yell out "Chipmunk at 2:00." Of course, by the time everyone put down their books or whatever they were doing, and began looking at 2:00 the "sighting" would already be at 4:00. The truth is that there is abundant wildlife in Alaska but it kind of like fishing—if you do it at the wrong time of day (i.e., not sunrise or sunset) it's unlikely you'll catch a fish. The same was apparently true for seeing bears or moose—they just don't hang out during the heat of the day which was exactly when we were would most often be out looking for them.

Jon also felt compelled to teach us the history of every town the train occasionally rode through, explaining that one city was voted by the state's Congress to be the next State Capital because it was half way between the State's two largest cities, Anchorage and Fairbanks. Apparently a lot of smart people hurried up to it and bought lots of property, expecting a land grab in the new Capital. Unfortunately, when the populace learned what the new city would cost ($20 billion) to replace Juneau the people voted it down. The location was today virtually deserted.

Arriving in Whittier we were all somewhat astounded at the size and majesty of our cruise ship, The Coral Princess, a boat that houses 1900 guests and 1100 crew members. After going through a fairly extensive security precautions (very much like today's airports) we boarded the ship and quickly found our stateroom, far nicer than most of the lodge rooms we had just experienced.

Getting on a ship like the Coral Princess is almost like returning to the womb. You will be nourished with abundance (food, entertainment, education, exercise and extraordinary views) to such a degree that it feels almost like returning to the cradle and you are gently (assuming you're lucky enough to dodge any major storms) rocked to sleep with the motion of the sea.

After the somewhat hectic pace of the early trip stage (constantly on and off buses, trains, rafts), our first two days on the ship were idyllic and almost overwhelmingly relaxing. Our group went its' own way, setting their own pace, doing various activities on the boat, the most exciting of which was observing the beautiful views of mountains, waterfalls, glaciers and the fjords of Glacier National Park.

At night we'd all meet at dinner and discuss what we had done and seen (i.e., whales at 3:00 and otters at 9:00. At one point the "Naturalist," who was constantly talking over the ships' intercom, noted a bear with her two cubs on a beach at 2:00 and I thought that the ship might capsize as everyone ran over to that side. Unfortunately most of us weren't fast enough as the mama bear quickly took her cubs into the forest because, as our naturalist would explain, the loud sound of her announcement "probably spooked her."

That night we would eat a quick dinner and later go to one of the ships' theatres to hear a comedian, named "Sarge." As soon as I saw him on stage I remembered seeing him and saying hello, while out walking around the deck. He was a big guy but, despite his girth, he looked in reasonably good shape. After absolutely killing us with laughter at his great gags, we ran into him in the lobby, where he was selling CDs of his show that he would give to the troops on his visit (a U.S.O Tour) to Baghdad later in the year.

When I walked up to Sarge he was telling someone else about an experience he had had with O.J. Simpson, when he had taken O.J.s' credit card and paid for a huge bar bill, unbenounced to O.J. I thought to myself that that might have been a dangerous mistake to make.

When he turned to talk to me, I said, "Hi, I used to 'hunt' O.J."

He stared at me and said, "So you played the game?"

"I used to play linebacker for the Pittsburgh Steelers," I replied.

"You're Andy Russell," Sarge said, reaching out to pump my hand.

"What are you—a sports trivia expert?" I said.

Sarge, an African American, raised by a white Jewish couple, would go on to explain that he had played nose tackle for Boston University and that he had gotten his start doing a radio show for Fox Sports and that on the weekends he would often be assigned to drive Terry Bradshaw around, which was not easy because Terry was seldom on time.

At one point the situation had gotten so bad that Fox told Sarge that if he didn't get Bradshaw to the station to tape a show on time that both he and Terry would be fired. As the story goes, they were in someplace where there were deer and Terry was fascinated watching the deer, not wanting to leave. Finally Sarge commandeered him and began driving him back to the Fox set up at the Stadium at over 100 mph. Soon they were joined in this race against time by a police cruiser who came up behind them with his lights on, clearly trying to pull them over.

Terry told Sarge to ignore the police and to continue into the city and to the stadium. Soon another cruiser joined the chase but Terry insisted that Sarge continue racing to make the set on time. Eventually, as the story goes, there were five or six police cars chasing Sarge and Terry, trying desperately to cut them off but Terry insisted that he drive right around the barriers and get to the stadium.

Finally Sarge pulled up to the stadium entry point and the six cruisers surrounded the car with the numerous police jumping out with their guns aimed at the car.

Terry, who was slowly putting on his coolest sun glasses told Sarge, "Don't worry about it—I'll handle this."

With that he slowly got out of the car and said "Boys y'all don't need those guns, just be cool and get yourselves in line and I'll autograph anything you want me to."

According to Sarge, the police all put their guns away and got in line, asking Terry to sign everything from their police badges to their gun handles.

Tuesday we arrived in Skagway. Our trolley car driver and entertainer was a cute, young lady, named Nicki Bunting. Nicki, wearing vintage (late 1800s) clothing, full of energy and spunk, gave us a story about each building in Skagway. The primary interest about Skagway was it was the kickoff point for all the gold miners who came and tried to get up into the mountains all the way into the Klondike, where they hoped to strike it rich. The Canadians were tough, requiring each miner to have at least 2000 pounds of supplies which, of course, meant that they had to buy a horse to transport the goods. Unfortunately, many of the horses died during this horrendously difficult journey, fighting their way through ten foot snow drifts, taking nine months to fight their way up to the Klondike, only to find that all the decent gold claims had already been taken. Of the 1800 miners that made their way up through the mountains only nine made it rich.

When we got out of the "Trolley" to visit the first Skagway site of interest, I asked her where she was from and when she answered New Hampshire, I immediately told her that my son had gone to Dartmouth. She too had gone to Dartmouth where she studied mathematics the first two years (you could tell she was very smart) and theatre/drama the final two years. With her degree she moved to Telluride (where we have a place) and then on to Skagway, where she had had three jobs: one as a waiter, one as a Cancan dancer in a show, and one driving the Trolley and explaining all the points of interest.

We would also learn that she and her "partner" were starting a new business to create "video-graphics," films showing various adventures and wilderness areas. Their first gig would be in Saint Kitts Island in the Caribbean as soon as the Skagway tourism season was over—the end of September. Before leaving she told me her brother had graduated the same year from Dartmouth that my son had (1988) and gave me his name, Derek Bunting. Incidentally, the only President to ever visit Alaska was President Harding and he went to Skagway.

Later that afternoon we were transported by van up to the top of White Horse Pass, strapped on a helmet and rode bikes back down the 15 mile route to Skagway—all down hill. Our guide on that trip was another vivacious, smart and interesting cute, young lady named Melissa from St. Louis (Chesterfield). We would later find out that she had also, like me, gone to the University of Missouri.

150

Asked what she studied there she responded with a scowl on her face, "Business—but I've figured out that I love the wilderness and want to be involved in education, helping disadvantaged kids." I told her to go with her passion.

As we approached the outskirts of the small town, Skagway (less than a thousand people live there in the winter) we asked her where she lived.

"Real estate is expensive in Skagway. See that little unimpressive 3 bedroom we just passed—they want $250,000 for that. If you want to rent an apartment it's $700 per month. If you want to rent a tent site in the camp ground it's $450 per month. I'm living alone, illegally, up on the mountain in a tent—costs me nothing."

One of our group said, "What if it rains?" apparently unable to imagine living out in the wilderness, alone, in a tent.

"That tent site is my little piece of heaven—I love it," replied Melissa. Before that she lived on an island with two other guides (one guy and a gal) and had to wade across the river to the town each morning. Apparently, as the snows melted and the water cascaded down, the crossing became too dangerous and she moved up onto the mountain.

One thing that virtually all the guides (Todd, Phil, Doug, Nicki, Melissa, and others) wanted to talk about was the high cost of groceries in Skagway. In addition the high priced bananas were bruised and nearly spoiled, as were most vegetables. Apparently, the grocery barge only came once a week (Tuesday) to Skagway and everyone raced over as soon as they could get off work to buy their groceries. Nicki joked that it was the only time that the locals were rude to each other, fighting to get first in line—grocery shopping was serious business.

That night, after having a drink at one of the many bars on the ship, served by Andre, a Rumanian tall and good looking young man who amazingly had remembered from a previous night that Cindy and I wanted Vodka and Cranberry, we ate at the ship's one Italian restaurant, Sabatini's Trattoria. The waiters were either Italian or Rumanian and served us 17 small servings in addition to our main course. It was a terrific dinner but we all staggered up to our staterooms totally stuffed, feeling guilty that we had broken our diets, knowing that there was a high probability that this cruise would cause us all to gain a minimum of 10 pounds.

The next morning we awoke in Juneau, the capital of Alaska, despite having no roads to it. It is accessible only by air and water—cruise ships and a reliable ferry service (twice a week). Juneau is the largest Capital city in the United States in land mass but the smallest in terms of population (only 35,000 people). Our tour de'jour was a Whale Watching excursion by boat up something called the Lynn Canal, actually a natural channel, running southwest away from Juneau.

Naturally, we had to be motor coached over to the dock to board the ship and so we were treated to another driver/comedian/lecturer—this young man named Eric.

"So, do you all think I'm a local?" Eric said.

"No way!" most of the bus responded.

"Can anybody guess where I'm from? He asked.

"Utah," a guy yelled.

"I'm shocked—how did you know that I'm from Utah?"

"Every driver we've had has been from Utah," the guy joked.

It didn't take a genius to figure out that most of these kids, working in Alaska, were bright, comfortable speaking to large groups and all had developed a sort of comedic way of educating us or entertaining us.

For example, Eric asked if any of us were on the cruise celebrating wedding anniversaries and sure enough a number of hands went up. Naturally Eric then asked for how many years the people had been married and the largest number mentioned was 37 years. Eric than proceeded to tell us a moving story about his grandparents whom had just celebrated their 50th wedding anniversary. Apparently, his grandparents had also gone on a cruise and on their wedding night they sat out on their private balcony overlooking the sea with a glass of champagne staring out at the beautiful scenery of Alaska.

But his grandmother noticed that his grandfather was tearing up, starting to cry and she asked, "Honey, what is it? You aren't going to cry because you're so overwhelmed at our good fortune to find each other and live together all these wonderful years?"

"No, that would be nice but that's not what I was thinking about," he said.

"Well, what's causing you to get so emotional, dear?" she said.

"I was just remembering how I felt the night before our wedding. I was unsure, nervous and afraid that we wouldn't be right for each other," he said.

152

"Oh Honey, I never knew that," She said. "What did you do?"

"Well, I went to see your father, as you know I always respected his opinion, after all he was the sheriff, and I told him about my fear, my hesitancy to get married, after all I didn't have a very good job and was afraid that I couldn't afford to be married," he said.

"What did my father say," she implored.

"He said that if I stood you up at the wedding the next day that he would throw me into jail and put me away for 50 years," he said, with tears running down his face and then he said, "and I just remembered that and realized that I would just now be getting out of jail and I'd be a free man."

The next port of entry was that of Alaska's fifth largest city (population 25,000) Ketchikan, the only port that required us to use a "tender," a smaller boat, transporting us for our next tour. Cindy and I had chosen a "Jeep Excursion" up in the mountains, coupled with a "War Canoe" trip across a mountain lake.

Our first driver/educator/entertainer was a young lady named Chessa who proceeded to tell us how to remember the five types of salmon by using your hand. First, your thumb, represented the "Chum" salmon, on that is not particularly tasty and often used for animal feed; second being your index finger which we use to point at things, such as your eyes, so that digit reminds us of the "Sockeye" salmon; third, our middle and largest finger stands for the "King" salmon; the fourth finger, or so called "ring" finger should reminds us of the "Silver" salmon and, finally, the so called Pinky signifies the "Pink" salmon. There it is and I write it down because I know that in a few weeks I will totally forget these five digit reminders of the various salmon species.

Chessa deposited us at a side yard containing about a dozen 4 passenger jeeps and we were introduced to our second guide/educator/entertainer of the day, a Ryan. Ryan was interesting because he was by far the least gregarious, most shy, of the week's guides. Ryan viewed himself more as a teacher rather than an entertainer.

Ryan and I kind of hit it off because I discovered that he was interested in climbing mountains and had done one of Colorado's 14ers, Longs Peak. I learned that Ryan was planning on working the following summer at a ranch in Gunnison, Colorado, from where he hoped to climb more of the 14ers, hoping to do the Slam (all 54) someday. Cindy recommended he try Uncompaghre Mountain, one of our favorites and very user friendly—a good starter mountain. We had climbed it with ten other couples out of Lake City, Colorado a well kept secret—a beautiful little town nestled amongst the mountains and streams.

After dislodging from the jeeps into our "War Canoe," a twenty person large boat (capable of handling 6 foot ocean swells) we met our next guide, a vivacious, young lady from Wisconsin, named Jamie. Jamie was a pistol, jabbering all the way across the lake, where we docked and walked up a wood chip strewn trail or a thirty foot circular, clear plastic covered veranda. Ketchikan is one of the world's wettest spots, getting over 160 inches of rain per year. After being served a lunch of smoked salmon sandwiches and a very tasty and warm clam chowder, Ryan took us on a "Nature Walk," around a 100 yard loop trail (more wood chips), giving us some sense of the second largest rain forest in the world (the Amazon is the largest).

Entering the rain forest I was overwhelmed by its' beautiful features—the canopy, as high above us as 280 feet, made it almost dark inside the forest; moss inches thick hanging on every rock, lichen onto every branch, due to the rain the forest floor was very squishy, as Ryan demonstrated by stepping out of the trail and his rubber boot disappeared immediately. We would learn that the largest tree was 600 years old, there before Columbus discovered America. An interesting fungus, called "Bear Bread," hung off many of the tree trunks which are actually poisonous to the bears but the plant does help decompose the tree once it falls. These trees can take up to 85 years to decompose.

There were also plants with huge leaves (similar to elephant ears) called skunk plants and they possess a little bud that the bears eat when they are constipated! Imagine how they discovered that.... These plants are so called as they put off an offensive odor in the winter thus naming them skunk plants.

After our lunch and tour we got back into our canoe and raced the other canoe (Ryan was the captain) while Jamie steered our canoe. Obviously they were more coordinated as our oars were not in synch and we lost. Always hating to lose, at anything, I found it irritating that our team was so out of synch with oars smacking into each other. The gentleman in front, just one of the guests, appointed as captain by Jamie was joking and laughing and not taking his role as seriously as I would have liked. We tried to oar as fast as we could but oars were flying everywhere and most of the people in the boat had no clue.

I couldn't help but reminisce about our competition after winning our first Super Bowl at the Super teams' competition in Hawaii. Being the captain of that little fiasco I had mistakenly put Fats Holmes on the war canoe race and he almost sunk it. I remembered a Hawaiian spectator coming up and saying "not a bad effort for a submarine."

By this time we had gotten to know a number of crew members on the ship. One, for instance, is Andres from Rumania and he is our waiter in the Wheelhouse Lounge we go to every night before dinner. He explained that the salaries are very small in Rumania and when I mentioned that I planned to go there on business he was very interested in what kind of business would take me to his home country. He again remembered what all of us had to drink the night before so when we come in he says, "Vodka and cranberry?" We threw him off last night by ordering a marquerita instead.

At dinner our head waiter is Jorge and he is very entertaining and fun. He is over the top when waiting on us. He remembers all our names and has to wait on a number of other people at the same time. Since we are a party of 12 we are all very impressed with him. He is from Mexico City, the largest city in the world. He is engaged to a lady from South Africa and will only be on board for two more years before they get married and settle down. We bought him a bottle of champagne and will give him a tip tonight. We all enjoyed him and his assistant (who doesn't speak as good English but works hard and smiles a lot).

There is also a naturalist on board who speaks through the intercom and tells facts and stories about the glaciers and the animals that inhabit them. The only problem was that her voice was so soft and melodic that she almost put me to sleep. She is very informative and we have learned a lot from her. I realized that had Cindy become a naturalist we might not have met as she would have loved that profession and probably would live somewhere like Alaska rather than PA.

In an effort not to gain too much weight, as we were eating far more calories than our norm, Cindy and I decided to go the whole cruise (6 days) without using the elevator a single time, forcing us to climb up and down the ships' 14 floors. Of course, we started every morning by climbing from our 8th floor stateroom up to the 14th floor 24 hour buffet breakfast. Instead of working out in the ships' exercise room we decided to stay outside, hiking around the ship (2.8 laps to a mile) and climbing all ten stories each lap, from the 5th floor to the 16th—there was no 13th floor. We started by doing 5 laps and 50 flights of stairs the first day, increasing that by one per day, ending with 10 laps and 100 flights—sort of like climbing the Empire State Building. What I liked the best about this work out is that part of it (the laps) were outside, enabling us to see orcas, otters and the spectacular scenery. Our teammates also stayed very active, some doing special classes in the workout room and others doing bicycle (spinning) classes.

The final day on the ship was at sea, making our way down the inter-passage way to Vancouver where our group would split up, some staying to spend one extra day in the beautiful city, others heading directly home. The journey down the inter-coastal route was blissful with more incredible scenery on both sides of the boat—numerous islands to our right (starboard) and the Canadian coast to our left (the port side), all covered by rugged, fir laden mountains. None of the mountains were very high, probably around 2500 feet high, but still impressive.

As this trip drew to a close I again found myself sad, not wanting it to end, not in a hurry to return to the demands of my business and personal life back in the Burgh. Of course, I also realized that without my outstanding business partners, who work so hard while we're gone, there would be no cruise type life style in our life. Life is certainly very very good for all of our group.

I also wanted to thank all those guides, drivers, lecturers for having added so much enjoyment to the trip. They entertained us, educated us, and made us laugh and appreciate more of what we were seeing by learning more about its' history. They were all extremely impressive young folks—smart, well-schooled, funny, enthusiastic and clearly loving what they were doing. In the end, we all concluded that our country will be in good hands when the next generation takes over, although I think we'd have a tough time getting that bunch out of Alaska.

Chapter 16

THE CONSTANT THREAD

Now that I am a "Senior Citizen," I find myself spending a dispro-portionate amount of time reflecting on my past, trying to make sense of all the choices made, both good and bad, all the changes in direction, and trying to understand how all the pieces of my life fit together, or, in some instances, don't. I'm sure that this is not par-ticularly unusual as I suspect most older people begin looking back, trying to understand their life's choices (their so-called legacy), and trying to make sure that all the most important people in their life, the ones they love, respect and admire, (parents, spouses, children, grandchildren, mentors and good friends) know how important they were in their life.

I am constantly amazed at how incredibly serendipitous the nature of life can be, the unexpected opportunities and choices made with-out much thought, that in the long run turn out to have had an enor-mous impact (both positive or negative) on one's life. The question arises, for all of us, was there a common thread, perhaps a genetic predisposition, which stands out in having influenced our decisions, our choices and, thus, affecting our lives in meaningful ways?

The one common thread for me was my passion for the world of sports. Even at an early age I loved to challenge my body with athletic moves, whether it was climbing a tree that the other kids in the neigh-borhood couldn't climb, running faster, jumping higher, winning vari-ous games, always trying my best, (of course, not always succeeding), to try to excel in whatever physical activity was at hand.

I don't know where this desire came from. My parents never really encouraged me to participate in sporting activities; they did not praise me for my sporting efforts as they seldom showed up to observe these contests. Since we didn't have a TV set until I was twelve, I wasn't try-ing to emulate something I had seen and admired on the TV. It was clearly something that I was born with, an innate drive, or need, to be the best that I could be athletically, and sometimes that wasn't all that good—sporting contests can sometimes be very embarrassing.

Now, so many years later, my greatest satisfaction (other than being with my family and friends) is still to challenge my body, bicycling up hills, hiking up or down steep trails and climbing mountains or trying to find my golf ball. Granted, I'm not really pursuing competitive sports anymore, but I still find that I am deriving the most joy/satisfaction from a physical activity. That's not to say that I never try and exercise the brain, as I love to read books and enjoy trying to write them and I force myself to do the crossword puzzle every day—got to keep the old brain functioning (use it or lose it).

As I look back on my life, the good and the bad, I can clearly see that the one common thread has been the positive impact that sporting challenges, especially from the game of football, have had on my life. Reflecting on my past experiences, I am somewhat astounded at how much football has influenced the choices I have made; personal choices, family and post football, business career, not just when I played the sport but afterwards and until this day.

I am, (as all my teammates are), still constantly being reminded of my Steelers experience; being asked frequently to do, and enjoying very much, interviews (i.e., "Where are they Now," kind of stuff), memorabilia signings, giving motivational/teamwork speeches and doing "meet and greets" at some corporate outings—somewhat amazed that anyone can still remember that long ago (Andy who, you played when?), as I retired from the game in 1976 at age 35.

Back then, if someone had told me that in year 2009 (33 years later) that I would receive more fan mail requesting autographs on photos or football cards and be asked to speak more often than I had during my Steelers career, I would have said they were crazy. Of course, the reason for this has little to do with my football accomplishments but far more to other factors, such as the NFL having grown hugely in popularity and many more people are aficionados and the Internet gives them easy access to even players low on their list.

More importantly, I am constantly amazed at how our company's (Liberty Tire Recycling) business contacts often seem to prefer to hear my football stories than our business stories. Whether I want to admit it or not, football has clearly been a defining event in my life and continues to be a common thread, weaving its way through many of the major choices I have made in this life.

For example, I joined the ROTC program at the University of Missouri. Why? It was because one of my football teammates and fraternity brother, Don Wainwright, urged me to do so, arguing that it was important that we learn more about leadership and that, since in those days (1963) there was a mandatory draft, why not go in as "an officer?"

Upon graduating from the University of Missouri (B.S. in Economics) with my Army commission (Lieutenant) I discovered that I was not scheduled to report to Fort Sill, Oklahoma until January of the following year, 1964, thus allowing me to play for the Steelers as a rookie in the 1963 season, a wonderful experience, as I got to start and hugely enjoyed playing pro ball despite often struggling to perform well. That choice, picking pro football over working, as a business intern in St. Louis that short time between my June graduation and reporting to Fort Sill, turned out to have an enormously positive influence on my life.

Then when I arrived in Germany (Nuremberg) for my military service I was surprised to find that there was military football in USA-REUR (United States Army Europe), selecting teams to represent each of the ten or so major Divisions (each having approximately 25,000 men) in the theatre. My commander in a 8" self propelled howitzer unit in Nuremberg, a Lt. Colonel, made me promise that I would not identify myself as a former football player to the VII Corp team (our unit fell under the Corp that oversees all those Divisions) because my artillery unit would be an officer short in "TDY," (temporary duty).

I honored that promise but a Captain Lindquist, the VII Corp football coach, diligently reading through thousands of Lieutenant's personal files, hoping to find Lieutenants who had played college football, found that under the heading, "Hobbies," I had written "Football," as there was no place to list one's athletic achievements. He called me from VII Corp Headquarters in Stuttgart and the conversation went something like this.

"Lieutenant Russell, this is Captain Lindquist and I'm the coach of the VII Corp football team, here in Stuttgart—I've been looking through officers in our Corps personal files and I see that you listed football as a hobby. Would you like to explain that?"

"Yes, Sir!—I have played some football."

"Did you play at the College level?"

"Yes, Sir—I played for the University of Missouri."

"Were you any good? Did you start?" What position did you play?"

"Sir, last year I played professional football for the Pittsburgh Steelers, I started and I made the All Pro Rookie team—I'm a linebacker."

There was a significant pause at the other end of the line and then Captain Lindquist said, "That's great news, you will be transferring this week to Stuttgart and you will play for our team, the Jayhawks (at Mizzou we hated the Kansas University Jayhawks), here at VII Corp headquarters."

"Sorry, Sir but my Colonel has already told me that I am not allowed to play football because it would hurt our unit—missing an officer TDY."

"Lieutenant Russell, you don't understand. The commanding officer of VII Corp is a four star General, named Truman (yes, a relative of Harry's) and he significantly outranks your Colonel. You will be transferred to Stuttgart tomorrow and be one of our defensive coaches and you will also play middle linebacker. That is an order, Lieutenant. General Truman is quite unhappy that last year our team came in last—he wants to see significant improvement."

"What about our personal goods that just arrived and are stored in our Nuremberg apartment that my wife and I just rented?

"Don't worry about your "stuff,"—we'll be sending a duce and a half (truck) to pick that up tomorrow as well.

We would go on to win the USAREUR Championship and I was lucky enough to stay healthy and be picked as the MOP (Most Outstanding Player) in military football, including those teams in Europe and the U.S.

After winning the Championship I spent a few months working in General Truman's office (as a back up General's Aide) before Coaching the Corp basketball, golf, track teams and running the gymnasium. Playing football had once again clearly altered my military experience, never returning to my 8″ howitzer unit in Nuremberg. I often joke that the most dangerous thing I did while in the Military (two years active duty) was to drive my Porsche on the Autobahn (that auto bought with my rookie "signing bonus—$3,000).

160

I would realize many years later that my football experience in Germany had made me a better player because I had been one of the assistant coaches, designing defenses and being aware of all the positions responsibilities—I came back with a different thought process with respect to the game and I believe it helped me perform better in the NFL.

Upon returning to the States, after my "military" experience, I found that the Steelers weren't particularly impressed that I had been the "MOP" of USAREUR football, thinking that I most likely had lost all my skills and couldn't possibly return to the NFL level of play after being "out of the game" for two years—at least that was their negotiating position when I tried to discuss a new contract, asking them to recognize my having made the All Pro Rookie team (granted, three years ago) and double my first year's $12,000. They finally, after months of negotiations, gave me a $2,000 raise.

Realizing that the NFL wasn't going to be the place to make "real" money, I spent the first two off seasons back from Germany, using my Steelers income to pay for my MBA at Missouri University, my Alma mater, something my good Army friend, Tom Graham, also a coach of the Seventh Corp team, had convinced me to do. Shortly after receiving the degree (June, 1967) and having worked one year for Oliver Tyrone Corp, I started my own company (1969), Russell Investments, a NASD licensed, SEC security broker dealer, began syndicating tax advantaged investments (real estate—mostly apartment projects) for DLJ, (a prestigious Wall Street Investment Bank) and made more money that first year of business in the off season than I did playing for the Steelers.

I quickly realized that I was playing professional football because it was my passion, something that drove me to challenge myself to improve; to learn how to better play the game that I loved and the joy of being part of a team—it was not about money.

Of course, it took me forever, into my mid-thirties, to really learn how to play linebacker, learning new techniques and thought processes every year. I viewed my business as every bit as important as football, driving myself to make it more profitable, having early morning business breakfasts and late night dinner meetings during the football season, working 7 days a week, enjoying the challenges of the business world and the contrasts with the world of football.

I convinced myself that if I spent all that more time analyzing game films that I would have so much information about the opponent to analyze and compute that, on the field, I might get "Paralysis of Analysis," the dreaded disease of the over-thinker, causing the player a moments hesitation that could cause failure.

Some might think that being an ex-Steeler might have been a big advantage in the business world, as people might be more willing to see you, thinking "I wonder what this dumb ex-jock wants—this guy probably has no clue about the business world." I realized that I needed to make sure to impress my prospects with my knowledge of my product and, as in football, took the memorization of details to an extreme. Many of the plays I would make on Sunday happened because I was memorizing the opponent's tendencies and watching game films at midnight during the week—the same discipline became just as important in the business world—success is in the details.

Of course, since much of my business success came overseas (Switzerland, South Africa and Saudi Arabia), with clients who had absolutely no knowledge of what it meant to play pro football in America and, frankly, didn't care, having that on my resume meant nothing. They didn't know a Super Bowl from a wash bowl. However, if it hadn't been for football, I probably would not have even sought out these international opportunities.

For example, in early 1974 (we had won our first Division Championship in 1972 and played well in '73) I got a call from my ex-Steelers teammate, Frank Atkinson, (a great friend from football) telling me that he had made a life altering decision, leaving his venture capital business and moving his family from San Francisco to Beirut, Lebanon and asking me to come visit in our next off-season.

My first wife, Nancy, and I had already been to Beirut in 1965 (before their civil war), flying down on a space available military flight (something I probably would not have been allowed to do if I had not been one of the General's favorites, again only because of football).

Beirut was described by many as the gem of the Mediterranean, and, being a Scot, having already been there and knowing that such a trip would be extremely expensive, despite being a great friend, I put Frank off, telling him I wasn't sure if I could make it, expecting not to. But Frank remained persistent, (probably one of his traits that helped him to start as a rookie for the Steelers and do well in business) and I finally, to get him off my back, agreed to come "if, and only if, we win the Super Bowl."

Since we had never even been in a Super Bowl, let alone win one, it was sort of like giving Frank the sleeves of my vest. Of course, we went on that year to win our first Super Bowl and off we, (two of my business associates, Peter Kalkus and Sam Zacharias), went to Beirut, making it a business trip, since most of the Saudi financial advisors resided in Beirut at that time. Our somewhat naïve idea was to sell some of our major investments (i.e., the Equibank building and DLJ deals) to Saudis who had huge supplies of money from their oil sales.

That invitation, from Frank, would go on to change my life forever, creating the opportunity to travel around the world, eight straight years, using the NFL's extraordinary marketing power and the Steelers new found fame, having won two Super Bowls in a row.

Ray Mansfield and I, helped by our pal and my working partner, Sam Zacharias (who served as our sort of unofficial agent who handled all the reservations, tickets and scheduling), gave media interviews, autograph signings, sports clinics and speeches with teammates Lynn Swan, Mike Wagner, Mel Blount, and Jack Ham (each on a different trip), in such places as Saudi Arabia, Kuwait, Singapore, Bangkok, Hong Kong, Osaka, Tokyo, Seoul (Korea), Vietnam, Bombay, Naples Frankfurt, Amsterdam, Zurich and London, meeting and greeting people all over the world. So, once again, football had changed my life, taken me to new places, making new friends, and offering me new opportunities.

We would finally hit the proverbial homerun when we sold a number of Appalachian Gas Drilling programs to one of South Africa's wealthiest men, Dr. Anton Rupert, a billionaire, owning diamond and gold minds, as well as tobacco plantations and wine vineyards. Of course, Dr. Rupert didn't know or care that I was a former professional football player but the NFL's enormous marketing power had enabled me to travel the world and get in front of him.

After retiring from the game after the 1976 season, deciding it was time to focus one hundred percent of my energy on my investment business (the Steelers offered me a two year contract but I felt it was time to "seek my life's work," one of Chuck Noll's favorite sayings), I would discover that my past football experience would continue to have a significant influence on my life.

I was asked by NBC if I would like to be a color broadcaster for their NFL games and I immediately accepted, thinking the experience might help me deal with the enormous impact of not doing something that had been such a huge part of my life for nearly 25 years. I didn't think of broadcasting as a potential new career but as a temporary activity that would help me "transition" from the game to the real world.

Despite thinking that I knew the nuances of the game very well, I would discover that broadcasting a game, fitting in with your play by play commentator, making concise analysis in only a few seconds, is a very difficult performance. I could get up in front of an audience and speak without notes for over an hour without boring them too much but as a TV analyst I didn't have that time to think, having your producer/director talking in your ear, telling you to wrap it up in the next ten seconds because they have to go to a commercial, which, of course, is what it is all about—without those advertisers the NFL couldn't afford to televise their games.

Despite working full time in my business (6:00 am to late—often past midnight, Monday through Friday) I would try to cram some study about the teams I was going to be talking about on the flight to the game on Saturday. We would then be briefed by the NBC director, reminding us of what were current topics of interest with each team (injuries, coaching styles, recent trends, etc.). I would then go out to dinner with the play by play announcer and we'd talk about the NFL and the next day's broadcast.

Despite all this, always feeling hurried, I was unable to deliver the kind of meaningful information to the listener that I had hoped to. Consequently, I would come home from the game on Sunday, ready to go to work on Monday, but often found myself thinking about what I could have said (if I'd though of it), instead of focusing on my business, which, of course, was far more important to the welfare of my family.

Football, in this case, frustration over not doing a better job broadcasting, was still a major driver in my life. Fortunately, (for NBC) I would only spend a few years trying to learn the entertainment business before NBC dropped me (that's right I was "let go" for the first and only time during my career) and rightfully so. I had stupidly done an interview with a national correspondent, essentially saying that TV color commentating was somewhat frivolous, since you didn't have time to say anything meaningful since you couldn't describe anything in detail. Obviously, NBC was unhappy about one of their employees bad-mouthing their industry, and I don't blame them. I was stupid and arrogant to make those comments but I wasn't all that upset about it, as I had only planned on broadcasting for a year or two anyway. Perhaps it also had something to do with my turning NBC down when they asked me to do four more games—employers don't want to hear the word NO!

I realized at that time that it was very important not to live too much in the past, to not have football continue to drive my life but it was difficult. One of my heroes, Reinhold Messner, arguably the greatest mountain climber ever, being the first man to ever climb the worlds 14 highest mountains, many without oxygen, theorized that a person is not what they did but they are what they do. In other words what you've accomplished in the past means nothing—it is over and of no value. Only what you are doing now is important—granted that is somewhat harsh but probably true.

So, when I was asked to be part of a national beer advertisement I declined, thinking that it wouldn't be the image that I should have if I wanted investors to take me seriously as a financial product provider. But, when I was asked to be the spokesman for Equibank, doing a series of Ads promoting the bank, and, since the company was in the financial services industry, I thought it would be OK relative to my image, not to mention that I was paid a fairly hefty stipend (nearly as much as my average annual Steelers salary all those years of playing) for doing those ads. In retrospect, I think my being a Scot (brought up to not spend and to save as much as possible), was the main reason I decided to do those well paying ads.

Living and working in Pittsburgh during those years I was not un-aware of the prestige of certain clubs—both country clubs and private dining clubs, like the Rolling Rock Club, Fox Chapel Golf Club and the Duquesne Club (granted there are many other quality clubs in our city) and I thought it wouldn't hurt my business career if I could get into those so fine clubs. When I asked one of my business mentors, Bob Arnold (my CPA and advisor) he told me "look, Russell, if you think you can get into the Duquesne Club you should do it right now because you're in the investment business and no one bats a thousand in that business—you're bound to piss somebody off when an investment goes sour and he could boycott you from the club—definitely go for it."

So, I started the lengthy process to get in by going to two of my other business mentors, Dick Means and Ernie Buckman, whom I had worked for at Oliver Tyrone, my first year out of graduate school. Dick was the head of the New Members Committee and he agreed to sponsor me and he got the other committee members to co-sponsor me, so I figured it was wired. Little did I know, as a month or so later, I got a call from Dick and he informed me that my admission had been denied. When I asked him why, he told me that the Club Manager, Melvin Rex, a crusty, but well respected gentleman, who ran the club with an iron fist but hugely effective, had vetoed me from membership. When I asked why, Dick didn't know, so I asked him if I could request a private meeting with Mr. Rex to find out the reason.

A week later I was in his office, nervous, wondering why I had been rejected, worrying about how to handle the meeting. After a short wait, Mr. Rex walked in with a scowl on his face and got right down to business.

"You're probably wondering why I vetoed your membership," he said.

"Yes Sir, you are correct. Have I done something wrong? Is there someone else you would have preferred recommend me?" I replied.

"Here's the deal. We don't let anyone in this club who is not a pure businessman. We don't let sports celebrities, people who are doing commercials on television into this club. For example, Bob Prince (the Pirates so talented and revered announcer) cannot get in this club—period."

"With respect, Mr. Rex, but I am primarily a businessman. Over 95% of my income comes from my business which is investment banking—doing commercials is less than 5 percent of my income," I said.

"Mr. Russell, you don't understand, that's like being just a little bit pregnant—we don't let any women into this club—period," he said. (The Club does have many female members today but not then).

"Well, Sir, if I stop doing those Equibank commercials would you let me in the club?"

"Absolutely—in fact, I'll sponsor you myself," was his answer.

166

Walking out of the Duquesne Club that day, I realized that once again football had impacted my life—this time in a strangely negative way.

One year later, Equibank, got tired of my mug and I went straight back to the Duquesne Club and became a member, a membership that I have enjoyed ever since—a truly outstanding club, where we have done a great deal of business and solidified some very strong relationships.

Later I would join the Rolling Rock and the Fox Chapel Golf Clubs, both very prestigious clubs that are tough clubs to get in to, neither of whom wanted their membership to include some dumb jock whose only claim to fame is that he played the game. Some how I was granted membership and have enjoyed the benefits of being a member of two such fine clubs. In both cases, however, I could feel a slight negativity due to my athletic career, the members of those clubs, being somewhat concerned (and rightfully so) that I might not comport myself with the dignity of their typical member. Football was again influencing my life, as we players took partying to a different level, not always being as dignified as one might hope but we certainly had a lot of fun.

Being an ex-Steeler would stay with me regardless of the success of our business. I joked that we could buy some huge company (via a leveraged buyout) and I'd still be stopped and asked "aren't you the linebacker." None of us were concerned with celebrity; only trying to be the best player we were capable of becoming, a challenge of the mind and body.

Being so caught up in my post football and around the world business experiences, one might wonder whether I had an ordinary life, having a family and raising our kids. My first wife, Nancy, the mother of my kids (son, Andy Keith and daughter, Amy Esther) and I believed very strongly that it was important that we not let our kids be affected, or negatively impacted, by all the Steeler/media/TV announcing mania. In fact we made a point of avoiding taking the kids to too many Steeler events, keeping them out of the lime-light and trying to instill in them the same old school values our parents had given us. Despite our efforts to shelter them from unwanted publicity they found themselves on the cover of the *Post Gazette* Sunday supplement.

Not wanting to be the classic "stage" father I would suggest to my kids that they play tennis or golf, safer games without any of that "are you going to be a football player like your Daddy? My son, despite my spending more time with him camping and hiking on the Laurel Ridge Trail than tossing him a football, ended up playing football at Fox Chapel H.S. and Dartmouth College and he was quite good. My daughter, a very strong runner and soccer player was on Fox Chapel's Western Pa. championship soccer team.

So, now at age 68, I am accepting this inherent unfairness and smile at the absurd popularity of those of us lucky enough to have played in the 70's. Hey, there is something about being in the right place at the right time—timing is everything.

Thank you, Steelers football, for giving me the thrill of a lifetime and opening up all kinds of new worlds I had no idea even existed.

Chapter 17

A GREAT PROFESSOR

The following chapter is written in the third person, talking about how some guy named Andy found his way through college being helped by his professor mentor, Paul Doherty. This was the first time I tried this concept (in the third person) and perhaps the last. This story was actually sent to Paul Doherty on his 70th birthday celebration, in response to a letter from Paul's children asking for a note from me congratulating their father for being such a fine professor—I'm sure that this essay was more than they wanted but Paul was an extraordinary mentor and I owe him a great deal—so here it is!

Once upon a time there was a young man, named Andy, attending the University of Missouri, on a football athletic scholarship, trying his best to survive the challenges of his game and, since he was just an average student, hoping he could remain eligible. This is a story about how Andy and his writing professor, Paul, became friends and how Paul made a major contribution in helping him realize his dreams. Please forgive Andy, now an old man, if this story is more about him than it is about Paul—Andy's memory is not what it used to be (after ten concussions) but he does remember clearly the powerful impact of Paul's friendship and tutelage.

To understand just how important Paul's mentoring was to Andy, we need to know something about Andy's childhood and what kind of young man he was when he first met Paul. Andy was just the typical nervous and jerky, insecure, overly self-conscious, somewhat nerdy (anti cool), neurotic undergrad that is the norm—however, his parents had taught him (true or not) that he was unique, special, gifted and destined to go on to bigger and better things (Andy is still working on modesty).

Athletically Andy had a strong self-image but scholastically Andy was a potential disaster, lacking the ability to concentrate (except on the athletic field), burdened by the dreaded Attention Deficit Disorder, an affliction unnamed in those days. Arriving at Missouri U. he had virtually no confidence in his intellect—how could he? He had never paid any attention in class, ignoring the teacher's lessons, thinking instead about scoring touchdowns and his academic record reflected this lack of attention. He definitely needed encouragement and found none, other than his mother's unbridled praise, until he met Professor Doherty.

Andy would discover that his mental talents were at best limited certainly stacked against Mr. Doherty (Paul's) wisdom, one would say that he was almost intellectually impaired and that he would only succeed if he committed all his energy and drive to whatever goals he had. He would also learn that luck would have a great deal to do with whatever good fortune his life had in store for him.

Andy had grown up a Corporate Brat, moving from city to city, as his father was promoted from one job to another. His parents explained how lucky he was to have the "opportunity" to make so many new friends and to learn to adapt to so many new environments. They pushed him to become independent, self reliant and to learn how to survive the "jungle" that is life with all its pitfalls, risks, and dangers juxtaposed against such wonderful opportunities, experiences and adventures.

During his first month as a freshman at Missouri, his parents moved to Brussels, Belgium and would be gone for ten years—it was time to grow up and be the independent person his parents always wanted (demanded) him to be.

One of the most important things Andy would learn was that it was critical to pick his friends and mentors very carefully, that there are a lot of very seductive people out there and despite their high intelligence, their charisma and other attractive features, these people can severely impair your ability to succeed or, worse, get you into serious trouble. Obviously, there is some degree of luck in who you find yourself spending time with, but finding Paul was one of Andy's biggest breaks.

Andy's English teaching mother, Esther, had mandatory family readings every Sunday evening, where Andy and his brother, Will,

170

would read out loud a chapter of a family book while their parents critiqued their pronunciations and questioned their understanding of the words. Andy's sweet supportive mother would take him to the New York City Library and spend hours hunting in the stacks to find special books about American Indians, a group of people that Andy had always found fascinating. He was particularly incredulous how they could exist in the wilderness with nothing but their wits, demonstrating amazing survival skills.

Esther even suggested (planted the seed) that someday Andy might write a book himself. But all of that was way back in his mind, hidden well behind his one overwhelming and almost neurotic need, to be the best athlete he could be. His body had subliminally told him, since he was a young child that he had been born with a gift, that he should be, first and foremost, an athlete. He could not even imagine writing a book.

Andy got very lucky in his journey, almost serendipitously finding strong and wise mentors to guide him on his way. In the world of Academia, his best luck was to be a student in a writing course taught by a graduate student, Paul Doherty, (eight years older than Andy), learning his trade.

Paul's contribution to Andy would be far more than his technical advice with regard to how to write but, more importantly, his praise and encouragement. Professor Doherty, despite giving him mostly "C to B" grades (because he really wasn't all that good), seemed to take a special interest in Andy (of course, he may have been that way with all his students), pushing him to read the great masters works, writers like Dostoyevsky, Faulkner, Hemingway, Salinger (Andy loved Franny and Zoey), Tolstoy and others. Andy would discover, and be amazed, that he could totally lose himself, selfless deep in a great book and frequently came away from those classics feeling inspired and exhilarated—as though he had found a whole new world.

Paul encouraged him to continue reading all the great works and to this day, Andy remembers savoring those wonderful books, finding the joy of reading. One vivid memory is when, during his college years, he was on a summer trip to Norway, with his parents, exploring the Fiords. One night he found himself reading *Crime and Punishment*, totally riveted and overwhelmed by Theodors' prose, late into the night and looking outside and seeing the northern lights and realizing that he was at the same latitude as the troubled Russian in the book. Could this midnight sun cause psychological problems, Andy wondered?

Paul Doherty had given Andy a tremendous gift, encouraging him to read the classics, and that night, reading the great Dostoyevsky in Norway, he was as high as any athlete had ever been and as blown away as if he was on a drug induced trip. No alcohol, hallucinogenic mushrooms, cocaine, LSD, heroin or marijuana needed for this boy. Nothing could have produced a more memorable trip—Andy was flying high and he owed it all to Professor Doherty, his new flight instructor.

Another time Paul, as part of a writing assignment, encouraged Andy to write an essay that was based upon "original" research and something that would feature one of Andy's favorite authors, Ernest Hemingway. Knowing that Ernest had written for the Kansas City Star when he was 19 years old, as a cub reporter covering accidents, (essentially an unnamed ambulance chaser), Andy dug deep in the University of Missouri Library and found that all the Star's issues, since the paper was founded, were on micro film.

Knowing the year that Hemingway was there, Andy read all the ambulance/accident reports written that year and felt that he could feel Hemingway's style grow as he wrote more accident updates. At first he ignored the Sunday supplements, (thinking Hemingway wouldn't be writing there), but eventually Andy decided to browse through all the 52 supplements and mid way through that process he stumbled across an article, written by the editor, that outlined the *Kansas City Star's* "Ten Rules of Good Writing."

Reading the article, Andy immediately could see how Hemingway's style might have been developed as a young writer. For example, the No. 1 rule was to "never use a long, complicated, pretentious word when you can use a short, simple word." No. 2 was "always use short, simple sentences." No. 3 was "Repeat, repeat, repeat." The rest of the rules all had to do with writing in a concise, brief as possible, almost simplistic way, with a premium on truth and accuracy.

Andy could feel his excitement increase as he realized that he had potentially discovered how Hemingway had developed his writing style, something that had never been mentioned in his well-documented biographies. Thrilled, by his first and only original research, Andy wrote his "original research" essay and got his first "A+."

Meeting with his new mentor, Paul, he felt his first flush of scholastic achievement—maybe, he wasn't such a dumb jock after all. Paul, knowing that Andy traveled every summer to Europe to visit his parents, amazing as this idea now sounds, suggested Andy take his essay and deliver it in person to Hemingway in Pamplona, Spain where the Running of the Bulls Festival occurred, a place where Hemingway was known to migrate to every year. Yes, it is clear that Andy did not learn how to write short simple sentences.

So, full of this new found academic confidence, encouraged by his hugely supportive professor, Paul, Andy (granted, naively) headed down to Pamplona to meet the great writer and show him his paper and, possibly, get confirmation that he had in fact discovered the mother lode of Hemingway's uniquely blunt style—a journalistic technique full of universal truths and prose that resonated with passion, honesty but deep simplicity, repeated often.

Stopping for a visit at the French Riviera on his way to Spain, Andy found himself, after a night of heavy drinking (Hemingway would have approved), sitting on a beach near Monte Carlo, and couldn't help but notice an attractive young lady, lying nearby, sunbathing in the nude, reading a newspaper. Wondering if she spoke English, (Andy knew no French other than how to order a glass of wine) his eyes moved away from this amazing feminine pulchritude to read the newspaper's headlines and he saw something about Hemingway and the word Merte, a word that Andy feared meant death.

Rushing to the closest newsstand, he found the *Herald Tribune*, where his suspicions were confirmed, reading about Hemingway's suicide from a shotgun shell he fired into his own mouth. Hemingway's father had also died of suicide and his mother had bizarrely given Ernest the weapon his father had used. Since his father's death, Hemingway had been fascinated by death, following ambulances in Kansas City, covering the war in World I (*A Farewell to Arms*), the Spanish Civil War (*The Sun Also Rises*) and arriving in his beloved Paris even before the Allies got there and holding out, ignoring the Nazis, drinking heavily in the Hotel Ritz Bar. Apparently, living between two places, Montana and Cuba, surrounded by his cats, unable to write, and drinking heavily he had become depressed over his failing health and decided to take his own life, as his father had.

Andy sat there stunned, reading about his hero's death, thinking how sad it was that the great man had passed and about the irony of his traveling to Pamplona to pay honor to Hemingway—his first experience in trying to contact a celebrity hero, as just a star struck fan and Hemingway taking his own life only a week before the festival. Andy would change his itinerary, returning to Brussels early and it would be a few years before he would travel to Pamplona and pay his alcohol-hazed respects to the great writer and the town that he loved.

This strange, but meaningful experience, happened only because of Paul Doherty's enthusiastic encouragement—chase your dreams young man, you can achieve whatever you set your mind to, go for it, use that brain, be the man you can become. Paul was clearly a blessing.

Later Paul and Andy would develop a relationship outside of the classroom, as Andy and his roommate and best friend, Jim Card, (one of Missouri's best baseball pitchers) would visit with Paul and his roommate in their third floor flat, where they would sit at the feet of these academic super stars, their first mentors to encourage scholastic achievement instead of athletic achievement. Paul would sit with these young students and dazzle them as he told stories of the great books and their writer's idiosyncrasies and lives.

As they got to know each other better, Paul and his friend let their hair down and showed them some of their favorite activities that almost always had to do with sports. One game Andy would never forget was a game where each player would be given the opportunity to drop kick an old raggedy football up onto a cot bed from across the room. Actually this was a very difficult thing to do, as the ball had to land softly without rolling off the bed—only a ball that remained on the bed counted. Since drop kicking was an anachronism, long gone from the game, no one had ever taught Andy and Jim how to do it. Astoundingly, Paul, clearly a natural athlete himself, set the record by kicking a half dozen straight successful kicks in a row—none of us were even close.

By this time Andy's football had progressed to where he was a starting fullback and linebacker but still falling woefully short of his lofty goals. He realized that while Jim and he wanted to listen to Paul and his friend talk about literature, the professors wanted to ask Jim and him about their efforts on the athletic fields. It was a mutual admiration society. Jim and Andy were infatuated with the professors for their wisdom and knowledge, whereas, they appreciated Jim and Andy for their success in performing well at the college level, certainly viewed by most as bigger than those crucial drop kicks, late into the night, onto a third story apartment cot)—but hey, Jim and Andy were not familiar with losing athletic contests and, admittedly, it stung that Paul could beat them so easily.

During Andy's junior year, not wanting to live in either the dorm or the fraternity house, he lived off campus the first semester with a couple of friends. Unfortunately, during the spring semester, they had a beer party on the porch of their rented home (Paul was probably in attendance) and apparently made too much noise, as one of the neighbors called the school and complained. Since they were living illegally (juniors were not allowed to live off campus—at least those that had grades as poor as Andy and his pals), they were called into the chancellor's office and given a severe reprimand and a warning—do it again and you'll be kicked out of school.

But Andy was a stubborn type, hating the idea of going back to the fraternity or a dorm; he asked Paul if he had any solutions to his dilemma. Paul suggested that he sleep on a small bed that they could wedge into the foyer, at the foot of the stairs that led up to their second floor kitchen, beneath their third floor apartment (on campus).

The apartment was only a block from the fraternity house, where he could store his stuff. Paul also suggested that he share the costs of food (approx. $20/month) with Paul and his pals, a group of graduate students, and live and eat with them, learning and absorbing their wisdom, at their feet, so to speak. This solution allowed him even more time to sit and be inspired by all these high academic achievers with his only responsibility to occasionally reciprocate by telling a sports story now and then.

In fact, it was the first time in Andy's life that he discovered that people were so interested in sports that they would love to hear stories of the battles on the field, or even silliness in the locker room. Sitting at those dinners, with a room full of professors or graduate student assistants, Andy would learn, by trial and error, observing how Paul would spin a yarn, to put together tales of his athletic challenges that were, hopefully, both interesting and humorous.

Later, in his adult life, Andy would take this new found ability to tell a story, learned with Paul's sage advice, encouragement and support, and use it to travel eight times around the world, giving speeches, (and hopefully entertaining people), in places like Tokyo, Seoul, Hong Kong, Singapore, Bangkok, Saigon, Bombay, Jeddah, Kuwait, Beirut, Zurich, Stuttgart, Frankfurt and London, before returning home. The purpose of these trips was to identify potential investors around the world that might participate in Andy's investment products (Andy had returned to Missouri and gotten his MBA—something he never would have considered himself capable of without Paul's earlier academic guidance and encouragement). The reason for the speech making was simply to finance the extravagant cost of traveling around the world, seeking more investors. Ultimately, Andy would land the giant whale of an investor, a billionaire from South Africa, who would buy, for years, virtually all Andy's products, enabling him and his partner Sam Zacharias to open an office in Zug, Switzerland—without Paul, none of that would have happened.

So, one can see, what a hugely positive and profound impact Paul had had on this young man's life—teaching, mentoring, encouraging, and always supporting Andy's goals, even those that, in retrospect, were definitely over-the-top, highly unrealistic (like even dreaming that Hemingway would be interested in Andy's sophomoric "original research").

Paul definitely gave Andy a wonderful gift, at an early stage in his life, which was teaching him to believe in himself, set his goals high, chase all his dreams, and to pay the price by working hard, dedicating himself to achieve whatever goals he set, regardless of how unrealistic they were.

This gift, showing Andy how to earn confidence in his own abilities, helped Andy make his way in raising his beautiful family (two great kids—son Andy, currently the Global Director of Transition Management for NIKE (living in Portland, Oregon) raising his own family, together with his wife, a German lady named Brigitte, and two boys, and, his daughter, Amy (living in Columbus, Ohio), who is now Super Mom (like her own Mom, Nancy) together with her husband and great Dad, Dave, with three kids. Nancy, now divorced from Andy, lives in St. Louis where she works giving psychological support, and takes care of her parents.

Senior Andy, his parents now deceased, now lives with his new wife, Cindy, a true sole mate, spending much of their time (when not working) traveling, bicycling in Europe, climbing mountains in Colorado and occasionally finding time to write stories like this.

Lessons learned from Paul also helped Andy survive in the tough worlds of professional sports (Andy played 14 years for the Pittsburgh Steelers) and business where he was lucky enough to achieve some of his personal and team goals.

Paul was a great mentor. He is still advising Andy after all these years. Just last year, Andy sent Paul a chapter of a book he was attempting to write, and Paul, just as he so many years ago, responded with a well thought out critique, red lining grammatical and spelling errors, and, more importantly, making helpful suggestions as to how the chapter might be improved. That chapter is now part of a published book, called *An Odd Steelers Journey*, Andy's second book, following his first, *A Steeler Odyssey*. Yes, the books are all about the journey of self-discovery all of us take, where Andy continued to follow Paul's advice—chase your dreams, pursue your goals and do it with enthusiasm and a lust for life.

So, as Paul turns 70 years old, he is still giving the gift of his knowledge, his enthusiasm and his encouragement to his pupils, former and current, his collegiate colleagues, now his friends, all over the world. Paul is a superb teacher, a gifted man, whose impact has changed the lives of so many people, in so many hugely positive ways. Like those great writers Paul asked his students to read, Paul has inspired, motivated, encouraged, pushed, and driven his flock.

HAPPY BIRTHDAY, PAUL—YOU'RE THE BEST,

Your friend always,

Andy

P.S. Paul, please don't feel the need to correct the grammatical and spelling mistakes above.

Chapter 18

AMAZING COINCIDENCES and SERENDIPITOUS SYNCHRONICITIES

I am constantly amazed at how serendipitous life can be, how truly astounding it is that unrelated events can come together in such incredible synchronicity, where it clearly appears, in some way, to have been destined. Do we truly have a fate that is somewhat out of our control?

It is said that there are only six degrees of separation from any of us meeting anyone we want to—perhaps we'd choose the most important, interesting, richest, smartest, famous, or special people/celebrities in the world. For example, let's say you wanted to meet the President of the United States, you could go to someone you know, perhaps in the world of politics, who would know someone else (perhaps located in Washington, D.C.) and so on for only six times and you would be sitting in the White House having a chat with a current or past President (or so the theory goes).

Not too long ago, it seemed that it no longer took six degrees of separation—more like two, as one of my college buddies is a good friend of George Bush's, as is Lynn Swann, my former teammate but back then I chose not to bother my old friends (asking for them to try and set up a meeting) with then President Bush, as he had enough to deal with. Of course having contacts isn't the same thing as serendipity but it is amazing what could be right around the corner if one seeks it out.

Regarding the serendipitous nature of life, things always seem to happen for a reason, as though they were destined. For example, one day a few years ago in February, I was sitting at my desk in Pittsburgh, and noticed my old Rolodex, hundreds of cards showing the addresses and phone numbers of people that had been part of my life, both friends and business contacts.

I realized that I had slowly been moving most of my current contacts into my computer and that I seldom used the old rolodex. So, I decided to go through it and discard names of people who I hadn't spoken to in the past five years and to put those still important to me into my computer contacts list.

Scrolling down the list, amazed at how many names I didn't even recognize and others that I clearly no longer had any connection with, easily discarding them, I found the name Tom Graham. Tom was an old friend. We had met as fellow Army Lieutenants in Germany, where we both coached the VII Corp football team in Stuttgart; the team won the United States Army Europe Championship.

Tom had played the game himself at Iowa State (where we had played against each other—his Cyclones versus my Missouri Tigers) but, because of a knee injury, he did not play in Germany—just coached, as Army rules only allowed four Lieutenants to play and Tom's knees were hurting. We had become good friends and I had the honor of being Tom's Best Man at his wedding, as Tom had met his spouse in Germany where she was working for the USO.

The old Rolodex card showed that he lived in Sioux Falls, South Dakota, where he managed his family automobile and tire sales businesses. I had not talked with Tom for at least ten years. We had gone our separate ways and our paths had not crossed, but I still hesitated, not wanting to throw his card away.

I realized that he had had an important impact on my life, influencing me on a key decision—in fact; we had both influenced each other in unsuspected ways. While in Germany, we often found ourselves debating (rather heatedly after downing some good German Ales), what path we should take after our military experience.

Tom felt that it would be best if we went back and got an MBA, before looking for permanent work. I argued that we would learn more meaningful business skills by working in a real business, not in academia.

This debate, between Tom and me, had lasted for nearly two years and it culminated in an unsuspected way—Tom went back to his home town, Sioux Falls, and went right to work in his family automobile business (no graduate school) and I, apparently convinced of the strength of Tom's arguments, went to graduate school, getting my MBA at the University of Missouri, each of us doing the exact opposite of our position in the two year long debate. Our debate and our decision to accept our friend's recommendation had turned out well for both of us.

So, I decided to pick up the phone and call the number—maybe he would still be there, despite the ten years lapsing from our previous conversation.

Dialing the number, hoping he would be there, the phone was answered by a secretary, "Graham Industries," she said.

"Yes, is there a Tom Graham still working there?" I asked.

"Chairman Graham is in his office, I'll ring you through," she said.

"Tom Graham—can I help you?" he said.

He, of course, was greatly surprised that I had called, not having heard from me for so long. After briefly describing our current lives (I had gotten divorced from my first wife, Nancy, whom Tom knew in Germany but later had found my soul mate, Cindy, now my second wife. Tom's wife had passed away of a stroke and he had remarried the widow of the South Dakota governor who had been killed in a plane crash.

"Tom, we've got to get together some time—it's been too long. How about coming out to Colorado this summer and spending some time with us climbing some mountains," I said.

"We'll be out in our place in Scottsdale in March and we'd love to see you—we could play some golf," Tom said.

After a short conversation we realized that because of both of us having busy schedules we wouldn't be able to get together until early Fall.

Before even looking at my schedule, I said, "Why don't we try and get together in early September?"

"Sorry, but we'll be in Europe then," Tom said.

I flipped through my calendar to the September page and saw that Cindy and I had scheduled a bike trip with our friends from St. Louis (and here is the freakish serendipitous nature of life) in Denmark that same month.

"Where are you going to be in Europe," I asked, thinking that we just might be able to meet some where, prior to or after our trip.

"We'll be in Copenhagen for a business meeting," Tom replied.

"When, exactly? I said, incredulous that he'd also be in Denmark.

"September 10th," he said.

"Tom, you are not going to believe this but we will also be in Copenhagen that same day," I said, excitedly, not believing in this extraordinary coincidence, having not seen him for a decade.

"Let's get together for dinner at Copenhagen's beautiful Tivoli Gardens," he said.

So, we met in Copenhagen and had a great reunion and resumed our friendship. We would later discover that we both had a connection with the former Vice Chairman of Mellon Bank, Mark Norby, (my investing in one of his venture capital transactions and Tom an old high school friend). Yes, it is a small world!

Another strange event involved my mother. I was fortunate enough that both my parents lived into their later years. With my Dad back at their condo in Florida, back in the 80's, my sweet mother visiting my brother's family, in D.C., had a stroke but came back from her paralysis after extensive rehab, and eventually they both moved to Pittsburgh, hoping, I'm sure, that I could figure out how to take care of them—they were in their 80's. After a number of false starts relative to housing, we found a place for them at Friendship Village, a superb old folks housing facility in Upper St. Clair, a suburb of Pittsburgh.

After struggling to regain her athletic form (she was a champion swimmer) and to regain her health and to meet new friends at the Village, she seemed very happy. But at first, having lived overseas (Brussels and Geneva) and having traveled the world, she had a difficult time adjusting to living with so many people who only wanted to talk about their lives in Pittsburgh (places like Monroeville, Mount Lebanon, Upper St. Clair, the Rocks)—she first thought they were somewhat provincial and unworldly but ultimately decided that they were very nice.

My father was in the same facility, but in the 24 hour care unit, whereas my mother was down the hall in her own apartment where she could, for the most part, take care of herself. Mom and Dad would see each other every day, and their lives seemed pretty good.

Since my mother was a lover of travel and art, I offered to have her come out to Sante Fe, New Mexico, where I had purchased a condo (50-50 with my business partner, Don Rea) off the city's famous "Canyon Road." She, truly a lover of travel, having traveled all over the world (my parents honeymooned in Europe after their wedding, sleeping in open fields, on the ground, with only an umbrella to shed the rain), an artist herself, was someone I was sure would just love Sante Fe.

Well, we had a wonderful long weekend, visiting all of the city's great art museums, galleries and fine restaurants and even driving up to Taos and appreciating the native Indian village and artifacts. That drive, up the mountain route, taking us through small villages, almost each of which had a famous old church and their own art galleries, made us appreciate this unique state.

Returning back to our condo in Sante Fe after a wonderful day of sightseeing, my mother informed us that Sunday we would be going to Sante Fe's Unitarian Church for it's services, because the Minister had been, "coincidentally," the minister of our church back in St. Louis many years ago.

At the service, my mother made sure that we met virtually every member of the church and we all sat in the front row of the church to listen to her friend's service. When he introduced us as his "guests" and old friends from St. Louis, I could see that my mother was very proud. As we left, she noticed that the Minister had displayed a book that he had written about local Indian legends, many of which re- volved around an animal they believed sacred, the coyote.

Later that afternoon, shopping along the plaza where the Indians displayed all their beautiful jewelry, I noticed that my mother was only buying "trinkets" of jewelry showing coyotes. During the fol- lowing year, after finishing her Minister friend's book, she seemed almost obsessed by coyotes, referring to them often, and buying more replicas of their beings.

So, the following year, our sweet mother lost her life to another massive stroke, and I was devastated. Here, one of the most significant women in my life had passed away and after giving her eulogy at the Village, I was content to follow her wishes—to deposit all of her ashes on Seagull Lake where she and Dad had built a cabin in Minnesota up against the Canadian border. The only problem was to figure out a time when both my brother and I could free up our schedules to make this trek to the Land of Lakes and fulfill our sweet mother's wish.

But later that year my older brother, Will, called and said that he believed, since Esther had also loved Sante Fe so much, that we should take half her ashes there and deposit them there. For some reason, the idea resonated with me, just knowing that our mother would feel good about Will's idea. Why not spread some of her ashes in another place she had come to love?

For some reason, Will and I were luckily able to easily find time in our schedules to fly out to New Mexico—perhaps because the travel was somewhat easier to fly to New Mexico than Sea Gull Lake, a place much harder to get to, requiring a rental car and a three hour drive from the airport in Duluth. Granted, it is ridiculous to be complaining about a slight inconvenience when talking about something so sacred as depositing one's mother's ashes in a place she held sacred, but it is my answer to why, to this day, we haven't been back to Sea Gull Lake, a truly wild and beautiful place.

So, off we went to Sante Fe (actually we flew into Albuquerque and planned to drive an hour to Sante Fe), having sold our condo we rented a condo there. Before leaving for this trip my brother and I had had a short telephone conversation.

"Where exactly are you thinking about placing Mom's ashes," I said.

"Don't worry about it—we'll figure out a good place," Will replied.

"What kind of a ceremony?" I asked.

"We'll figure something out that will make Esther happy," Will said. I hung up the phone, realizing once again how often I had taken my so very smart brother's advice.

Later, on the plane out to Albuquerque where we planned to play golf at the University's golf course near the airport and the Motel where we were to meet Will and Mary Lee, my wife, Cindy, an incredibly intuitive person, said "I think there is a high probability that we will see a coyote on this trip."

"Why do you say that?" I asked.

"Because it will be the way your mother will return," she said.

I sat there absolutely blown away, wondering if we would see a coyote and concluded that it was unlikely, unless we saw one on the golf course.

After another frustrating round of golf (it truly is an experience in ego reduction) without seeing any coyotes we had a quick dinner and, because of the time change, went quickly to bed.

The next day we met up with Will and Mary Lee and drove up to beautiful Sante Fe and walked around town, visiting the Georgia O'Keefe museum, one of our Mother's favorite artists and a former resident of Sante Fe. Having a good lunch where we started to focus on our Mother's ceremony.

"So, where do you think we should conduct our sweet Mother's ash deposit rite?" I asked.

"I was thinking we should drive up high on the ski mountain and conduct our 'ceremony' as the sun goes down, with each of us giving a short tribute, telling our favorite Esther story, and then toasting her wonderful life with a glass of champagne," Will said.

Of course, this meant that somebody, (probably Will since I had relied on him to handle the details most of my life), would have to buy some wine glasses and a good bottle of Champagne and someone else would have to figure out the route up the mountain and how much time it would take to drive from our condo to our spot on the mountain.

Naturally everything took longer than expected and we found ourselves driving way too fast up a mountain road as the sun was nearing the western horizon, worrying that we would lose the beautiful view. Driving up through the tall trees it was already getting dark. Slamming around a curve, I was stunned to see in our headlights a huge, beautiful coyote crossing in front of us. Right in the middle of the road, as we slowed down to avoid running into it, the coyote stopped and, believe it or not, smiled at us, before darting into the forest, apparently heading up towards where the next switch back would take us. Fortunately, as the sun had almost disappeared, right around the bend, we found a perfect parking spot overlook and walked slightly down into an opening surrounded by beautiful Aspen trees (our Mother's favorite) and a gorgeous view of the western skyline as the sun went down—the resulting glow being what the Indian's call Angel Fire.

We stood in a small circle with our arms around each other and each told our favorite Esther story. Mine was how she had always supported me and encouraged me to chase my dreams, telling me that all I had to do was "Think Big, Work Hard and Have a Dream." She always encouraged me to seek out challenges, claiming I would be successful if I just made the effort.

When we were all finished, with tears in our eyes, we broke open the bottle of champagne and toasted her wonderful life. As I took my first swig I heard a sound in the woods and just knew that the coyote we had seen running across the road was there, observing our ritual, truly the embodiment of our sweet Mother.

Driving back down towards Sante Fe I felt more bonded to my brother and his wife, and didn't want to drive back into the city but preferred to spend time out in the wilderness, so appreciated by our dear Mother. The bottle of champagne was gone, so we decided to stop at a mountain resort, (where I had once played in a tennis tournament between the Steelers and the Cowboys, arranged by a local charity), and each of us had another glass of quality red wine to again toast our mother.

So, is it possible that our mother came back in the body of a coyote? I have chosen to believe that it is very possible (reincarnation) and that our sweet mother chose to come back and enjoy the reverence of her children in the body of a coyote.

Of course, if that is really possible, it would be more than just serendipity, more like astoundingly fateful but I am constantly amazed at how people and events come together, from all over the world, as though there is a master plan. What can we learn from realizing that such events can happen? Perhaps, we should constantly be aware that amazing synchronistic events can very positively impact ones life and, therefore, one should always remain open to new experiences and consider all possibilities.

Chapter 19

HAM AND LAMBERT

I am sometimes asked to describe Jack Lambert and Jack Ham, to contrast their very unique styles, to compare their abilities, to stack them up against today's fine linebackers. They were, of course, both brilliant players, now enshrined in the Hall of Fame, as they should be.

If I was a current Steelers player reading this, I might respond with, "What about our great linebackers today—Lamar Woodley, James Harrison and James Farrior? Why not talk about them?" This chapter is in no way meant to be disrespectful to our current line-backers, who are clearly very talented. Frankly, I am not qualified to judge them, because I have not watched them on film, studied every play, and observed mistakes versus successes as I did often, late into the night, with the two Jacks. I just applaud the current linebackers' good plays, and when they make a mistake, I remember the times I made the same error. The game of football can be very painful at times and not just to your body but also your psyche.

It is also nearly impossible to compare athletes from different eras anyway, because rules change and so do strategies. For example, the 1970s Steelers linebackers, allowed to jam receivers until the ball was in the air, frequently covered wide receivers man to man underneath, denying them the route they wanted to take, but also having deep help. Because of that rule we seldom blitzed, instead relying on our "Steel Curtain," our great front four, to generate all the pressure we needed on the quarterback, which they did in spades.

Today's schemes often blitz the linebackers and virtually never place an outside linebacker over a wide receiver, because defensive players are allowed only one jam within 5 yards of the line of scrim-mage and nothing after that. Frankly, today's rules seem bogus to me, not allowing the defense to cut, jam, re-route, take out of bounds, all maneuvers previously allowed before the ball was in the air. I know—there's nothing worse than an old fart complaining about today's game.

Obviously, today it is much more difficult to play pass defense than it was back in the 1970s, and apparently what the NFL wants is more scoring. Granted, part of that has to do with Bill Walsh (one of the NFL's all time most brilliant coaches) creating the so called West Coast offense, designed to give the quarterback many short options, allowing them to be able to hold the ball for a shorter period of time. But, there is no question that the rule changes made a significant difference.

Today's receivers, taking advantage of the rule changes (as they should), frequently make contact with the defensive back because they know the defender cannot respond. Wide receivers today can attack a safety or cornerback past five yards down field and if the defender responds they'll likely get a flag—to me it just doesn't seem fair.

Also, it is unfair to compare Ham and Lambert because they played two different positions, outside linebacker and middle linebacker, positions that are dramatically different in the challenges each presents.

I have always taken the position that the quintessential, most exciting, most important position on the football field is the middle linebacker. Having played the position in college and in the military and during one NFL game (versus the Houston Oilers when our middle backers were injured, where I made more tackles in a quarter than I would make in two games on the outside)—having played the position I know enough about the position to state that if you truly love the game of football, the challenges, the hitting and the strategies, there is no position, none close, to middle linebacker. Forget quarterbacks, because they don't block and tackle, the two most fundamental aspects of the game.

The middle linebacker should be in on almost every tackle, ranging sideline to sideline. Unless the opponent is running right up the middle, opponents typically try to block the middle linebacker with the center, trying to cut him off from the pursuit, almost an impossible task for the center. Sometimes they would bring a tackle down on the middle linebacker, but when this happened Lambert, anticipating the play, was too quick, penetrating up field, denying the tackle a shot at him. It was also amazing how well Lambert could deal with the block of a much larger lineman, nullifying the opponent's size advantage with great technique, use of leverage and, yes, his surprising raw power (being barely above 220 lbs.).

I have also always taken the position that Jack Lambert is the best middle linebacker of our era. I know that's a big statement to position Lambert above such players as Willie Lanier, Ray Nitscke, Dick Butkus, Tommy Nobis, Lee Roy Jordan, Mike Curtis and Sam Huff (all players I admired greatly), but I believe I can make a good case for Lambert's superiority.

Lambert was the best of the 1960s and 1970s, not because of his macho style (which, granted, was true to his nature because he is a genuinely tough guy) but primarily because of his ability to cover receivers man-to-man by utilizing his 4.7 speed, quickness, agility and quality techniques.

I know everyone gets excited over the devastating hit on a running back but, since the game was about 50 percent pass, our Steelers defense was able to use strategies where Lambert covered running backs out of the backfield (normally covered by outside backers), which allowed Ham and me to help jam and cover the wide receivers, thus helping our cornerbacks. He also often covered the tight end man-to-man. The Chicago Bears could never have dreamed of playing those defenses, because Butkus lacked the speed to do it forcing them to run simplistic zones instead.

Granted, Butkus, being almost 30 pounds heavier than Lambert, might have had a few more impressive collisions with running backs but Lambert would have been there to make the same tackle, and Lambert never was accused of hitting someone too softly. None of the greats of those two decades could match Lambert's ability to cover—remember his fourth quarter, essentially game-clinching interception against Los Angeles in Super Bowl XIV.

Jack Lambert's superiority had less to do with his feisty attitude than with his intelligence, his ability to anticipate plays and his ability to cover backs or tight ends. I know that many fans loved his natural combativeness, his aggressiveness, his confrontational style, but in the end Lambert beat opponents with his head. Jack was very smart.

Many people remember Lambert's knee-jerk reaction in Super Bowl X, when he roughly threw Cliff Harris to the ground after observing Harris making fun of Roy Gerela after a missed field goal. Some people, even the announcers, thought that was the turning point of the game, inspiring the Steelers on to victory. Forget it. I ran onto the field and chastised Lambert for a silly move that could have gotten him tossed out of a Super Bowl. But that was Lambert, true to his own nature, reacting with his gut instinct, as nobody was going to ridicule his teammate without facing Jack Lambert's wrath.

Of course, Jack Ham and I, playing on the outside, had a different set of challenges, because some of the best teams favor one side, usually because of superior offensive linemen on that side. For example, when we played the Buffalo Bills and O.J. Simpson, Ham, L.C. Greenwood and Joe Greene had their hands full, because the Bills definitely favored their right, running to our defensive left.

On the other hand, when we played the Oakland Raiders, they rarely ran to the right, instead running to their left, behind their Hall of Fame lineman, Art Shell and Gene Upshaw, keeping Dwight White, Ernie Holmes and me very busy. Once, Jack Ham actually asked me, (tongue firmly in cheek, of course), during the AFC Championship Game, against Oakland, if he could take a few downs on my side because he was getting bored.

During those two decades, Hammer was the finest linebacker I ever saw. Fortunately for Lambert and me there were three linebackers on our 4-3 defense, because if there had been only one linebacker (like there is only one center or one quarterback), Jack Lambert and I would have been on the bench cheering for Jack Ham. Could Ham have played middle linebacker? Absolutely.

When Jack Ham came in as one of our top draft choices in 1971 we veteran linebackers cynically wondered just how good he would be. But after the first drill, a drill that I had struggled with my entire career—one where you first had to read the tight end blocking down (someone who could hook block you if you were too focused on others), then the depth of the guard's pull and then the threat of the fullback's block—Ham absolutely nailed it the first time.

Since he took the job of our good friend, Jerry Hillebrand, it might have been difficult to appreciate Jack Ham, but it wasn't because he was so gifted, so smart, so talented, and such a very nice person as well. Even Hillebrand, despite knowing full well that Jack was going to take his job, liked Ham.

Well, you might wonder how the two superstars differed and how they got along. Ham, a Steelers linebacker three years before Lambert, was very focused, driven, always in the right place at the right time, a true professional, but yet, somehow laid-back, cool, detached, calculating. Lambert, just as committed, was completely different: Hot, impulsive, explosive, combative and instinctive. But in many ways, they were similar, both driven to excel, completely absorbed by the game, two totally unique players that the Steelers were lucky to have playing at the same time.

To explain their different styles, I remember one incident where Ham came into the huddle, during a critical game and asked Lambert, "What time is it?" Lambert, never having been asked this question during a game, in a huddle, thinking Ham was asking how much time was left in the game, snarled, "three minutes left." Ham looked at him, as though he was on Mars, and said, "No, right now—what time is it?" Lambert ignored him, knowing intuitively that Ham was just having fun with us, letting us know that this wasn't life and death, just a football game. Of course, despite this apparent coolness, Jack played with an enormous intensity.

In the end, no one had a greater commitment to excellence than Jack Ham. His preparation was always complete, his concentration and intensity pure, coupled with incredible physical tools. In fact, I believe that in a 10-yard sprint, Jack Ham would have been the fastest player on the team. Ham was so good he made difficult plays appear easy, made nearly impossible tasks appear routine. Again, Ham was just the best I ever saw.

So how were they similar? They hated to be blocked, hated to make mistakes and hated to lose games. They were proud, confident, fearless and intelligent. Their styles were different, but their effort and performance were near identical and very special

So what was it like for me, an old-timer, who started in 1963, eight years before Ham and 11 before Lambert? It was fantastic to be part of that trio. I had liked and respected all my fellow linebackers during my career. Myron Pottios was a very good, Pro Bowl, middle linebacker in 1963; Hillebrand had been the Giants No. 1 draft choice with a big forearm hammer (I had discovered this trying to block him in college—my Missouri Tigers against his Colorado Buffalos); Bill Saul, an overachiever, but always rough and ready; Rod Breedlove, a smart old pro, taught me how to think; Chuck Allen was a hardnosed, smart player (he taught me how to work an injury), acquired by Chuck Noll, who had coached him at San Diego; Henry Davis, traded from the Giants', played very well before Lambert; and Ray May, later traded to Baltimore, could really play. John Campbell played the other side in the sixties with passionate and thoughtful aggression.

But playing and working with Ham and Lambert was a very special way to end my career. They certainly made my job easier but, at the same time, their outstanding performances inspired me to be better. Teaming up with two such great linebackers was an extraordinarily meaningful experience for me, and I respect not only their awesome talents but also the quality of their character. They were consummate team players, and I am both proud and fortunate to have played alongside them.

Sometimes people try and rate the best linebacking corps ever; trying to compare statistics, such as tackles, interceptions and sacks, but that is very difficult because each team had different strategies. As mentioned, we rarely blitzed. Interceptions were rare (although Ham had a lot) because our man-to-man technique gave little opportunity to intercept. In fact, Coach Noll often told us he didn't want any heroes (those who might gamble for an interception but hurt the team when unsuccessful), just solid players who did their job.

One-way to compare, one obviously to our advantage (Oh, that devil ego), is to use the cumulative pro bowls of the trio. I doubt many Steeler fans know that the three of us hold an NFL record for the most cumulative pro bowls (24—Lambert 9, Ham 8 and me 7), being far ahead of the runner up Kansas City trio of Bobby Bell (8), Willie Lanier (9) and Jim Lynch (1) who had 18 Pro Bowls between them. I am very proud to have been a part of that threesome.

Chapter 20

LETTER TO MY BROTHER WILL

February 12, 2004

Dear Will,

As you may remember, (from our Xmas trip in Colorado), I have been writing to those people who are most important in my life and, as my only brother, you certainly fall into that category. I have recently completed long, impassioned, and admittedly over the top letters to Amy, Andy, Nancy and Cindy, all incredibly important people in my life, as you are.

These letters have been my effort to figure out the ways in which I have wronged these so very critical figures in my life and then to apologize and ask for their forgiveness and, if they have wronged me, which is seldom the case, I have forgiven them. The letters have also been my effort to get in touch with my feelings (I know they are in there somewhere), to understand what I really think I think, and to take into consideration all the bad and even sometimes take a little credit for the few things I've done right.

Obviously, of all those precious people to me mentioned above, you and I go the farthest back. As I sit here, poolside, hearing the Pacific Ocean surf pounding the beach, feeling the warm trade winds caressing my body, in the beautiful country of Costa Rica (tough life, huh?), I can see in my mind's eye the photos of you holding this little baby (me) back in 1941—Wow! Time sure does fly by when you're having fun—where has the time gone?

In Pat Conroy's new book, *My Losing Season*, he writes about how, as we grow older, all of us suddenly realize the absolutely quicksilver nature of life, all amazed at the age we find ourselves. It seems just the other day that you and I were playing in the sand box in Pleasant Ridge, our first Detroit home. I always joke that from there we moved to Royal Oak, which wasn't far from the Zoo, and how all my friends find that appropriate—suggesting I'm some kind of animal.

I have so many fond memories of our childhood: walking to school; singing Broadway hits as Mom played the Piano (hearing Dad's so powerful tenor); our being required to work in the yard on Saturday mornings, and then eating Dad's home made soup (from leftovers) and listening to the mandatory Opera (I eventually learned to like at least one of those—soup); the family readings on Sundays; (granted, we didn't always follow that family ritual as Dad was frequently out of town); playing various sports with neighborhood kids; climbing the biggest trees and steepest roofs in our neighborhood; playing with our beautiful boxer, Lady; traveling, camping, fishing and occasionally even eating in a real live restaurant where I was allowed to order Fried Chicken, my favorite food at the time.

I'm sure you could add many more memories (things I've forgotten—hey, I had ten serious concussions—at least those are the ones I can remember) and, of course, I realize that some of my memories wouldn't be so interesting or even relevant to you but many were experienced together.

However, it occurs to me that you might remember our childhood very differently than I do. In my recollection, our parents were quite strict (old school), but fair; we were not allowed to complain (ever); we received modest gifts on special occasions, like Xmas (an apple and a comic book in our stocking) or Birthdays; we were expected to follow their rules (granted, simple stuff—like, wash the dishes, pick up our clothes, make our bed, mow the grass, rake the leaves, eat everything on our plate, do all our homework, etc. etc.) and, if not, deal with the consequences (like getting spanked by Dad's belt)—he once spanked me for confiding in Mom that I didn't love him. Well, with that said (of course I loved him), I never felt as though I was living in a tough environment, nor did I ever feel abused. I understand that you may have some very different perspectives and I would be interested in hearing about that.

Obviously, you and I were very different in our likes and dislikes, our interests, our passions—yes, we were, and still are, very different but in some ways that was a positive.

So many young siblings grow up too competitive, always trying to out do each other, frequently to gain their parents attention. I don't believe we did much of that. First of all, we were engaged in totally different types of activities—hard to compare a basketball player with a ham radio operator or an airplane pilot with a football player.

Secondly, Esther always seemed totally impartial, fair and equally interested in all our activities, encouraging us both to chase our dreams. Dad was so tough that we probably didn't even want him to get too interested in what we were doing or he might become critical, something I think we both wanted to avoid. On the other hand, you may have wanted more attention from Dad—I didn't.

You, being the first-born, certainly received more attention (perfectionism, direction, rules, advice, criticism, etc.) than me. I'm sure my daughter, Amy, received less attention, focus, scrutiny than my son, Andy, and, my guess, is that it was the same with your boys—slightly tougher (not intentionally) on Bill Guy than Wyott. It's definitely more difficult to be the first—a lot more pressure and higher expectations.

I always secretly admired your intellectual toughness, your independence, your strong willed, objective, honest self—refusing to accept trivial inaccuracies, like your unwillingness to agree with Dad when you knew, or believed strongly, that he was wrong. At the same time, I dreaded those confrontations, knowing that it was not going to work out well for you.

Dad was always going to win those arguments, crushing you with his big voice, even if he was wrong and you might even receive a smack on the bottom, despite often being correct. It was horribly unfair, totally insecure and old fashioned of our father (I always made a point of praising my children when they were right and I was wrong—which happened often, as they have their Mom's smarts) but we forgive him now because we know how he was raised—talk about a tough Grandfather.

You always had a stubborn integrity, a quiet confidence about you, always willing to stand up to the neighborhood bully even when he was bigger and a more gifted fighter. But you were more determined, and you wouldn't quit, and those bullies, despite often landing solid punches on you, almost always quit when they discovered that you were not going to—you were always unrelenting.

I always admired that, Will, and later in my life that "mentoring," granted unintentional, probably helped me deal with my sporting challenges. I would not quit, nor would I allow myself to be intimidated, perhaps subliminally trying to match my big brother's mental toughness. You can't imagine what an advantage that gave me all those years, as the challenges grew bigger and harder through High School, College and the NFL. So, thank you—your determination, toughness, integrity, and your unwillingness to concede, to succumb, to ever quit helped me immensely in my chosen field.

When I think of you and me I do not have any negativity. You never wronged me, cheated me, took advantage of, nor abused me and, therefore, I do not have to forgive you for anything. You were a damn good brother and I will always love you with all my heart. Wait a minute; I should forgive you for being smarter, tougher, and straighter—well, just about better at everything, which made you a tough act to follow. The only thing I could do better was to run and jump better and it's hard to take any credit for that because it came so naturally, some kind of genetic gift, not something I worked hard for, as you did to develop many of your skills.

I realize also, that when it comes to the Russell family (kids and ex-wives excepted) you are all I have—no one else is left, except Lucia and our cousins, Grant, Arthur and Mary Beth (none of whom I have seen in the past thirty years—shame on me). I just made a mental note to invite Lucia to our wedding (perhaps you could pick her up and drive her to Aspen—don't worry, we'll figure something else out if you can't).

I have put a small collage of old photos of you and me and our parents, in various poses, as we grew up, in one of our scrapbooks. Of course, our true memory of those days is forever etched in our minds.

You have mentioned a few times that it would be nice if you and I could spend some time talking together about our childhood and our parents—perhaps putting into perspective, after all these years, the good and the bad, the rough and the gentle, the right and the wrongs of our "old school" parents and our unique (everyone's life is unique) upbringing. But we never seem to get around to it when we are together—perhaps, because we feel it would bore Cindy and Mary Lee or maybe because it might be more painful for you and me than we would suspect. But, as I write this now, I don't believe that would be the case.

When it comes to me trying to remember the ways I wronged you, in any meaningful way, I don't remember specific moments of lying or cheating, wronging you (not that there probably weren't some) but I focus more on perhaps how certain aspects of my life might have been negative or unfair to you.

For example, I have often wondered why I was invited (told to go) to bicycle through Europe at age 15 with Jan Hein instead of you. You were older, (18—same age as Jan Hein if I recall correctly) and it would have been much more logical for you to go. Of course, for all I know, you couldn't go because of some other commitment you had already made—like learning how to fly a plane or something. Maybe, because you were more technically inclined they thought that I would appreciate the bicycling more than you. Or frankly, maybe they thought that you were already independent, self reliant and capable of making the right decisions and that such a trip wouldn't be as meaningful to you.

That trip was epic for me, Will, as it was the first time I had traveled alone (Jack Schneider pretty much followed my lead) and I didn't have you along to make all the correct decisions—I had to do it myself, find my way, make choices, pick alternatives, stumbling along from Glasgow to Naples—admittedly, Jan Hein mostly led the way from Amsterdam to Milan (but even there I found that I asserted myself more often, giving Jan Hein my opinions) and I learned from his leadership.

That trip was clearly a journey of self discovery and one that changed me forever—I came back dramatically more independent, more confident, intellectually and mentally tougher, having learned that I could also make the right decisions/choices.

So, thank you, sweet brother, for allowing me to go on that trip because I'm sure they would have let you go if you had wanted to. Of course, they probably had correctly judged that I needed those adjectives mentioned above more than you.

It also occurred to me that it might have been more than slightly irritating to have a brother whose chosen field (sports) was unfairly given so much more public acclaim than your chosen interests (ham radio and flying airplanes)—not that either of us were particularly interested in receiving publicity or celebrity.

I remember the first big play I made my Sophomore year (catching a pass to beat John Burroughs, late in the game) resulted in me getting a head line on the St. Louis Post sports section and all of sudden Dad started getting real interested in my sports career. I'm sure that I wasn't any more gifted in sport than you were in what you chose but sporting success has always received an unfair and absurd amount of praise and publicity in our society.

So it must have hurt (at some level) to have your little brother getting headlines and watching your father clearly loving it while you were being equally successful in your choices but not receiving the same kind of attention from Dad or the community. I'm sure he tried (as I'm sure Mom would have urged him to) but Dad just loved all the attention that I was getting (of course, so did I) and I think he received a vicarious thrill along with it. He also probably believed that he could understand sports (after all, they are pretty simplistic) better than he could comprehend what you were doing.

Of course, Dad really didn't understand sports but still felt the need to criticize, to point out my mistakes. I will never forget my senior year, after playing Clayton in the last game, where I scored five Touchdowns and an extra point to win the St. Louis scoring championship by one point and my teammates were hoisting my jersey up the Ladue High School flag pole, with Dad standing there, staring up at the United States flag and my jersey flapping in the wind, with a huge smile on his face (hey, we all love to be appreciated) I approached Dad and he said, "You missed a block in the third quarter." That was our Dad—but, for the first time, I knew he was just bluffing and that he was proud to his toes. From that point forward he treated me differently, giving me some slack, listening to my opinions, praising my actions.

Frankly, I can only try to imagine how it must of felt (of course, you were off to college when the above occurred) to feel and see your Dad's joy for your brother's success and not feel the same kind of support and praise for your own accomplishments. I am finding it difficult to apologize for being me but I certainly can attempt to feel, to sympathize with, and to understand this unfairness.

Later in life, I would tell Dad that he should tell you how much he loved you and apologize for giving you such a hard time, things he admitted to me about how he felt about you—he had tremendous respect for you. He would sit there, saying nothing, and nod his head in agreement but I suspected that he never took my advice and actually voiced his praise for you.

Of course, who knows? You might have been a very good athlete had you tried a sport but you chose a different path. Maybe, you went another direction because you observed that I was a faster runner, better at ping-pong, or catching a ball in the back yard when Dad found time to play with us (granted, that was a rare occasion, as I can remember only a few times when this happened).

Conversely, I might have been far more interested in technical things (like Ham radios, electricity, etc.) had you not been so obviously gifted in such areas. I clearly didn't think I was as smart as you, nor did I believe that I could be as good as you in understanding those technical interests.

Bottom line, however, I believe we both went with our hearts and did what came most naturally, not really caring about praise or recognition, just loving the thrill of participation in those activities—you the band (a great clarinet), the stage/lighting direction of the high school plays, Ham radio operation and flying (I'm sure I'm forgetting something)—me the world of sport.

Naturally you and I fought on occasions; about various silly things I'm sure. I remember Dad attempting to teach us how to box in the Royal Oak's living room, when I was around six and you were nine. Of course, you trying hard to please Dad, went after me and I remember receiving some pretty good whippings until I learned to avoid your blows—actually those evasive tactics probably helped me immensely to survive in the NFL so many years later, trying to avoid those giants who were hunting me.

Of course, I remember our fight in Ladue, while Mom and Dad were away, being baby sat by our Scottish cousin, Jack Russell, where I finally decided not to run away, not wanting to embarrass myself in front of Jack. I remember that Mom and Dad were quite upset with Jack for letting us fight (lots of broken furniture) but he replied, "It seemed like a good idea to let them work it out."

That was the last time we resorted to fists to solve our problems/disagreements and the timing was appropriate. Again, I don't think either of us should apologize for the occasional fights over silly issues—it goes with sibling territory.

Of course, that fight was more important to me because my habit had been to avoid violence, to flee, to be evasive and I would later go on to make my living being the opposite of those—I needed to learn how to be confrontational, aggressive, attack, and, yes, violent—I needed to find the warrior inside of me and it was there and that fight was the beginning of my journey to discover it. It had nothing to do with whether I fought well, only whether I stood my ground, refusing to submit to your aggressiveness.

Well, I guess I should apologize for not being a better brother all these years, seldom visiting your family, infrequent phone calls, and I don't remember the last time I wrote you a letter—in fact, this may be the first. Maybe, a lot of that is understandable since we have not lived in the same city since 1957, our parents moving to Europe my Freshman year at Missouri and your Junior year at Northwestern and our paths have just not crossed that often since but much more often recently.

Some of that might be because our first wives weren't particularly interested in visiting anyone other than their own families and I clearly loved the Tusseys. In fact one of my many shrinks said that I married my sister (I do not agree with that). I always loved that family; Ed and Betty, Bill and Betsy Comfort, Nancy's brother and sisters and all their other relatives—I kind of felt, in a weird way, sort of adopted and I miss them now. This probably wasn't any solace to you, as you might not have had the same feelings for Charlotte's family.

Feb. 19th—I'm now on the plane, flying back stateside, non-stop U.S. Airways to Charlotte.

February 27, 2004—Regarding the 2.19 flight, we missed our flight because of the delay out of San Jose and were lucky to get home at all that night (after midnight).

Anyway, where was I—running out of steam, so to speak, searching for any other issues you and I may have to discuss and iron out. Actually there probably are others, things that you might think of and I have overlooked or can't even imagine.

I am now on another plane—this time Cindy and I are on a Friday night flight to Los Angeles where we are being paid to go to a party for a bunch of rabid Steeler fans, a group called the Black and Gold Brigade (Sat. night) and return Sunday—what a crazy life.

It would have been nice if our kids had gotten closer but it never happened. Andy and Bill Guy had an opportunity to connect, on their trip to Scotland with Mom and Dad, but that trip seemed to divide them more than help build a relationship.

Where do I find myself right now—on the usual roller coaster that has been my life, chasing too many deals, closing too few of them, and trying to determine the right amount of time and energy to spend in my five favorite categories (family, business, fun, charitable work and spirituality). I've got the fun figured out but the proper balance on the other four has remained elusive. Oh well, life is a journey and you never arrive. Remember, the journey is the destination.

Well, brother, as an old teammate once said, when discussing the secret of having a happy and productive life, "Just try hard and do good." I think the best advice I've gotten lately is from a famous Japanese psychiatrist around the time of Freud, named Morita, who said to figure out what you should be doing and then — "Just do it."

Love ya, Bro.

Chapter 21

AN APOLOGY TO MY FAMILY

Sometimes my two children (now adults) kid me about some of the stupid and dangerous things I had them do as they grew up, anyone of which could have ended up a disaster. Looking back on a number of those "adventures" I took them on, I must admit that I'm truly embarrassed about the risks that I just assumed we could all handle. I guess it was part naiveté, part stupidity, part arrogance, but also part wanting to teach them to be bold, believing in themselves and their abilities and not letting them grow up being afraid to seek new adventures and to deal effectively with risks.

Their mother, Nancy, my first wife, has said that she gave our children roots and that I gave them wings." Nancy, a great mother, (and a very supportive wife) gave them a lot more than "roots," as she taught them many of the old school values, such as being responsible, reliable, respectful and accountable. But I wanted them to be willing to accept risks, face challenges, feel the joy of overcoming fears and appreciate our so beautiful wildernesses but, now in retrospect, I think there were more than a few times that I was irresponsible, asking them to face unrealistic challenges and unacceptable dangers.

Now my children, as adults, married with kids (I love those 5 grand kids) they are probably dramatically more careful with their kids then their crazy Dad was with them and, (perhaps it's age, now understanding the dangers better), I'm far more careful with my grandchildren than I was with my kids.

My daughter, Amy, is 40 years old, married to a wonderful husband and a great Dad, Dave Zemper, with three kids, two girls, Molly (15) and Jackie (12) and one boy, Derek (9). Amy is a gung-ho athlete, running the Columbus, Ohio marathon and working out every day. Dave, a good athlete himself, and Amy have encouraged (actually required) their kids to participate in sports (mostly soccer, rowing & basketball) and they are all in great shape, enjoying the challenges of sports—obviously I can appreciate their efforts. I believe in the power of sporting activities to help teach children the old school values and also to keep young people out of trouble, primarily because you don't have time to get in trouble, as you have practice after classes every day and are too exhausted afterwards to get in any trouble.

My son, Andy (age 43) is married to a great, German lady, Brigitte, whom he met while working in Frankfurt. They have two sons, Carsten (10) and Finn (7) and both of them are engaged in various sporting activities, as both Andy and Brigitte are good athletes, (Andy played football at Dartmouth—once being named the Ivy League Player of the Week) and Brigitte is a very good skier, learning in the German Alps.

But I would doubt that either of my children has allowed their children to face real danger, teaching them well to understand risks and to be cautious, unlike what they grew up with. Below is a list of some of the scariest moments in their childhood with their dumb and dumber Dad. These are not in any order and I'm not sure which one I feel most foolish about but they were certainly all stupid things to ask your children to do, fraught with danger.

For example, once down in Hilton Head, staying near one of its' great golf courses, I decided, late in the afternoon, to take the kids out along some of the creeks, hoping for them to get to see some wildlife—frogs, turtles and such. Parking the car, and walking through the trees, coming into an opening with the creek, out in front of us, with a row of very nice condos on the other side we observed, right in our path a very large alligator, about 50 yards away. For some idiotic reason, I had no fear of this alligator so I suggested the kids get closer (say around ten feet) to the gator so that I could get a good photo.

But as the kids walked towards the gator, they looked back at me as though they finally understood that their Dad was truly nuts, as I followed them with my camera. When they got about 20 yards from the beast, we all saw a woman, across the creek, come running out of her condo, waving her arms frantically and shouting to get away from the gator, who did seem much bigger now that we were so close. I immediately came to my senses and we ran back to the car, with me feeling very sheepish—"Gee, Dad, did you think we should pet that Gator?"

Another, even more dangerous, thing I did with my kids and wife, Nancy, was on our first trip to Africa when we were down in Kenya, creating our own tour, as I was too cheap to hire a guide. One of the best places to view animals in Kenya is near the southern (Tanzanian) border, the Masai Mara Game Reserve, but when we first arrived in Nairobi we learned that there had been an attack by a group of heavily armed renegades from Tanzania (shall we say "Terrorists") who crossed the border, entered the Park, had gone into one of the tented Safari camps and roused all the sleeping tourists, dragging them outside, robbing and beating some of them and injuring a few of them seriously. It had happened on a Monday.

Since we were planning on going to the Masai Mara in a couple of weeks, Nancy asked (no demanded) that I call the U. S. embassy to see if they would recommend that we stay away. After a week of traveling, north of the area (climbing Mount Kenya, sleeping in the famous Tree House and other fabulous sights), we were almost ready to head south to the Masai Mara where all of us wanted to see the animals but, of course, didn't want to deal with potentially lethal human aggressors.

But before dealing with that problem we had to cross over the mountains where in the old days the Kenyan rebels (known as the Mau Mau) had hidden in their effort to get rid of the British rule of Kenya. On the map it appeared to be a major highway (Hwy A1A) but it turned out to be nothing more than a dirt road starting up through the jungle and into the highlands. After driving nearly an hour and a half through the wilderness, without seeing a single other car (we had no water, food or survival gear), through a few small towns (actually native villages with wooden huts—no gas stations or restaurants, electric or phone lines, or hotels) we found ourselves facing a part of the road (miles from the nearest village) that had deteriorated into deep, wet, and muddy tracks. Obviously, I didn't want to have to re-trace our route, causing us to go all the way back down to Nairobi and around—an additional twenty more hours of driving, causing us to not show up for our hotel reservation (not reserved past 6:00 pm) and, of course, those were days way before cell phones.

So, ignoring my fear of getting stuck out there in the wilderness, so far from help, I told everyone to hold on (this was before seat belts) and drove the 4-wheel drive Range Rover as fast as it would go, through the mud, hitting huge ruts causing the car to bounce wildly up and down, so violently at one point that Nancy bounced up and hit her head hard on the roof of the car, causing her to let out a huge scream. Insanely intent on getting through this mud I had to ignore her pain until we finally made it across the dangerous muddy track—it would have been a true disaster if we'd not gotten through that mud—as we were twenty miles from the nearest town and in a mountain forest with plenty of dangerous animals.

Upon reaching the other side, free of the mud, (venting my fear and frustration from taking such a stupid risk and feeling forced to do so) I yelled angrily at Nancy, saying, "Do not scream unless you've broken a bone and need to immediately go to a hospital." Now how unfair and insane is that? Come on Russell, get a grip!

But still in the north, reading the paper Tuesday morning we learned that Monday night the rebels had again come across the border and attacked another lodge, again robbing and beating some of the guests. When I finally got through to the Embassy they surprisingly told me that it was safe to go because the Kenyan Authorities had sent an Army of their soldiers down to this park to protect their biggest industry—Tourism. "Probably be the safest place in Kenya," they said.

So, down we drove, expecting to see large numbers of Kenyan troops all over the Park. Unfortunately, as we entered the park, going through its' gate, we noticed only a few soldiers acting very bored and barely paying attention. Driving down towards our reserved hotel, nearer the border, I noticed that there were very few cars and we saw no troops and no tourists—the Park seemed deserted—well, of course, Dummy, the place had been raided by murderous thugs the past two Mondays, Duh!

Checking into our hotel, not far from the border, we saw no cars in the parking lot and when we checked in the lady at the desk seemed surprised that we had come. Nancy, was not happy, saying "this place gives me the creeps!—are you sure this is safe?" Too late to return to Nairobi, assuring her it was safe, I worried that we might have made a terrible mistake visiting this Park.

Checking in, I asked the female attendant, "Did you have any trouble with the outlaws these past two attacks?"

"No problem at all—those incidents were down the road," she answered.

"How far away was that?" I asked

"Oh they were almost five miles away—they won't be back," she assured us, unconvincingly.

After she had given us our room key, telling us that she was upgrading us to a bigger mud hut, changing us from one hut to another, we walked about a hundred yards to our really cool mud hut, a Yurt like structure made of sticks for walls with a mud roof, copying the tribal structures that the Masai tribes build.

After dinner at the hotel (besides us only one twosome dining), I continued to worry about potential marauders storming into our hut, dragging us outside and stealing all our stuff and potentially worse—giving us a good beating or killing us. So, really out of my mind with worry, I walked back to the desk and asked the woman how many people were staying at the hotel. When she replied that there were only a few of the 30 or so huts being rented, I asked her to please show us on her books as registered into our original booking and not the actual hut we were using, figuring that, if the bad guys came, they would storm into the hotel, look at the guest list and go to the rooms that were occupied.

I figured that the least we could do would be to be in a hut that was shown on the register as "vacant." Now, how desperate is that? Naturally, I laid awake all night; worrying about my family getting attacked by a bunch of wackos with machetes—talk about feeling helpless!

Now here is where I really have to worry about my sanity—talk about taking risks. So, after surviving the night without any attacks, we got the kids up early to go down to the big river (on the border of Tanzania) where, we had read, there are many crocodiles and hippos. Using our guide book, we found the turnoff for the river "viewing" and pulled into an absolutely empty parking lot in the jungle with a small dirt path leading down, hopefully, to the river.

Now we had read that Hippos kill a lot of people every year (the second most in Africa, Water Buffalos being the worst), typically by just running over them. In other words, if you disturb a hippo in the jungle as they are eating their "greens," they will bolt for the water and if you are between them and the water it is not a good thing—it would be like getting in the way of a tank.

So, down the four of us went, weaponless, walking down this narrow, dirt road, listening to wild birds and the sounds of the jungle and as we approached the water, we were actually tip toeing, trying not to disturb hippos that might have been on land. Frankly, it was insane, as the jungle was so dense there was no way you could possibly see a hippo before you were right on top of him, or her—hey, they are all giants.

Not to mention all the other animals that could become a threat— Rhinos, Water Buffalos, Crocs, various cats (Lions, Leopards, Cheetahs etc). But somehow, by the grace of God, we got down to the river (no other people there) and walked out on a small wooden bridge out to a small island that had a ladder going down into an underground/ underwater viewing area, from where we observed hippos walking on the bottom of the ten foot deep river. They were monstrous in size and I worried about the return trip to the car, would there be Tanzanian bad guys or animal dangers?—this African tour was not doing much in the way of peaceful relaxation. Fortunately, thank God, we made it safely back to our car and back to Nairobi, where we went to a stadium to watch a major soccer match, before flying home.

Another insane thing we did was on our trip to New Zealand, and, yes, I should have known better, as I was the adult adventurer who should have been making better decisions and my wife was naively confident that I knew what I was doing but obviously I didn't.

We wanted to see Mount Cook, the tallest mountain in New Zealand, and we drove up to the entrance to a park, having heard that you could ski down the Tasman glacier that flowed below the peak. Again the place was empty but all you had to do was rent this plane and they would fly you up to the top of the glacier, drop you off, and guide you back down to the bottom (approx. 14 Kilometers or 9.8 miles) on skis and then a flight back up for a lunch on the glacier and another run down—there was no mention of how good a skier you should be (obviously they wanted the money). So, naively we signed up, jumping in the plane, (the only ones) with a guide and a pilot and up we went.

On the way up, after grilling the guide about his mountain climbing experience, (he offhandedly admitted he had climbed Everest), he finally asked me what kind of skiers we were.

"Oh, I'm a half assed intermediate but the kids are pretty good but my wife is really a beginner," I replied.

"You mean on a groomed ski slopes at a resort in the States?" he asked.

"Yes," I answered.

"Well, that makes you all beginners here because this snow is really treacherous," he said.

Irritated that we hadn't heard about this prior to signing up, I asked "What's so bad about the snow—looks like there's plenty of it?" I replied as I looked down at the huge glacier, as we flew up it.

"Well, the latest heavy snow fall, about two feet, was about a week ago (we were there during their winter, our summer) and the surface has frozen about two inches thick—your kids might stay on top but you are going through it," he answered

"How do you recommend we deal with it?" I asked.

"Best thing to do, if you can, is to do a "kick" turn, which is to jump completely out of the snow and turn in the air," he informed us—a skill that none of us had any clue how to execute.

So, we get out of the plane, slap on our skis and the guide takes off, telling us, cavalierly, to follow him. Within a few turns I realize that it is impossible to turn in these snow conditions and, in fact, the only way I can change direction is to fall down and turn my skis and then get back up—not pretty but effective. After falling numerous times I catch up with the guide who is impatiently waiting and the kids pull up beside us but their Mom has disappeared.

We look up the slope and see Nancy heading directly towards an enormous crevice in the glacier and we all start screaming for her to turn but she is too high above us and the wind is too strong for her to hear us. Fortunately she sees the crevice and purposely falls down and turns her skis towards us and gets down. I honestly think that if she would have fallen into that crevice that I would have strangled that guide right on the spot and then someone should have strangled me for being so stupid to sign up for that crazy adventure as we were essentially novice skiers, at least in those conditions.

Now we are down off the top of the glacier and have a relatively nice wide open slope, granted still the icy conditions, to ski down about 9 miles. When we hit the bottom, near exhaustion, Nancy and Amy (being the smartest of the four) decide to not return up but Andy agreed to accompany me (as there was no way that I would not use something I had already paid for no matter how insane it was—

207

granted, there are problems caused by being a cheap Scot). Hours later, Andy and I arrived at the bottom, both totally spent but exhilarated from the effort.

Later that week Andy and I would ski one of New Zealand's finest ski resorts, in a very foggy blizzard, skiing down super steep ungroomed slopes, without being able to see ten feet—it was absolutely over our heads and extremely dangerous but somehow we made it out with no injuries.

Another adventure I naively encouraged my kids to do was to climb Castle Peak (considered a relatively easy climb) in Colorado, the Elk Ranges' highest peak near Aspen on a summer vacation—in this case Nancy was smart enough not to join us. Anyway we drove up a very steep road in our rented Jeep, crossing two streams (and me stalling the vehicle in one), worrying about turning the Jeep over, before we made it up to a parking area near an old abandoned mine.

The problem was that below the peak was a big bowl full of snow and we didn't have any crampons or ice axes. Nevertheless, I told the kids that it would be no problem and we would be able to deal with it because the snow had warmed up enough so that we could kick our feet into it to build a step—if it had been icier we could not have proceeded. What I didn't mention is that if one of us fell we might pick up speed so quickly that it would be difficult, if not impossible, to stop our accelerating slide down the steep (i.e., 60% in places) slope.

Anyway, we made it up just fine, climbing out of the snow onto a fairly gnarly rocky ridge on up to the top at around 10:30 am and got off the mountain, after hydrating and eating some energy snacks, well before the deadline of 12:00 (to avoid afternoon lightning) and we arrived back down the ridge onto the snow. Naturally, I suggested that we sit down in the snow and glissade down, using our elbows (instead of ice axes—which we didn't have) to alter our route and, if we got going too fast, we could self arrest by rolling over and punching our fists and kicking our (crampon-less) boots into the snow which had become fairly soft and slushy.

Well, we tried that and it became somewhat of a disaster because of the steepness, we picked up too much speed and had trouble self arresting, not to mention the equipment that fell out of our backpacks becoming strewn across the slope. Amy going last, dutifully (as I yelled up to her) picked up the stuff, and started down and before I knew it she was flying by me (I had intended to jump in her way and stop her), but she blew by my son and myself, heading for a small pond down by the car. Fortunately, she was able to stop herself and we were able to get down safely with no injuries.

You'd think that I would have learned from these mistakes but just a few years later, vacationing in Telluride, Colorado, with Amy's boy friend (now husband) Dave, I decided we should climb Wilson Peak one of Colorado's most photographed 14ers. Not far from the car, about a half hour into the climb, we found ourselves crossing a large, steep, snow slope—the problem being the frozen snow condition (much like the Tasmin Glacier's frozen surface). The only reason that it was even possible was that there were some deep tracks made by a previous climber, obviously when the snow wasn't frozen.

Again finding ourselves without proper gear (crampons and ice axes) we climbed up this potentially dangerous slope. About half way up I suddenly felt how severe and imminent the danger was—if one of us fell, he or she, would fly down the icy slope, picking up speed, down to the huge boulders below. Certain that such a fall would cause, at best, serious broken bones or worse, death. I stopped and informed the kids that "You cannot make a mistake here. I want maximum concentration, total intensity, putting your feet into these tracks, maintaining your balance—a fall here could be life threatening." There was no response.

Well, some how we made it up that slope, and higher up we avoided another serious exposure to a major fall (the climb's crux) and made the summit. Arriving at the top, my future son in law, exhausted and somewhat angry about the risks he and his sweetheart had just been exposed to, said, "Mr. Russell, with all due respect, you are a frigging lunatic!"

On another occasion the four of us were on a family vacation (spring break for the kids) at the Caribbean island of St. Maarten, staying at a nice hotel that offered "scuba" classes in their swimming pool. Since we had done some snorkeling (the Red Sea, Indian Ocean, Hawaii, etc.), and having enjoyed that experience, we signed up for this so called class which gave us about two hours of information about how to scuba—understanding the equipment, how to take turns using your mouth piece if your partner's oxygen tank is malfunctioning and so forth. Of course, this was down at the bottom of a ten foot deep pool, so there was no danger because if things didn't work properly you could easily rise to the surface of the pool without worrying about getting the bends.

After the very simplistic "course" was over the instructor asked me if we would like to go out on the hotel boat to a special diving site, going down nearly 100 feet down to some interesting coral formations.

"Do you think we are ready for such a dive with only one two hour course where we learned only the basics," I asked.

"No problem—all you have to do is remember to breathe," the guide replied.

Since we had some friends who had worked hard in the States to get their diving license, having many hours (like over 100 hours) of diving time and instruction before becoming "Certified" I was skeptical but, feeling the excitement of this new adventure, I signed up my son and myself, as the two females (Nancy and Amy) were far too intelligent to be sucked into another poorly thought out and potentially dangerous Russell challenge.

So, later that same afternoon of having received our two hours of simplistic instruction, off we went in a boat with the guide and his assistant guide (a rather attractive young lady who appeared to be his girl friend) and another guest at the hotel.

As we motored out to the diving site, our fellow diver, asked, "So how long have you been certified and have you ever gone this deep?"

"Well, we aren't exactly certified and this will be our first dive ever," I responded.

Our fellow diver, acting as though we were totally out of our mind, said, "What? It took me over 100 hours to get my certification—this is dangerous stuff and you better know what you are doing! This will be my deepest dive, having only been down 50 feet once."

"Hey, there is no problem—this is an easy dive, only about one hundred feet down," explained our guide, as we arrived at the dive site (about five miles off shore in heavy swells) and connected to a buoy and started putting on our gear, apparently going to go down a cable to the location of the coral formations with some small caves. The first person to be ready was our 100 hour expert but as he fell off the boat backwards, (the preferred way to enter the water), his harness came over his arms and he rose to the surface, struggling to right himself, being carried away from the site by the surf, appearing to be in real trouble, as he struggled with his equipment. Our "guide" who had been mostly flirting with this girl friend, as he took puffs of his marijuana, restarted the boat and retrieved (saved) our so called expert.

The guide then says, "I'll be your partner and my friend here will be your son's."

"No, I'm going to be my son's partner and you three can follow us down," I arrogantly respond, not wanting my son to be partnered with some pot smoking bimbo.

So, my son and I now have our gear on and we are the first to exit the boat, swim over to the buoy and, seeing the guide wave us down, we begin to descend the 100 foot cable down to the area of interest. About half way down my son taps me on the shoulder and takes his mouthpiece out and gestures to me to take his and to hand mine to him, so that we can practice what we had learned hours ago in the hotel pool. Frankly, I was incredulous that he would do that but had no option but to trade my mouthpiece for his, practicing this technique as we waited for our 100 hour expert and the two pot heads. When they arrived we gave each other back our mouth pieces and headed on down.

Well, it was a spectacular experience, swimming in and out of small caves (trying not to have our tanks bump into the ceilings) and seeing a very unusual coral formation. After what seemed like a long time, I glanced at my watch and realized that we were slightly past the time that the guide had said we should return to the boat. So, I tapped him on the shoulder and pointed to my watch. He appeared OK but gestured that we should go back to the cable and begin our ascent which had to have orchestrated stops in order not to get the bends—you just can't charge back up.

So, anyway, my son and I had a super experience, diving over 100 feet down, with absolutely no training, but we were fortunate there were no problems. Frankly, scuba diving is only difficult when you have an equipment failure and fortunately we had none. This was another classic example of addiction to adventure, having potentially endangered my son's life and my own but we were again lucky. Believe me, I am not proud of this story, although I must admit I have an incredibly great memory of such an exciting event, despite not having the training required to attempt such a deep dive.

I guess if the grandkids would like to do some climbing, or diving, or skiing that I will insist that we be far more careful, teaching them the proper techniques and using the right equipment.

Thinking about these "dumb and dumber" episodes with my kids, I wonder what I was thinking at the time. One possibility (although I find this hard to believe) is that my experience with the Steelers, fighting off and evading huge monsters, might have had something to do with my cavalier attitude about dealing with the unacceptable risks? After all, my job, for so many years, was to avoid 300 pound giants who were trying to knock me down and wipe me out. Did I subconsciously think I could elude, dodge, avoid, or attack animals (i.e., Hippos) that could be far more dangerous?—what an idiot!

I remember being told back in High School, by a pugilist, that dogs have "glass jaws." When I asked what he meant, he explained that dogs act real tough until you hit them in the face and then most of them will run, surprised that you resisted their attack.

Many years later, when I was still playing for the Steelers, I was jogging through my neighborhood in Upper St. Clair and I passed a house with a guy mowing his grass and a huge German Shepard lying next to him. As I jogged by, I waved at the man, just as his large dog, (probably around 130 lbs.) jumped up and ran towards me, barking loudly and growling, causing me to go into a backwards trot (something linebackers do every day), as the dog rapidly approached, apparently planning on an attack. I remembered when Nancy had turned her back on an approaching German Shepherd and gotten badly bitten on her thigh.

I waved to the dog that all was OK, that I was not a threat, using soothing words, but he kept on coming. As he lowered his head, driving in to bite me on my bare legs, I stopped and threw the most perfect punch I had ever thrown and caught him right between the ears with all my 225 pounds—granted a mismatch in weight.

The dog's jaw bounced off the pavement, as his legs flew out beneath him and his huge chest landed hard. The stunned animal immediately jumped up and ran back to his master, with his tail between his legs, whimpering as he ran.

His owner, probably amazed that his dog wasn't as ferocious as he had thought, yelled at me, "Hey, what do you think you are doing?"

"What am I supposed to do—allow him to bite me? I was just defending myself," I replied and continued my jog. Obviously, a dog isn't the same threat posed by a Hippo or Croc in the wild.

Since I had spent a lot of time in black bear territory (Minnesota, Canada, Colorado) I was disappointed in the advice that was originally given, which was to "play dead," if approached by a black bear. Later, the expert advice became that you should stand tall, holding your arms high above your head (making yourself appear larger) and act weirdly aggressive but to not look them in the eyes. If they kept coming you were instructed to fight for your life, by punching them in the face—perhaps they too had a glass jaw like most dogs.

So, now so many years later, I wonder what it was that gave me so much confidence that nothing bad was going to happen when asking my family to "indulge" in such haphazard adventures/risks. Perhaps, I was just naïve, hoping all would be well. But, maybe it had to do with having made a living fighting off opponents—I guess if you make your living avoiding huge and aggressive athletes (who were clearly attacking me), a 130 pound dog doesn't seem too intimidating.

As a young child growing up, I would not have described myself as a very tough kid, having an older brother who could easily whip me in the little boxing matches my Dad (who tried to teach us how to protect ourselves) had us conduct in our living room when I was 6 and my brother 9. In fact, my main skill was conflict avoidance, finding it easy to out maneuver my brother by dodging his punches, and to escape his attacks.

Obviously, football forced me to learn how to deal with men who were bigger, faster and probably tougher but, hopefully not smarter (although I'm sure many were)—the game had forced me, over my twenty plus years of playing it, to learn how to deal with overt aggression through technique and using my quickness and agility to my advantage—toughness had little to do with it.

This experience had apparently subliminally (this was never a conscious thought—had it been I would have realized how ridiculous it would be) caused me to not have the fear I should have had when dealing with wild animals—they're quickness, size, agility and aggression clearly being significantly better than an old linebacker's, who apparently wasn't very smart or he wouldn't have asked his family to participate in such outrageous adventures.

Maybe, after all those years of dealing with giant, smart aggressive athletes, football had somehow given me an unrealistic sense of invincibility, coming out of the game, believing that I could withstand threats from certain animals and from the dangers of the wilderness itself—i.e., falling down steep icy slopes. Unknowingly, perhaps, I then took my children out into the wild, without the proper respect for those dangers.

So, I hope my kids accept this sincere "apology," and I hereby promise to be much more careful with my grand children, who I can't wait to take up a 14,000 foot mountain and, maybe, we can dodge some wild animals at the same time—oops, there I go again.

Now, at age 68, not having to avoid any monsters for over 30 years, my attitude about such dangers has changed significantly and I believe now is far more sensible.

Chapter 22

GIVING BACK TO THE COMMUNITY

One of the things we learned early from the Rooneys was that if you are going to be a Pittsburgh Steeler and live in the great city of Pittsburgh, you needed to give back to the city, to get involved in charitable events and to give some of your own money and time. We were often invited to various charitable efforts that the Rooney family supported and we could see the tremendously positive impact that they were having on the city, helping the poor, the sick, the homeless, the arts and even the country of Ireland (and now so many years later Dan Rooney is the Ambassador to Ireland).

My first real invitation to get seriously involved in charitable fund raising, other than just making personal appearances at various charitable events, was something called The Press Old Newsboys, where a number of Pittsburghers (Corporate Executives, Politicians and one Pittsburgh Steeler) were asked to involve themselves in a competition to see who could raise the most money annually for Pittsburgh's Children's Hospital, an effort organized by the *Pittsburgh Press* newspaper. Believing it was a very good cause and always enjoying the challenge of a competition, I signed on and had lots of fun over the years figuring out different ways to use our Steeler successes to help raise money.

For example, one year we had a Pittsburgh Steelers bar night where we got five or six of the city's top bars to let us (me and a number of my teammates—i.e., Ray Mansfield, Bruce Van Dyke, Mike Wagner, Rocky Bleier, Jack Ham and Jack Lambert) be the bartenders with the net profit of the evening going to Children's Hospital. You can only imagine the fun the customers (charitable givers/drinkers) had asking Jack Lambert to make them some exotic drink he'd never heard of and then listening to his outrageous reply.

We would have a limousine outside waiting to take us to the next bar and then at the end of the night to take everyone home—obviously we were taking advantage of the drinks being on the house for the Steelers. This event only lasted a few years, as the bar owners realized that they were losing a lot of money picking up the tab for the 4 or 5 Steelers taking advantage of their hospitality. Nevertheless, that event enabled, us one year to win the Press Old Newsboy challenge of who could raise the most money—something of which we were quite proud.

Another year, after Ray and I had retired, we decided to play a flag football game against the Dallas Cowboys who were still very unhappy that we had beaten them in two Super Bowls. We invited a dozen or so Cowboys (Roger Staubach, Leroy Jordan, & Cliff Harris, to name a few) and flew them up to our beautiful city and played that game in Three Rivers Stadium. Unfortunately, we didn't realize how angry and serious the Cowboys were after those two losses and also how difficult it is for former pro football players (who are used to going full speed, head to head, with full pads) to play flag football which requires a certain level of caution, the result being we had a number of serious injuries (a number of concussions and a torn Achilles tendon—mine).

The Cowboys brought a current player, (a wide receiver), who was, of course, in much better shape and way too fast for our retired Steeler defensive backs—no blitzes were allowed, giving Roger forever to throw the football. Roger, perhaps frustrated with the fact that during those Super Bowl losses he was required to run the ball (which usually resulted in little yardage) came out throwing every down and we were beaten soundly, in front of only about 10,000 gung-ho Steelers fans—way below what we had hoped for but, once again, we'd had fun raising money for Children's Hospital. A few years later we Steelers were invited to Sante Fe, New Mexico to play those same Cowboys in a tennis tournament for a local charity and the Cowboys won again but I guess I would rather win Super Bowls instead.

About that same time, my good friend, Walter Bent (the General Manager of Xerox in Pittsburgh) convinced me and my great friend/business partner, Sam Zacharias, to start a golf tournament with the proceeds going to Children's Hospital. He also arranged the first two years of the tournament to have Arnold Palmer be the Celebrity

Chairman of the event and we played it at his course, the Latrobe Country Club.

This was great fun for me because I got to drive Arnie's golf cart around the course, while he hit one shot with each 5-some (one "celebrity" athlete and 4 paying participants). Doing that I discovered that Arnie is a very enthusiastic Steelers fan and had many questions about what it is like playing in the NFL. Since I am a huge fan of Mr. Palmer and the PGA I bombarded Arnie with even more questions between his shots (which were often drives and approach shots but sometimes putts).

I think Arnie got a big kick out of watching these much larger NFL players, some over 300 pounds, hitting the golf ball only about half as far as his shots. Of course Arnie would have had quite a problem trying to tackle Jim Brown or Franco Harris. I think we both came to appreciate the challenges of both sports.

Arnie turned out to be an extraordinary host, taking everyone to his garage to show how he made his own clubs, giving a clinic on the tee and speaking at the award ceremony dinner. He is a true gentleman and we all have enormous respect for him. Over the years we were very lucky to have a number of famous golfers follow Arnie: Hale Irwin, Fuzzy Zoeller, Tommy Armour, Tommy Bolt and Chi Chi Rodriguez , to name a few.

That golf tournament is now in its 34th year, (yes, my favorite number) and we have raised over $5,500,000 for many different charitable efforts. But after ten years of running the tournament, about to quit (frankly, I was tired of asking my friends for money) I received a call from a Gail Balph, someone I would learn is a super smart and hard working fund raiser who worked for UPMC, and she asked if I would be "willing" to let UPMC take over the tournament and run it for us. Despite being absolutely amazed at the serendipitous nature, the irony, of getting this call, as I was about to announce it's termination, I started negotiating and ultimately agreed to "allow" UPMC to take over but I earmarked 25% of the net revenue to go to Children's Hospital, assuming that amount was equal to the full amount given to Children's Hospital the previous year and, if not, the percentage would increase until it hit that number. Gail and UPMC exceeded that amount the first year they took over.

Now so many years later, UPMC owns Children's Hospital, and 25% continues to go to the Russell Family Charitable Foundation which makes donations to various children's charities—i.e., EconomicsPennsylvania, children's medical issues, funding trainers for the inner school sports, helping Dapper Dan with their effort to support the Boys and Girls Clubs in Pittsburgh, Animal Friends (my wife, Cindy, is on their board) and, on the adult side, helping fund prostate cancer research, since our dear friend and founder of the tournament, Walter Bent, died from that horrible disease. All and all it's been a great run and we are equally excited that our upcoming 34th annual tournament at Nevillewood, still supported by UPMC and so many corporations and citizens here in Pittsburgh, will take place in 2010.

Many of my charitable involvements have come about from being invited to other charitable events, often being golf tournaments (this seems to be everyone's favorite venue), but some times other interesting sporting events as well. Many of those events also gave me the wonderful opportunity to meet and get to know people from other sports.

For example, for many years I participated in the American Airlines Golf Classic (an event primarily to thank their customers but with some money going to charity) where my partner was Bill Mazeroski and we'd often find ourselves up against some interesting characters. The first year, after 54 holes, we found ourselves in a playoff for the Championship (Maz is a great golfer) against two huge celebrities; former N.Y. Yankee Joe Dimaggio and Cleveland Brown QB Otto Graham. Maz won it for us (we split $10,000) by sinking a nasty birdie putt on the first playoff hole. Another year we were teamed up against two celebrity lightweights (just kidding), Mickey Mantle and Joe Namath, and had great fun getting to know those two famous athletes.

On another occasion Joe Greene and I were asked to fly to Paris, France to play in an "All Star" football game, a golf tournament and a baseball game to raise money for the American Hospital in Paris. Prior to teeing off I was introduced to my favorite comedian, Bob Hope, who had also flown over to back this important charitable effort.

Another year I found myself in Las Vegas playing in a tennis tournament and during the pre-tournament dinner names were drawn out of a hat to arrange who would be your playing partner for the first day.

218

When they pulled out my partner I was thrilled to learn that I would be playing with Doctor J, the NBA's MVP. Meeting the "Doctor" minutes later I learned that he had never in his life played the game of tennis and asked that I meet him a half hour before our first match so that he could "get the hang of it." Not being a seasoned player myself I worried that I wouldn't be a very good instructor but he learned how to play in those 30 minutes and got better every set, actually winning a couple of sets—absolutely amazing athleticism.

Later in that same tourney, I was teamed with another famous NBAer, John Havlicek and we ended up going out on a boat in Lake Mead to water ski, giving my two children their first chance to water ski since John's wife was an expert.

One time I received a call from Tony O'Reilly, H.J. Heinz's CEO, asking me if I would be willing to fly (in the Heinz private jet) with him and my former boss, Dan Rooney, to N.Y.C. for a dinner to raise money for the newly established Ireland Fund. He also asked if I could give a short speech to "entertain" the audience. Obviously, this was a no-brainer, as I thoroughly enjoyed myself and felt honored to be invited.

Once again in the sporting world I was asked to participate in a charitable ski race event at Copper Mountain, Colorado which was backed by the Denver Broncos. Flying out there I worried that I wasn't a very good skier, certainly not capable of ski racing but, what the heck, it was for charity. Meeting all the Bronco participants the night before, guys like John Elway, I thoroughly enjoyed getting to know athletes that I had only played against, knowing their athletic skills but nothing about them personally. The next day, without a single practice run, I raced down between the flags and as I went down, almost out of control, I thought that I was going very fast and that maybe this could have been my sport, but upon arriving at the bottom I learned that my time was the second worst of all the skiers, only better than another former Steeler, Ernie Stautner's, time (Ernie was skiing with two bad knees or I'm sure he would have also beaten me).

Another time I was asked to participate in a fly fishing tournament in the streams and ponds at Copper Mountain. Flying out to Colorado I didn't worry at all about whether I could "compete" well in a fishing tournament—I thought of it as a joke. But when I got there I learned that my team was made up of all very serious fishermen, wanting to win and they needed me to perform well. One of the key requirements was that every member of the team had to catch at least one fish during the morning contest ending at 12 noon. If one member didn't catch a trout the team would be severely penalized and I found myself the only person without a fish at 11:45 am. Our team's guide took me in a golf cart, racing up the creek to a spot he knew were some fish—"anybody can catch a trout here—even you," he said.

Well, it wasn't really that easy and I found myself stepping in holes, falling into the current, catching my fly on bushes over hanging the creek and with only a few minutes left I hooked a nice trout but it got away a minute later. With only a few seconds left, the guide, thinking I was truly the worst fisherman he had ever coached, yelled at me "if you get another bite like that just yank the fish out—don't bring him in slowly." Well, I got a bite and flung a tiny trout (about 8 inches long) way over my head and back in some dense underbrush. The guide made me crawl back into the underbrush to retrieve the fish—poor thing. I would discover later at the awards dinner (we lost) that many of the athletes invited, unlike me, were very serious fishermen.

At another event, again in Colorado, I played in Ed Podolak's (former Kansas City Chief great) golf Tournament (The High Country Shoot Out—if you win you don't get invited back) in Aspen where I met Kevin Costner, (who owns a ranch near Aspen) a famous actor that I had always appreciated because of his many outstanding movies being about sports: i.e., Field of Dreams, Tin Cup and his classic, Bull Durham.

My Steelers heritage gave me another amazing opportunity—an invitation to be part of a charitable event (I forget the cause) that was a boat race between an NFC team versus an AFC team at a Super Bowl in Miami. What made this such a special event is that the two greatest American sail boat racers, Ted Turner and Dennis Connor (both of whom had won the America's Cup—one of the World's most respected sailing races) were to be our Captains. Unfortunately we AFCers, (both teams sailing huge catamarans that were so fast we could have towed a water skier) lost when our Captain, Dennis Connor, fell off the boat (he didn't know how to swim but fortunately had a safety vest on) and we had to retrieve him before continuing the race but the NFC and their cocky captain, Ted, won the event. As a young boy living in Westchester County, New York, I did quite a bit of sailing in the Long Island Sound so I found this event very exciting.

Another favorite event that I've been involved in is the annual Taste of the NFL, at the Super Bowl, an effort to stop hunger in America. The event is held in a large venue (i.e., a Convention Center) and all 32 NFL teams have a food station (hosted by some famous chef from that city) and one former player representing his team. I have had the good fortune to represent the Steelers at the Taste of the NFL for the past 12 years. The Chefs do all the hard work, cooking up their specialty, serving thousands of people, while we former jocks just sit there having fun talking with the guests, taking photos and signing a few autographs.

Going to the Super Bowl every year (not something I had anticipated doing) has been great fun, as it also gives me time to participate in other charitable efforts—i.e., Franco Harris' annual golf tournament and dinner held at every Super Bowl with the funds going to the local Children's Hospital. It's always fun to see Franco and watch him sponsor such a successful event, giving back to the community.

Of course, it's also important to support our country, not only our wonderful city of Pittsburgh. I was lucky to have gone through ROTC at the University of Missouri and, graduating with a commission, I was fortunate to serve (after my rookie year with the Steelers) two years as a Lieutenant in the Army in Germany in 1964 & '65. Unlike Rocky Bleier who fought in the jungles and rice paddies of Vietnam, being wounded badly before returning to football (described in his great book, Fighting Back), my service was pretty much a piece of cake (in peace time) where the most dangerous thing I did in the service was to drive my Porsche on the Autobahn.

However, I was very fortunate to be invited by the NFL to participate in a USO trip to Vietnam in 1968 where I was accompanied by Jack Kemp, Bobby Bell (HOF), John David Crow (Heisman Trophy) and Bill Brown—four outstanding athletes and had the great opportunity to thank our soldiers for their so extraordinary service.

Years later, post retirement from the Steelers, I would put together another USO tour (Jack Ham, Bobby Bell, Ray Mansfield and myself) to thank our soldiers and sailors serving in the Mediterranean Sea off the coast of Italy. A few years later I was given the Byron Whizzer

White Award for the NFL player who did the most for his City and Country. Frankly, I'd like to be able to give all those soldiers, sailors and fighter pilots we met on those USO trips that same award, as their service is dramatically more significant than mine.

Obviously meeting famous actors, super successful businessmen (i.e., Tony O'Reilly and Ted Turner) and famous athletes is great fun and these charitable "efforts" (golf, fishing, bowling, skiing, baseball, flag football, tennis, etc.) have certainly never felt like a burden. Again, what a lucky guy I am to have all these experiences in the name of charity.

Now, after all these years, I find myself at age 68 as energized and excited as I have ever been about raising money for meaningful charities and part of that is because of having met one of the most driven and effective directors, Fritz Heinemann of a very meaningful non profit educational effort called EconomicsPennsylvania.

Sam Zacharias, its Board Chairman, my long time business partner, introduced me to Fritz and EconomicsPa., an effort to teach our young people the values of the Free Enterprise System and Capitalism, something I'm afraid our country is in danger of losing, as the current economic meltdown has caused our government to print more money, bail out more businesses, many of which don't deserve to be bailed out, and gotten way too involved in regulating and even partially owning and running businesses which has started, I'm afraid, a dangerous path towards socialism, something that has never worked anywhere in the world. This is why I believe that EconomicsPa. is one of the most important organizations in the State that we can and should support, to teach our children the old school values and freedoms that our forefathers wanted them to embrace. Capitalism/Free Enterprise work (granted, it's not without it's challenges), Communism/Socialism does not.

EconomicsPa's President, Fritz Heinemann, is a man driven to teach children the advantages/strengths of Capitalism. I soon learned that Fritz is one of the most aggressive (in a nice way), unrelenting and driven pursuers of what he wants/needs for EconomicsPa—he defines persistence. For example, within minutes of our first meeting he asked me if I would be willing to become a member of his state board. Knowing that I already was dealing with too little time to give to our own charitable efforts, I told him no and thought that would be the last of it. Little did I know, as Fritz continued to bombard me, always with a smile on his face, with information and requests to get more involved.

Then a few months later, I ran into Fritz and he informed me that Roger Staubach, the former Dallas Cowboy QB, was thinking about joining his board and wouldn't I reconsider. I was impressed because I know what an outstanding businessman Roger has become since his playing days (of course, I also admired his spectacular NFL career), so I started to seriously consider becoming a part of EconomicsPa. Well, Roger and I are now both members of Fritz's board and I'm not sure which one of us agreed to join first, not that it really matters. We are part of what I believe is one of the most important educational efforts we have in our State.

Later, I would learn more about the irrepressible, unrelenting, driven intensity of Fritz's efforts to develop the programs and raise the money necessary to teach those programs. I now believe he is one of the most successful, flamboyant, and dedicated non-profit Directors I have ever met—he is clearly a fund raiser extraordinaire! For example, I am often asked to give Steeler memorabilia to various charitable efforts and have found, over the years, that one of the best items is a Steelers helmet signed by the three linebackers of the 70's, Jack Ham, Jack Lambert and myself. Of course, the two Jacks are in the Hall of Fame and very deservedly so, as both of them were incredibly talented and totally driven to succeed—in a way much like Fritz.

Anyway, Sam Zacharias and I were at the Dapper Dan Ray Mansfield Smoker event where they had a live auction of one of our Linebacker helmets (signed by the three of us) and Sam was the "winner" for $1,000, a number that I frankly found somewhat disappointing. Sam decided to give the helmet to EconomicsPa. to see if Fritz could raise even more money from it. Well, you would not believe how much Fritz sold that same helmet for.

When Sam gave it to him, as a gift to EconomicsPa. Fritz said that he would go out and raise at least $50,000 and, knowing that there was no way that the helmet was worth anything close to that number, I jokingly told Fritz that if he could raise 50K for that helmet that I'd give him a half an hour to draw a crowd in Mellon Square and I'd kiss his butt. Fritz thought about that for a moment and said, "I can get even more for that."

Well, Fritz went out and sold 50 $1,000 raffle tickets and in the process, one of his supporters said that if Fritz could raise the 50k he'd match it with another 50k—thus coming to the full $100,000 which he accomplished. When Fritz asked when I wanted to do the Mellon Square butt kissing, I told him that he might want to rethink that because "you'll have to lower your pants and take a half hour to draw a crowd and you just might get arrested for indecent exposure." Fortunately, for me Fritz has not required me to live up to my offer.

Economics Pa. has programs to help teach our young people the values of our free enterprise/capitalistic system, such as stock market games (much enjoyed by the students) and entrepreneur business plan contests, as well as other meaningful programs. Personally, I am very committed to the cause and will make an effort to speak with the young people as often as I can, as well as to provide some backing from our Family Charitable Foundation.

Some people today, while experiencing this global economic meltdown, might challenge the wisdom of our free enterprise system, but we must remember that no where in the world has socialism worked. One of the great strengths of our system is its freedom for all of us to pursue our dreams, whereas in other countries (like China and Russia) people are channeled into vocations that the government thinks best suit their skills. We Americans, on the other hand, are allowed to pursue what might be considered unrealistic personal goals, to seek our dreams, to take risks that perhaps the government would deem foolish.

When people risk their own money, instead of the government's money, they tend to work harder and longer, pushing themselves way beyond the normal 8 hour days, making a 24/7 commitment to bring their dreams to fruition. Governments don't create companies that hire people and, granted, the Capitalistic system is not perfect. People can make a pretty good case that Wall Street leaders were greedy and that banks created risky (toxic) assets that they sold all over the world. Also, that banks made loans to people whose incomes couldn't justify such debt (something encouraged by our liberal government officials) but Capitalism is still clearly the best economic system ever designed because it gives people freedom and hope and allows them to seek their dreams which I believe causes them to drive themselves with greater energy and efficiency.

Being a committed believer in the strength of our system, I have made many investments into venture capital opportunities where I'm betting on the entrepreneur's commitment, energy, skills and ideas. Obviously, some of these investments will fail but there should be no government standing by to "bail" them out, as our system doesn't work that way. Many of those failed entrepreneurs, having learned the hard way, may go on to start another business that makes better decisions, employs more people and goes on to be a success.

Now that I am retired from the business world, except to follow our various investments, I am spending most of my time trying to help our charitable efforts to be more successful, such effort being somewhat more difficult than in the past because of this economic crisis but American's are very generous and my belief is that private economic help to those who need it is far better than the government trying to redistribute wealth and giving only to those causes they deem in need.

Frankly, we need more people like Fritz Heinemann out there with a passion for their cause, raising significant money to help support these efforts and drive to teach their message.

When I think about life and what is most important I would list the following values: health, family, friends, work, spirituality, sharing and giving. Perhaps those important issues are not necessarily in the right order (this is certainly debatable) but they are all extremely important in one's life. Without good health we cannot have the other so important life conditions and without meaningful work we cannot have significant sharing and giving. Without work (career) we will struggle to support our family and such a condition could negatively impact our health and our ability to have quality relationships with our friends. Spirituality (religion) also plays an enormous role in our lives because without it we might not be able to have the family values and work ethic required to have those other values.

Chapter 23

WHAT I LEARNED FROM THE GAME

This will be the last chapter I ever write about football. Why? Because it is time for me to move on, thank the game and all the people who supported me (my parents, mentors, trainers and our great fans and, of course, all my coaches through high school, college and pro) for all it did for me and focus in my remaining years on the people and tasks whom I now care most about—family, friends, business partners and charitable efforts.

As mentioned in the other chapters I am frankly incredulous that people still associate me with the game of football after all these years (having retired from the game 34 years ago). Perhaps that continued Steelers association is due to the fact that I never quite (despite trying) made the same commitment to anything as I made to football, never having quite the same drive, the same passion and unrelenting spirit for my post football business ventures as I had on the field. However and more likely, it has more to do with the tremendous support of our fans—the Steeler Nation.

First, I'll start with thanking my coaches through all those years—from Bob Davis, my Ladue High School coach (St. Louis), Dan Devine my College Coach at the University of Missouri and my Steelers coaches Buddy Parker, Bill Austin and the great Chuck Noll. I thank them all for giving me a chance and then continuing to believe in me despite my playing some very bad games (we always remember the mistakes more than the successes), always giving me the chance to redeem myself.

There are also too many assistant coaches to list who helped me tremendously to learn the basics (techniques and fundamentals) and kept me focused on the intricacies of the game. However, Al Onofrio, the great Mizzou defensive coordinator, was the first coach to teach me to memorize the opponent's tendencies/plays, particularly ones that would attack my position, and then to anticipate when they might run those plays before the ball was snapped and then attack those plays upon the snap of the ball—not wait for post snap keys. Coach Noll didn't like this strategy because he believed it was guessing but the tactic worked for me through out my pro career.

Looking back on my career, I realize how lucky I was, not only to have such wonderful coaches but also to play for such a great organization (family) as the Steelers (the Rooneys). Art Rooney Sr., the Chief, would be at almost every practice (rain, snow or in miserable heat) and then visit with us in the locker room, patting us on the back, encouraging us and always being supportive. His sons Dan and Art Jr. were also always there for us and very supportive and they passed that on to their kids.

I was also extremely fortunate to never sustain the devastating year ending injury (i.e., breaking a leg) allowing me to never miss a game in my entire football career (high school, college, military or Pro)—granted, I once childishly (wanting to keep that record intact) put myself into a game for one play as a blocker for an extra point despite Coach Noll's refusal to play me, wanting me to get healthy and not risk further injury.

I am often asked, by both fans and the media, whether I think I should be in the NFL Hall of Fame and my answer is always the same, "that's for other people to decide—it is not my call." But, frankly, I never played the game for awards or even for the money, as it was always about the passion, yes, the love of the game. I played to earn the respect of my coaches, teammates, and fans, as well as my own self respect, expecting to play at a certain level of effort and quality anticipation and execution of proper techniques. Our team mantra was "Intensity, focus, concentration, commitment, accountability, maximum effort, responsibility, passion, and an unrelenting determination." Yes, those are just words but we tried to live by them.

Regarding the HOF I am extremely proud of my teammates who have been granted that honor, all very deserving of that so special distinction. Frankly, I am honored to have played along side of them, witnessing their brilliance from a very close distance. When I think about my NFL career I do not think in terms of awards or honors received, instead I think about the challenges met and those that weren't—the game of professional football can be very challenging and humbling. However, I realize that the HOF voters, knowledgeable sports writers around the country, who follow the game closely, primarily will focus on one's statistics, awards and honors.

Basically, it doesn't matter to me whether or not I ever get accepted into that lofty organization, as what matters most to me is whether I had the respect of my coaches and teammates. Did I execute quality techniques? Did I use my knowledge of the opponent's tendencies to properly anticipate the next play and then help stop it? Did I play hurt? Did I give my maximum effort on every play? Did I keep my ego out of it and not make silly mistakes that hurt the team because I was trying to be the "Hero?" Did I overcome my tendency to be too impatient, too aggressive and too often stupid? Did I help lead the team in difficult times? These are the questions that are important to me and many of my teammates demonstrated those same qualities every day, inspiring me to do better and often I didn't get it done, falling short of meeting those objectives. HOF voters wouldn't have a clue as to the answers to any of those questions but my coaches and teammates would and they are the ones I really care about.

My attitude concerning the HOF is that if I got in nothing would really change. Being elected into that organization would not change a single play I made or didn't make, did well or did poorly—it is over and done with. There are other things on my resume that would mean nothing to those HOF voters that mean a great deal to me. For example, I was the Steelers captain for 10 years out of my 12 years of playing. In those days the captains were not chosen by fellow players but by the head coach and I am proud that Bill Austin made me captain in 1967 (in my third year as a Pro) and also in 1968 and then Coach Noll picked me as captain for the next 8 years I played for him (1969 to 1976)—ten years total.

I am also proud that Jack Ham and I, at the insistence of Chuck Noll, worked hard to develop a new pass coverage technique (mentioned earlier in the Steel Curtain chapter) which we called "the Hug-em-up" which was very effective against the so called "halfback option," a play used by most pro teams on third and short, the offenses wanting to match up a quicker running back to come out of the backfield and attack the typically somewhat slower linebacker by breaking outside if we over played the inside and taking the inside if we overplayed the outside—having his option. Previously we would just play it safe, making the tackle after the reception but they would move the sticks—a first down.

Our new strategy essentially had us penetrating quickly into the backfield, denying the back the opportunity to take an inside route (because he would run into the defensive end) and then forcing him on a very flat route towards the sidelines. This technique took away the halfback's option.

When I worked for NBC for a year as a broadcaster (my theoretical transition from a player to a full time businessman), I was surprised that so many coaches came up to me to ask how to teach that technique—the one that Hammer and I had developed, with Chuck Noll's strong encouragement.

I guess in a way I'm explaining about things I am very proud of but that the HOF voters would probably not even be aware of and probably would have no interest in anyway, as such a technique is illegal today. Rather, they'd want to know how many sacks, interceptions or tackles I had, rather than how many times my anticipations, techniques and positioning forced the opponent to punt.

Well, once Chuck Noll got there we rarely blitzed because we had such a strong defensive front four who were quite capable of putting lots of pressure on the QBs, so Coach Noll wanted us linebackers to be busy covering all the receivers—tight ends, flankers, out ends and the running backs. The game was different then, so many of today's voters may not be familiar with what linebackers did back in those days, judging them as linebackers are judged today. I had a lot of sacks in the '60s (all linebackers love to blitz) but they didn't keep sack stats back in those days.

I am also very proud of having never missed a game having played in my pro football career (12 seasons × 14 games equaling 168 plus 12 post season games and 7 Pro Bowls =187 games. That fact in a way pays my respect to the players of the 1950's, guys like Ernie Stautner, Brady Keys, Tom "the Bomb" Tracey and Myron Pottios (whom I played with in the early 60's) who taught me that the biggest badge of honor in the NFL (at least in those days) was to play hurt. HOF voters today would give little credence to that stat, (one that is very important to me) because today's players often miss games due to what we players of the past would consider relatively minor injuries— i.e., mine were broken fingers (all of them) two broken thumbs, a punctured lung, torn knee ligaments, high ankle sprains, etc.—these were only some of my injuries and I was lucky I didn't have the worse ones that so many of my teammates had.

Actually, it seems to me that the media (or is it the statisticians), often in the broad perspective, gives more credit to players who may not be so deserving. For example, they will make a big deal about someone who fell on (recovered) a fumble when, in my opinion, we should applaud the fellow who caused the fumble with his big hit.

When I set my only NFL record (the longest fumble recovery for a touchdown in NFL playoff history, 93 yards—yes, saved by Ben Roethlisberger's great tackle when Bettis had fumbled on the one yard line in a playoff a few years ago) the credit should have gone to Jack Ham who had executed a successful blitz causing the fumble where I had been blocked at the line of scrimmage and the fumbled ball just happened to bounce up into my arms—lucky me.

Of course, my teammates had a lot of fun talking about that fumble recovery because they claim it actually has another record attached to it—"the most elapsed time in any single play in NFL history," referring to my lack of speed. Hey, I considered myself a smart player and it was late in the game, we had the lead, so why hurry—why not run out the clock? My teammates had knocked all the Baltimore Colts down and, having a sore knee, I decided to run down the field the best I could (granted it was very slow). Normally, I would have considered lateraling the ball to a faster teammate but both of my wrists were injured and wrapped tight in plastic casts, so I figured to hold onto the ball and not give it back to the Colts. Granted, Jack Ham worried that the Refs might call delay of game and Ray Mansfield claimed that NBC cut for a commercial and came back in time to catch the end of the run. Randy Grossman jokes that the team had time to go into the locker room, shower, dress and come back out to see the end of the run.

There are, of course, other situations where the credit goes too much to the wrong person. For example, there are many interceptions on miss thrown balls where the QB had to release too early, under severe pressure from our front four. In this case the defensive linemen don't get a sack and often very little credit for really causing the interception. Or how about when one defensive back makes a great play and deflects the ball back to one of his teammates who was out of position. The stat guys give more credit to the interception stat and not the breakup guy.

Don't get me wrong, I'm not suggesting that I didn't get my share of credit, as I do believe I often got too much credit, i.e. when coming in for an easy tackle because of Dwight White's and Fats Holmes hard work, stripping away the blockers.

Frankly, there are a number of outside linebackers who I think should get into the HOF and they are Chris Hanburger (a great player with the Washington Redskins), Dallas Cowboy Chuck Howley, picked as the MVP in a Super Bowl and Maxie Baughan who played for the Eagles, Rams and Redskins in his stellar career.

So excuse me for going on and on about this HOF situation but I just wanted to respond to people who are constantly asking me that question and, perhaps, put my career into a different perspective.

Let's get back to what I started to do in this chapter and that is thank the game for all it did for me, all it taught me. All my coaches from high school to pro demanded that we play every down as hard as we could and to never give up. They taught us that nothing replaces plain old hard work. That it is critical to always be a smart player (success is in the details) and that what we learned from the game would help us go forward in our "life work" (Coach Noll's favorite phrase) outside of the game.

Today, we observe how the NFL is trying to make the game safer, fining players for late hits even when no penalty was called during the game. Hines Ward, our super receiver, has had numerous fines for doing exactly what he should be doing—blocking the opponents, protecting his teammates. This is a difficult issue for the NFL and I'm reminded how Jack Lambert thought they should put the quarterbacks in skirts because of how the new rules were becoming so protective—guys like Johnny Unitas, Bobby Layne, Bart Starr and Y. A. Tittle would not believe how the new rules protect the QBs, as they had to play when defensive players could roll off a block and spear their knees, or go high with helmet to helmet collisions. Obviously, the new NFL is trying to eliminate or reduce the injuries to their players, as well as penalizing those who are deemed to be taking "cheap" shots.

Please understand, I am not accusing Hines Ward of taking cheap shots, as his hits may occasionally come from the blind side but they are legal hits/blocks. When I played linebacker I always paid attention to where potential blockers might be coming from and rarely got blind sided—granted, it will happen on occasion. It is difficult for a defender to defend himself from a blocker coming from the blind side (even if he knows he's there) when he is facing a running back directly in front of him—if you turn to play off the blocker the running back could go right past you—very embarrassing.

There were many times that I was forced by the ethic of the game, which I respect, to ignore a blocker, although I knew he was there, and, when I did that, was often hurt, sustaining bad high ankle sprains caused because I refused to defend myself against the blocker, putting the importance of tackling the runner ahead of my own safety—all defensive players have to deal with that awkward situation at times.

I think the NFL must be very careful that they don't take the violent nature of the game out of it, as most fans appreciate that it is a very tough game. Cheap shots should be heavily penalized but clean, legal hits, regardless of how devastating, should remain.

The problem is that by telling a defensive lineman, or any blitzer, that he is not allowed to hit a QB below the knees, he is essentially eliminating the possibility of rolling low off a block and scrambling on the ground, on hands and knees, towards the QB—something that happens quite often but now is not allowed.

One should also note, as discussed in earlier chapters, that it is impossible to compare the statistics of players today versus the one's in the past because the game has changed so much. For example, one cannot compare Lynn Swann's and John Stallworth's statistics with Hines Ward. First, because Noll preferred to run the ball, believing that when you throw the ball there are three things that can happen and two of them are bad—incompletions or interceptions.

Second, and more importantly, because the new rules allow Hines to run down the field without fear of being hit prior to the Quarterback releasing the ball, unlike Swann and Stallworth who had to deal with defensive backs taking shots at their heads before the ball was thrown. Jack Ham and I, (when playing man to man on wide receivers, having them short with deep help from the safety), spent a lot of the game trying to "re-rout" receivers, as we were allowed to keep our hands on a receiver (not hold him) until the ball was in the air forcing him (as deep as 15 to 20 yards deep in the secondary) to go in a direction he didn't want to go. Today's rules only allow one "chuck" within the first five yards and then you must release him and let him run free making it dramatically more difficult to play pass defense today.

While playing zone defenses, Hammer, Lambert and I would drop to the hash mark, 10-12 yards deep, and then look for receivers crossing our zones. If we spotted one we were allowed to stop him in his tracks by hitting him in the head, or by cutting him at the knees or just by delivering a good forearm shiver in the chest (our preferred strategy), stopping his route dead. Today's receivers do not have to worry, when 6 yards deep, about these kinds of tactics—which were very effective. My point here is not to take anything away from today's receivers, as I believe they are outstanding receivers, but their statistics simply cannot be compared with players of the earlier days. Obviously, Mr. Ward, regardless of this issue, will be joining Mr. Swann and Mr. Stallworth in the HOF, five years after his retirement—as he should.

Personally, I do not like it when today's referees always seem to call defensive interference when there is any contact between a receiver and a defensive back—even when the contact was initiated by the offensive player. Defensive backs probably have the most difficult job on the field, as they are trying to cover speedy and shifty receivers who are running forward and know where they are going, whereas the defensive backs do not know where he is going and they are running backwards—perhaps one of the hardest thing to do in the game, on a level with the difficulty of open field tackling or blocking.

Other rule changes that I don't like are the fact that offensive lineman today are allowed to grab the defensive lineman's jersey (HOLD), as long as his hands are inside the opponent's shoulders—in the old days that would have been holding. Clearly, the NFL is trying to reduce the number of sacks but are finding it difficult to do so, as today's linebackers and defensive linemen are just so strong and powerful, overcoming the offensive lineman's "holding."

Defensive lineman used to be allowed to use head slaps (hitting the offensive lineman in the side of the head with one hand and using the other one to jam the opponent under the chin, making it extremely difficult for the offensive lineman to block his man. Believe me, offensive linemen who played across from Steeler greats, Ernie

Stautner and Joe Greene, were often beaten to a pulp and bleeding profusely but all of that was within the rules in those days.

Obviously, the NFL is working hard to make it easier to block defensive lineman and easier to run pass routes, the objective clearly being to have more points scored, as they apparently believe that defensive battles are boring or at least thought so by the fans. Personally, I love to see a three nothing game but they rarely happen, as defense has been made more difficult and offense easier. Granted, the new rules also reduce the number of serious injuries—obviously a good thing.

With all these rule changes to increase scoring, I do not believe that the NFL should be fining players for minor contact which often happens accidentally because the defender is judging when to lower his head (knowing that he is not allowed to hit the opponent in the head—something we did regularly) and, all of a sudden, the opponent (QB or runner) makes a move that was unexpected (i.e., stepping towards the defender) and their heads collide—why is it the defenders fault?

Okay, there is nothing worse than an old player, an old fogie like me, criticizing today's game, complaining about the new rules—I can just hear today's fans saying, "Hey, things change, Russell—get over it".

I don't want to end this chapter complaining about today's game, as I have great admiration for today's players, their exhaustive training regimen, (much bigger, faster and stronger that those before them), their commitment, talent and community service. Also, the league has obviously made some good changes, as the game is far more popular today than it ever was in the past—hats off to the NFL Management and owners.

I want to end this chapter/book by saying thank you to the Rooneys (they truly created a family atmosphere and always demonstrated class), the Steelers Nation (our wonderful fans—the most incredibly enthusiastic supporters ever), that I have met all over the world, all my teammates and the NFL for giving me such a wonderful experience. I will never forget the powerful bond our teammates had, forged by our collective drive for perfection, our refusal to quit, our respect for each other and our love of the game and each other.

I feel like the luckiest man alive, for the opportunities I was given to play such a challenging game, the wonderful support of the entire Steelers training and locker rooms, the outstanding coaching from my pro-head coaches (Buddy Parker, Bill Austin and Chuck Noll—yes Noll was my favorite and clearly the most successful) as well as the many excellent assistant coaches who put up with my arrogance (I often debated them when I disagreed with their strategies), but I feel that we always ended up respecting each other.

As I'm sure all my Steeler teammates also feel, we do not need any more awards, trophies or media recognition, as the reward was just being part of such a wonderful game and team experience.

Thank you Steelers Nation (Rooneys, coaches, players and fans)— I will always love you!! Sayonara—Number 34! Hey, life is good and thank you for reading this book, as I hope it inspires you to challenge yourself and be the best you can be.

P.S. Thanks Mom and Dad!

ACKNOWLEDGEMENTS

As in my previous two books, *A Steeler Odyssey* and *An Odd Steelers Journey*, there are virtually too many people to thank. I appreciate all the encouragement my business partners and friends gave me during the three years it took to write this book. Many of them read parts of this book and gave suggestions and the supportive comments I needed. I have found writing to be very humbling and tremendously challenging and rewarding—in a sense very much like playing football.

I would like to especially thank Sandra Stevenson for coming up with the name—*Beyond the Goalpost*. My best friends Jack and Susan Musgrave, Jim Card, Fritz Heinemann and Sam Zacharias were always supportive and willing to give me constructive criticism. My writing professor, Paul Doherty, at the University of Missouri edited this book and gave me many helpful ideas and suggestions, making the book much more readable. Family members who read these chapters before they were edited and resisted criticizing my fledgling efforts to write are also to be thanked: my wife, Cindy, son Andy, daughter Amy and ex-wife Nancy all gave me meaningful feedback. I also want to thank my good friends and business partners, Jeff Kendall and Don Rea who also gave good counsel.